CASEBOOK SERIES

PUBLISHED

Trollope

The Barsetshire Novels

The Warden
Barchester Towers
Doctor Thorne
Framley Parsonage
The Small House at Allington
The Last Chronicle of Barset

A CASEBOOK

EDITED BY

T. BAREHAM

M

First published 1983 by
THE MACMILLAN PRESS LTD
London and Basingstoke
Companies and representatives throughout the world

ISBN 0 333 27554 3 (hc)
ISBN 0 333 27555 1 (pbk)

Printed in Hong Kong

CONTENTS

ACKNOWLEDGEMENTS

The editor and publishers wish to thank the following who have kindly given permission for the use of copyright material:

Ruth ApRoberts, extract from *Anthony Trollope: Artist and Moralist* (1971), by permission of Chatto and Windus Ltd; Elizabeth Bowen, extract from Introduction to *Doctor Thorne* (1959), by permission of Houghton Mifflin Company; William Cadbury, article 'Character and the Mock-Heroic in *Barchester Towers*', from *Texas Studies in Literature and Language*, v, No. 4 (Winter 1964), by permission of the author and University of Texas Press; Anthony Cockshut, extract from Introduction to *The Warden* (Collins Classics 1952), by permission of William Collins Sons & Co. Ltd; P. D. Edwards, extract from *Anthony Trollope: His Art and Scope*, by permission of the author and University of Queensland Press; M. A. Goldberg, article 'Trollope's *The Warden*: A Commentary on the "Age of Equipoise" ', from *Nineteenth Century Fiction*, xvii, No. 4 (March 1963), copyright © 1963 by The Regents of the University of California, and reprinted by permission of The Regents; Pamela Hansford Johnson, extract from Introduction to *Barchester Towers* (Collins Classics, 1952), by permission of William Collins Sons & Co. Ltd; Ronald Knox, chapter 'The Barsetshire Novels', from *Literary Distractions* (1958), by permission of the Estate of the late Ronald Knox; Laurence Lerner, extracts from Introduction to *Anthony Trollope: The Last Chronicle of Barset* (Penguin English Library, 1967), Introduction copyright © 1967 by Laurence Lerner, reprinted by permission of Penguin Books Ltd; Frank O'Connor, extract from *The Mirror in the Roadway* (1957) by permission of A. D. Peters & Co. Ltd; R. M. Polhemus, extracts from *The Changing World of Anthony Trollope* (1968), by permission of University of California Press; Arthur Pollard, extract from *Anthony Trollope* (1978), by permission of

Routledge & Kegan Paul Ltd; A. Quiller-Couch, essay in *Charles Dickens and Other Victorian Novelists* (1965), by permission of Cambridge University Press; Geoffrey Tillotson, extract from 'Afterword' from *The Warden* by Anthony Trollope, 'Afterword' copyright © 1964 by The New American Library Inc., and reprinted by permission of the publishers.

While every effort has been made to trace and acknowledge copyright, in one case this has proved unsuccessful. The publishers apologise for any infringement of copyright and shall be glad to include the necessary correction in subsequent printings.

TO

WENDY AND THE BOYS

GENERAL EDITOR'S PREFACE

The Casebook series, launched in 1968, has become a well-regarded library of critical studies. The central concern of the series remains the 'single-author' volume, but suggestions from the academic community have led to an extension of the original plan, to include occasional volumes on such general themes as literary 'schools' and genres.

Each volume in the central category deals either with one well-known and influential work by an individual author, or with closely related works by one writer. The main section consists of critical readings, mostly modern, collected from books and journals. A selection of reviews and comments by the author's contemporaries is also included, and sometimes comment from the author himself. The Editor's introduction charts the reputation of the work or works from the first appearance to the present time.

Volumes in the 'general themes' category are variable in structure but follow the basic purpose of the series in presenting an integrated selection of readings, with an Introduction which explores the theme and discusses the literary and critical issues involved.

A single volume can represent no more than a small selection of critical opinions. Some critics are excluded for reasons of space, and it is hoped that readers will pursue the suggestions for further reading in the Select Bibliography. Other contributions are severed from their original context, to which some readers may wish to turn. Indeed, if they take a hint from the critics represented here, they certainly will.

A.E. Dyson

INTRODUCTION

The history of Trollope criticism and the problems implicit in his work present a comparatively simple outline in most critical commentaries. After the unjust neglect of his two first Irish novels and the false start with historical romance in *La Vendée* (1850), he 'found' himself with *The Warden* (1855), confirmed his promise with *Barchester Towers* two years later, and by the time *Doctor Thorne* appeared, in 1858, he had established himself and Barsetshire at the forefront of public taste. Thackeray's invitation to him to provide the major serial for the first issue of the *Cornhill Magazine* gave Trollope the opportunity to assert his popular standing through *Framley Parsonage* (1860–61). His status as a novelist was then, supposedly (in the received opinion of many literary historians), sustained unabated through to *Phineas Redux* in 1874, after which a decline set in, with even novels as good as *The Prime Minister* (1876) and *The Duke's Children* (1880) failing to win back the changing taste of a fickle readership.

A few words of caution are due, however, lest the pattern appear too obvious or too simple. *The Warden* by no means took the reading public by storm. If it was a new start, it was also in many ways a tentative or even a misdirected departure. Its immediate sequel, *Barchester Towers* (1857), was more assured, less pointedly local and specific in its objects of satire, and hence more 'Trollopean'. But each of the subsequent Barsetshire novels appeared interspersed among other novels quite unconnected with the famous cathedral town and its county. Several of these non-Barsetshire books received a justifiably cool reception, for they certainly do not represent the best of Trollope. *Castle Richmond*, for example, appeared (in 1860) sandwiched between *Doctor Thorne* and *Framley Parsonage*; and *Miss Mackenzie* (1865) was published between *The Small House at Allington* (1864) and *The Last Chronicle of Barset* (1867). Thus, though it is customary to see a steady progression in depth of treatment and subtlety of technique within the Barsetshire series, this, if a true view, cannot be correlated with an overall steady improvement.

Indeed, it may be worth questioning whether steady progress is a concept at all applicable to Trollope. Many of his more discerning commentators have found reasons for not correlating an order of excellence with the order of composition even within the Barsetshire cycle. And, on a broader scale, while his first two novels – *The Macdermots of Ballyclorah* (1847) and *The Kellys and the O'Kellys* (1849) – are extraordinarily good, two of his latest works – *The Fixed Period* (1882) and *An Old Man's Love* (posthumously published in 1884) – are among his most feeble. It is much easier to trace 'development' in, say, Dickens or Hardy than in Trollope. One could indeed argue that it is by chance rather than by any innate sense of literary architectonics that *The Last Chronicle of Barset* proves to be the most powerful and profound of the 'clerical' series.

Usually coupled with the hazardous and perhaps ill-founded view of Trollope's steady development up to about 1868 is the undoubted fact that his general popularity expanded until about that date. In the 1950s, there gradually came to prevail a judgement that the novels written from about 1870 onwards were less affirmative in tone, that the writer's essentially benign and quietist view of society was disturbed, and that his hitherto almost monotonous belief in the eventual triumph of young love was shaken. The tone of his work from the 1870s was declared to be more doubting, more satirical – a tone epitomised by *The Way We Live Now* (1875). Anthony Cockshut's study (1955)[1] – part of which is excerpted in this selection – was influential in turning attention to the work of Trollope's later period. Dividing the novelist's life into three phases, Cockshut sees the first as one of 'suffering, self-reproach, and daydreaming', followed between 1847 and 1868 by years of literary and social success, and covering the period of the Barsetshire novels. The last phase, from 1868 to the novelist's death in 1882, is seen as one of 'retreat, questioning and satire'. Cockshut believes that Trollope's greatest achievements were made within this last period. Yet it must be acknowledged that this is the very time when his popularity began to decline.

It is well to remember that Trollope was already forty when *The Warden* appeared, and that when he died, in his sixty-eighth year, he had completed forty-seven full-length novels, several collections of short stories, biographies of Thackeray and Palmerston, and five substantial travel books. He had, in the meantime, served as an energetic and devoted administrator at the Post Office, engaged in literary editorship, and led a more than usually active social life. A carefully charted consistency of development in his art may be too much to expect on top of all this. Nor may some increase in acerbity of temper, if actually present in these later novels, be surprising. The natural conservatism of advancing years will often take that turn. Thus, whether the spirit of the age or natural hardening of the arteries was the cause of any change discernible in his artistic output must remain highly speculative.

What Cockshut's theory of encroaching pessimism achieved for Trollope studies was to move Barsetshire towards the periphery of interest for a generation or so, by its insistence that there is more to him than genial yarns of clerical storms-in-teacups: a falsely cosy view which a previous preoccupation with the ecclesiastical novels may have provoked. Cockshut's study forced a distinction between popular acclaim and literary excellence – an issue which is never far beneath the surface when we are dealing with Trollope. The extreme form of such a viewpoint is an insistence that the novels by which the 'general reader' has most readily approached Trollope are inferior to the later ones; and that it is by these later works that he should be most esteemed.

The usual argument, then, has it that, from his death in 1882 until about 1930, Trollope was in eclipse. The waning interest is attributed variously: to his affirmations in *An Autobiography* (written about 1876 but not published until 1883); to a shift in aesthetic sensibility which was taking place in the last years of the century; and to a general revulsion from mid-Victorian attitudes which Trollope is seen to epitomise. The essays in the present collection by Sir Arthur Quiller-Couch and by Frank O'Connor are typical in their forthright expression of irritation over the novelist's apparently mercenary and mechanical attitude to fiction, attested in *An Autobiography*. Certainly,

Trollope's affirmation of the primacy of persistence over inspiration, and his open insistence on the financial motive in writing, are stated with an aggressiveness highly characteristic of the man:

> . . . big, broad, and bush-bearded . . . scarcely giving himself time to think, but spluttering and roaring out an instantly-formed opinion couched in the very strongest terms. . . . 'I differ from you entirely', he roared out once to the speaker who preceded him at a discussion of . . . [Post Office] Surveyors. 'What was it you said?'[2]

Doubtless his insistence on pecuniary reward is tactless, perhaps ill-bred:

> It will not, I am sure, be thought that, in making my boast as to quantity, I have endeavoured to lay claim to any literary excellence. . . . But I do lay claim to whatever merit may be accorded to me for persevering diligence in my profession. And I make the claim, not with a view to my own glory, but for the benefit of those who . . . may intend to follow the same career. . . . Let their work be to them as is his common work to the common labourer. No gigantic efforts will then be necessary. He need tie no wet towels round his brow, nor sit for thirty hours at his desk without moving, – as men have sat, or said that they have sat. . . . I have never been a slave to this work, giving due time, if not more than due time, to the amusements I have loved. But I have been constant, – and constancy in labour will conquer all difficulties.
>
> It may interest some if I state that during the last twenty years I have made by literature something near £70,000 . . . I look upon the result as comfortable but not splendid.[3]

This is downright silly. 'Sit down for five hours a day, turn on the tap, and out will come the Reverend Josiah Crawley' is the implication. Behind the rodomontade, however, lies the essential Trollope. He was proud of his self-made achievements; he had even out-written the famous mother who had neglected him; and he valued the good things that financial success made possible. Disproportionately assertive as his emphases may appear to be, thinly as they may cover the raw, hurt interior scarred by his miserable childhood, they draw attention to the fact that, from a start in life which would have turned many men into absolute delinquency, Trollope achieved virtually everything he seemed to want from life – and entirely by his own efforts. And it is possible, of course, to share his contempt for the wilting-violet school of creative writing without condoning his stridency of tone.

A careful reading of the *Letters*[4] and of *An Autobiography* demonstrates how much he really did care about the imaginative, creative and didactic sides of his craft. He gave the game away when he confessed, of *The Warden*, that 'as regarded remuneration for the time, stone-breaking would have done better'. Had he been the verbal hurdy-gurdy he pretended to be, had he been avid only for money or popularity, he would never have persevered. There are, in fact, more passages in *An Autobiography* which deal with imaginative spontaneity, with the duty for revision and with the demands of and love for craftsmanship, than with money. Most of these have been excerpted for this volume. Something in his frenetic work-rate may indeed reflect a constant need to obliterate the early years of sloth and self-neglect; yet most of us who boggle at his rising at 5.30 a.m., writing by the stopwatch, adding up words to the page and pages to the volume, surely do so with a tacit sense of rueful envy. For well over a decade, this fierce devotion to regular habits enabled Trollope to produce at least one popular success every year, to fulfil an exhausting and important public office, travel over three continents both for business and pleasure, go hunting twice a week, play serious clubman's whist, and chair the financial committee of a major literary periodical. The vigour with which he declares and defends his interest in money is part of the total energy which sustained this phenomenal tide of activity.

Though some of the distaste which we are told was felt for the literary attitudes of *An Autobiography* by the generation succeeding Trollope's own may have coloured criticism of the novels, all the elements of the attack had indeed already been manifest in the reception of his work from as early as the 1860s. Frederic Harrison's retrospect of 1895 (part of which is excerpted in Part Two below) gives only half the truth: '. . . for the moment poor Anthony represents . . . all that was banal and prosy some thirty years ago. The taste of our youth sets hard for a new heaven, or at least a new earth. . . .' Yet we must not forget that it was the critics of Trollope's own generation who first castigated the repetitiveness, the lack of intellectual adventure, the stylistic

gaucheries of the middle-period books, and who hung Barchester round his neck like an albatross. Often they simply would
not listen when the novelist tried to break free of the cathedral
close. They resorted to unthinkingly invidious comparisons, or
forced his new wines into the old Barsetshire bottles:

> . . . the art and mannerisms which have pleased one generation are by no
> means certain to captivate the next. . . . The same strength and the same
> weakness distinguish *John Caldigate* and *Barchester Towers*. The same characters
> with which we have been so long familiar reappear in the later story, though
> under different names. . . .[5]

Whatever force there may be in the argument that a shift in
aesthetic sensibility destroyed Trollope's status, there can be
no doubt that the decline in popularity set in well before his
death, and that the contributory factors were numerous and
complex.

Lance Tingay has traced the putative decline forward into
this century.[6] His statistics show a falling-off in publication
figures immediately after Trollope's death, but thereafter a
steady level of activity – much below that of his creative
lifetime, but healthy enough. The concept of a dramatic decline
in popularity, followed by a rise in the middle years of this
century, lacks support from Tingay's figures. My own correspondence with publishers suggests that the modest but steady
support for Trollope continues. *The Warden* and *Barchester
Towers* remain the most popular of his novels among those
currently available, though the presentation of the 'Palliser'
novels on BBC Television in the 1970s boosted sales of those
books for the duration of the serialisation. No doubt a similar
effect could be observed, to the advantage of the Grantly-
Proudie stories, in the Barchester dramatisation on television,
beginning in late 1982.

Yet there *was* a degree of falling-off in the 1880s and 1890s.
Though the argument may flow back and forth, pro and contra,
over Anthony Cockshut's contention that Trollope's 'greatest
achievement' lay in his last period, it is, conversely, manifest
that most of his worst books also stem from this period. Or,
more charitably and cautiously, one might say that the bulk of
his most experimental writing was done in his last fifteen years.

Trollope is not often enough given credit for the restless energy with which he tried out new forms and modes for his fiction. The extremes of this are his venture into near-Wellsian fantasy in *The Fixed Period* (1882) and into anonymous 'foreign tales' in *Nina Balatka* (1867) and *Linda Tressel* (1868). Having made the full-length chronicle almost his own genre, he began to experiment with the exigencies of the short novel, almost to the point where it merges with the short story proper. Once, in *Sir Harry Hotspur* (1870), he achieved a masterpiece of starkly simple tragedy within this medium; but essentially it did not suit him. Popular coolness to the later books may indeed arise partly from disappointment that the mixture was not as before; but it may also be that the mixture is no longer satisfactory. Only one of his last ten novels has a claim to thorough excellence: *The Duke's Children*. Written in 1876, it has, comparatively slowly, established itself among the most respected of his books. With this one exception, talent and energy may in truth have begun to flicker in Trollope's last ten years, with at the same time a change in his novelistic purpose.

This is precisely the period in which he wrote *An Autobiography*, though it was not published, of course, until the year after his death. 'Now I stretch out my hand, and from the farther shore I bid adieu to all who have cared to read any among the many words I have written.' With this uncharacteristically emotive peroration, *An Autobiography* ends. It seems a curiously premature valediction to have written in 1876, though its tone is consistent with the enervation of the will displayed in *An Old Man's Love* – and very remote from the vitality which had endeared Barsetshire to so many.

If, then, the decline in Trollope's reputation and achievement is rather less clear-cut than is often asserted, so too is any permanent sense of major revival. Elizabeth Bowen has written an attractive critical fantasia[7] suggesting that the dark days of the Second World War fostered a new relish for Trollope's evocation of a placid, morally stable world: a kind of mid-Victorian idyll. But, beyond the special impact of the televised novels, publishers provide no evidence of much strikingly upward movement in the sales of Trollope's works in the post-war years. There has been, it is true, a substantial increase in the number of academic books written about him, but this is of little significance since literary industry is in our day deployed on virtually every feasible figure, with ever-increasing productivity. It remains inexplicably true that Trollope is the least read of all the major Victorian novelists among undergraduate students of English literature. Perhaps one should slightly provokingly add that much of the best criticism of him has come, not from the academic desk or rostrum, but from his fellow-practitioners in the craft of writing. Quiller-Couch, Frank O'Connor, Ronald Knox, Elizabeth Bowen, Pamela Hansford Johnson – all practitioners – are represented in this volume; and Hugh Walpole and C. P. Snow are likewise cogent in their appraisals,[8] albeit not so readily susceptible to excerpting in our format.

★

Trollope's critics have been constant in the reproof of certain mannerisms, attitudes and stylistic tricks in his work, while the nature, function and quality of his 'realism' have been a continuing source of debate. David Skilton's study of 1972 has an invaluable section on the subject.[9] The insistence on Trollope's realism has meant that much criticism has been cast in terms of analogies with mechanical trades or with photography. The novelist may have only himself to blame for this. In several letters and in *An Autobiography*, he likened his craft to that of a shoemaker – and, at least once, to that of an upholsterer! Perhaps the *Saturday Review* had first put the cobbling analogy in the novelist's mind: '. . . an excellent literary workman . . . he makes a novel just as he might make a pair of shoes . . . (19 May 1860: cited in the excerpt in Part One below). The *Westminster Review* complained that his novels were 'manufactured like Manchester goods'; and, putting it another way, R. H. Hutton protested that Trollope lacked the 'agony of meditative travail'.[10]

Two schools of thought, in fact, can be seen at work on Trollope in the 1860s: one approved of the comfortable factuality which it saw as the proper basis of his popular success; while the other deplored his lack of passionate, interior imagination. After a first flush of enthusiasm for him, the influential *Saturday Review* became the principal foe to his realism. Its reviewers found him 'monstrously prosaic'. As early as *Doctor Thorne* (1858), the *Saturday* protested against his 'mechanical skill'; and when *Rachel Ray* appeared in 1863 (sandwiched right into the middle of the Barsetshire series), its critic wrote: 'Mr Trollope . . . has not much straw to make his bricks with, but he has taught himself to turn out a brick that really almost does without straw, and is a very good saleable brick of its kind.' Underlying this is the assumption that this kind of work was easy to turn out. This led to a frequent deprecation of his facility, epitomised in a *Saturday* witticism of 1860: 'Mr Trollope is in the position of a man who, after becoming the father of a vast family in a very short time, takes at last to having twins.'[11]

Such jocularities gradually fostered an unease about the writer which turned in the 1870s to dismay or plain distaste. Given the comparatively unsophisticated state of photography at the time, it may not be surprising that the analogy was made between Trollope's actualising eye and the camera's lens. The *Athenaeum* in 1859 observed, neutrally enough, that 'Mr Trollope writes always with a plain photograph-like reality'.[12] A few years later, Henry James was to make a much more loaded use of the analogy (see his 1865 comments in Part Two below). Donald Smalley's *Trollope: The Critical Heritage* indexes twenty-eight instances of analogy between Trollope's fiction and photography[13] – and this is only among reviews appearing contemporaneously with the first publication of the novels.

The photographical analogy nearly always suggests a belittling criticism, as in the *London Review*'s article on *Framley Parsonage*:

Mr Trollope has not the qualities of some of our ablest writers. He has not the intense humour, nor the sweetness and pathetic tenderness of Dickens; he has not Thackeray's inimitable irony; he has not George Eliot's breadth and boldness; nor Kingsley's earnest genius; but he has his own special qualities of strength and soundness, which make him as charming a companion as any novelist extant. . . .

We are made to feel that 'charm' is a lesser, more bourgeois quality than the virtues enumerated for the other novelists.

Such comparisons with mechanical trades and with photography continued after his death,[14] usually in conjunction with confused argument about 'realism'. Frank O'Connor thus does a great service when he points to the importance that Trollope attached to the 'heart': 'This . . . rather than realism, represents [his] true quality as a novelist' (see excerpt in Part Two below). And, significantly, it is since this liberalising tendency began to make itself felt that studies of Trollope's technique have developed. The strategy and tactics of his rhetoric, for instance, as discussed by Ruth ApRoberts (Part Three below), help to lead us away from the photographer and towards the literary artist.

Thus, the quality and kind of Trollope's imagination may now be seen in a more favourable light (though still often suffused by the author's own apparent denigration of the imaginative faculty in passages of *An Autobiography*), and his selection and manipulation of verbal registers have come to be better appreciated.

His insistence on coining 'humorous' names has been a continuing source of disquiet. First mentioned in a review of *The Three Clerks* as early as 1857 – 'names which of themselves destroy much of the merit of some passages, by reminding us at every moment that we are reading a purely fictitious story' – the classic statement of distaste at the practice is that of Henry James, reproduced in our selection. Quiller-Couch, too, found the habit 'distressing'; and though a couple of modern apologists have argued that the basis of the habit stems from Trollope's reading of Jacobean drama, source is less relevant than effect, and it is difficult to find any commentator who expresses conviction in an approbation of this mannerism.

Trollope's social and political ideas have often been called 'conservative' in contexts which suggest an implicit link with the prosaic nature of his creative imagination. The work of critics like John Halperin has been valuable in re-exploring the relationship between politics and art in the fiction of Trollope.[15] Though not included in this selection because his major work centres on the 'Palliser' novels, Professor Halperin typifies the new directions taken since the 1950s which have approached the novelist through ever-widening perspectives. Both Arthur

Pollard and R. M. Polhemus (represented herein) derive maximum benefit from these extended backgrounds. Pollard enhances our understanding of the text of *The Warden* by documenting the social and political contexts from which the book grew, while Polhemus relates changes in Trollope's art to the flux of Victorian life. Sharp awareness of the novelist's acute sense of time, place and change also shows clearly in the closing paragraphs of Ronald Knox's essay of 1958 (excerpted in Part Two).

The opinions of Trollope's critics in this area of enquiry reveal how complex the case really is. While Frank O'Connor believes Trollope disliked reformers, Ronald Knox finds in the novels an anti-clericalism which is motivated by a reforming zeal. A. O. J. Cockshut believes Trollope, for all his liberal asseverations, to be innately conservative; yet Laurence Lerner dubs him a liberal, and other of my selected critics stress his appreciation of change and of the 'Victorian compromise'. M. A. Goldberg's claim that the novelist is sympathetic to *both* Bold and Grantly in *The Warden* epitomises this complexity. Bill Overton's study of 1982 – published too late for inclusion in this volume – seems to have found the reconciling element in a dichotomy between the 'official' face of Trollope, the civil servant and Establishment-man, and the private, careful, intensive artist who shaped his fiction from 'unofficial' standpoints.[16]

The most uniform praise of Trollope has been for his skill in depicting the character of his heroines. It is difficult to think of any male Victorian novelist who excels him in the sensitive and totally convincing representation of ordinary unheroic young women – though Mrs Proudie is there to remind us that he also had remarkable insight into the more mature female character. Contemporary reviewers instantly took to Trollope's heroines. Mrs Oliphant's outrage at the celibate fate meted out to Lily Dale (see section 2 of Part One) is typical of the sympathy this and other female characters created.

'Trollope settled down to the English girl; he took possession of her', remarked Henry James; and though Leslie Stephen found the young ladies to have 'a small allowance of the romantic' and, indeed, to be 'commonplace', most commentators have followed Quiller-Couch's high praise for Trollope's sympathy and understanding of the female heart, while Elizabeth Bowen shares with Henry James a belief that the heroines have 'something of the fragrance of Imogen and Desdemona'.

★

During the hundred years since Trollope's death, then, the emphasis of criticism has shifted from theme to theme and from attribute to attribute.

So it has been with the status of individual novels within the Barsetshire cycle – indeed, within the Trollope canon as a whole. Recent emphasis has tended to push the clerical novels to one side in favour of either the political or the satirical works. Attention has shifted from the novelist's iteration of normality towards his studies of deranged or disturbed mental states. This promotes a healthy sense of adventure in encouraging the reading of some of the hitherto neglected novels, but it would be quite deplorable if this tendency were to overshadow the massive achievement which constitutes the chronicles of Barsetshire.

The consistent popularity of *The Warden* often nonplusses the academic critics. As the first of the Barchester series, it is certainly the most tentative and the least achieved of the six novels. Yet, as *Emma* is the critics' Jane Austen while *Pride and Prejudice* remains the popular choice, so, whatever Trollopean work the experts may advocate, it will be pretty certain that the average layman who claims to have read only one of the novels will go on to name *The Warden* as that one. Flawed, and in some ways a-typical, it may be – Trollope himself declared that 'it failed altogether in the purport for which it was intended' – yet he took great pride in the imaginative achievement represented by its characters; and something of the simple strength with which they are drawn and with which the plot unfolds catches the general reader's sympathy as none of his more elaborate structures does.

Contemporary critics saw the novel's faults and merits clearly enough. The Warden of Hiram's Hospital himself has been the subject of praise since the very first reviews, and the

Archdeacon was recognised from the outset as a powerful character-study. Much of the subsequent praise of the Venerable Theophilus Grantly, however, comes with the wisdom of hindsight, for the prelate first appearing in *The Warden* is by no means the rounded and complex figure presented so admirably in *Barchester Towers* or *The Last Chronicle*. Indeed, Trollope's satirical animus comes close at times to killing interest in the character in the first novel of the cycle. 'Want of earnestness', 'half-sneering', 'lack of moral clarity' typify contemporary reviewers' reactions to the book. Much of this satirical tone fades away in the later Barsetshire novels as time, and plot, remove them from close association with the real-world ecclesiastical squabble in which *The Warden* had its genesis: a genesis entirely untypical of Trollope's normal practice.

However, other objections raised by the novelist's contemporaries have continued to trouble late critics. The burlesque portraits of Carlyle and Dickens 'are in very bad taste', declared the *Examiner*. Its reviewer found the Archdeacon's three hideous children acceptable, however – though many, more recent critics have not. The *Leader* pinpointed an even more basic bugbear, which is to recur from book to book and from generation to generation: 'Mr Trollope speaks far too much in his own person in the course of his narrative.' (See excerpts in Part Two.) This was a habit he never grew out of – one which to many readers is an irritating mannerism and a threat to the dramatic impact of his narrative. E. S. Dallas, Henry James, Quiller-Couch have all made the same point. 'This pernicious trick', 'these little slaps at credulity', as James described them, had to await a defence from twentieth-century academic ingenuity, and for most readers the mannerism remains unwarrantable.

Some recent estimates have striven to set *The Warden* to one side of Trollope's main achievement. Frank O'Connor's remark (in his excerpt in Part Two) is typical: 'I suspect that if it stood alone, it would be read only by fanatic admirers.' And Ronald Knox's judgement that this novel is not even typical of the series it initiates, being a satire conceived by an author without real satirical bent, draws some sanction from Trollope's own comments in *An Autobiography*.

Anthony Cockshut represents the main stream of critical opinion in finding the book's true centre in the character of the Warden, the Reverend Septimus Harding – 'one of the most appealing of Victorian heroes'. In him Trollope achieved that most difficult of tasks: the portrait of a man who is totally good, yet never dull. Or is there a tinge of satire in the portrait? – as M. A. Goldberg believes. Does Mr Harding's instinct to retreat into a vanishing 'age of equipoise', to disengage from the strife his office has created, give the book an acerbic undertow? Assuredly, *The Warden* is the work of a man who himself appreciated the values of conservatism, the qualities of quietude and decorum. They are values frequently met with in Trollope's fiction. R. M. Polhemus pursues these qualities through the historical moment, to the point where he believes that 'Barsetshire . . . makes the phrase "Victorian compromise" come clear through a healthy and essentially comic juxtaposition of the old and the new'.

Hence *The Warden*, 'small', 'a-typical', 'unsatisfactory' as it may be, can yet provoke thoughtful and fruitful debate. And for anyone prepared to push this novel from the centre of Trollope's achievement, there remains to take account of David Skilton's introduction to the revised World Classics edition (not represented in our selection since it is readily available elsewhere). Skilton claims the novel to be not only vital to the Barsetshire series, but also the germ of the epic achievement in the 'Palliser' novels.[17]

With the writing of *Barchester Towers*, Trollope extended the range of his imagination. Setting and plot here are on a bolder scale than in *The Warden*, and the character-drawing is perhaps as rich as any he ever achieved. It is a novel simply full of excellencies: the henpecked Bishop and his dominating wife; the Thornes of Ullathorne, who so perfectly represent the Trollopean ability to mock and sympathise conjointly; the Stanhope menage. More than with any other single figure, however, it is the remarkable and highly imaginative development of the Archdeacon into a rounded and complex character which marks Trollope's development between the two first Barsetshire novels. The author's 'great delight' in the writing of

Barchester Towers is reflected in the book's sense of poise and achievement.

The satire here is less local, and more genial, than in *The Warden* – neither seizing on a particular episode from contemporary affairs, nor venturing into those contentious attacks on fellow-writers which had marred the earlier novel. Yet no single review was unequivocally laudatory. The areas of unease may not coincide, but, for all the praise accorded the book, they are always there. Trollope narrows his range; he deals only with 'what may be called the second class of good people', said one article. In a few years' time this will harden into an accusation of imaginative deficiency. The *Westminster Review* critic raises what is to become a principal indictment among the anti-Trollopeans: 'Mr Trollope seems wanting in certain of the higher elements that make a great novelist. He does not exhibit much sway over the emotional part of our nature.' Henry James's stricture (of 1865) that 'he has diminished the real elements of passion' is prefigured here – as are the repeated claims that Trollope lacks imagination which takes powerful shape in Leslie Stephen's essay of 1901.

Stephen even objected to Archdeacon Grantly. Few others have been prepared to join him in this stand. Ronald Knox and Frank O'Connor are much more in the mainstream in noting the deepening subtlety of the characterisation in *Barchester Towers*.

The Stanhopes have been a bone of contention ever since Longman's reader turned up his nose at the character of Madeline. Yet for Ronald Knox they are the making of the book; while the tight-knit quality of its plotting is admired by Pamela Hansford Johnson. She is able to show how this 'beautiful and intricate fabric' places the infamous Madeline at its very centre.

William Cadbury (in the excerpt in Part Three) examines the architectonics of *Barchester Towers* even more closely. He argues that in this novel Trollope, almost uniquely, made the attempt to 'present a unified world without involving us so deeply in any of his characters that they monopolise our attention'. An uncharacteristic distance thus exists between author and characters: an opinion which leads Cadbury to the

ingenious and cogent defence of Trollope's intrusive narrator-
ial voice.

'At the proud apex of the pyramid of Trollope fiction the tale
of *Doctor Thorne* [is] perpetually enthroned', declared Michael
Sadleir. Nothing in its author's own account of the book quite
justifies such hyperbole. Indeed, gratified as he was by its
financial success, Trollope expressed surprise at its popularity.
Early reviewers found less fault this time, though the *Leader*
once again reproved him for the habit of taking his readers into
his confidence in so obtrusive a *propria persona*; and the *Saturday
Review* (beginning to lose its initial approval of Trollope) made
this point even more strongly. Most of the contemporary critics
seem a little disturbed even amid their enthusiasm. The book *is*
good – but isn't it time that the new master-novelist did
something excellent rather than just good? This bewildered
irritation grows more and more discernible over the next five or
six years, until many of the reviewers end by giving up Trollope
in disgust or amused despair. He simply refused (was unable?)
to develop the role of entertainer into that of sage.

Doctor Thorne divides his admirers more radically than any
other of the Barsetshire novels. If Sadleir typifies one camp,
Frank O'Connor speaks for the other: 'a book I find extremely
dull.' Significantly, perhaps, there is no good modern criticism
of this novel, outside the introductions in some editions to the
novel itself. Elizabeth Bowen's (excerpted in Part Three) is the
best of these. Admitting the novel's apparently disastrous
tactics in its first two chapters, she is yet able to demonstrate
how Trollope's love of honour, grace and courage irradiate the
book and make it, for her at least, one of his most endearing
achievements.

Trollope can at times be gruff and self-deprecatory about his
own successes, as we have seen. So it is with *Framley Parsonage*,
which he termed 'a hodge-podge . . . nothing could be less
efficient or artistic'. Most reviewers liked it, however – though
again with reservations which our selection attempts to typify.
It has been a favourite, too, with most twentieth-century
commentators, from Quiller-Couch to P. D. Edwards. The
latter (excerpted in Part Three) points to the excellence of
characterisation in Lord Lufton as well as in Lucy Robarts as

a unifying principle in the novel. His praise of Lucy as worthy of consideration as a 'Shakespearean' heroine would have pleased Trollope, who thought her his best-drawn study of a young woman.

Yet there has been some feeling that the intellectual daring which so nearly broke through in *Barchester Towers*, and even the satirical animus of *The Warden*, are missing, and that the lack of them leaves *Framley Parsonage* in danger of being swallowed up in its own middle-class blandness. It is debatable whether the tentative forays into the world of politics, through the Harold Smith episodes, achieve that variety of tone and temper they seem intended for. They were not much liked by contemporary reviewers, and few critics since have spoken positively in their praise. The interest in these chapters lies in their revelation of an increasing concern with politics, which was to receive a much fuller and more balanced treatment in the parliamentary novels a few years later.

Though Trollope much admired Lucy Robarts, he always declared that Lily Dale in *The Small House at Allington* was 'a female prig'. Yet for many readers she is one of his most moving characters. It certainly seems artistically right that she does not marry Johnny Eames; but it is so unusual for Trollope, in the 1860s, *not* to reward his heroine with a comfortable home and husband that Lily's case has struck readers as particularly hard. The rights and wrongs of her response to being jilted occupy the centre of critical debate about the book.

The character of Eames has caused wide divergence of opinion, too. Bradford Booth (whose study of the novel we select for presentation in Part Three) is of the Eames camp – unlike his fellow-Americans Richard and Lucy Stebbins, who found Eames 'loud-mouthed and boorish'. Even Crosbie finds his advocates: surely not a point of view Trollope would have agreed with. The degree of disagreement is surprising in so apparently uncontentious a novel.

Which ever is the 'weakest' of the six Barsetshire novels – and in the end it is Bradford Booth's conclusion that this description fits *The Small House at Allington* – there is not much doubt about which is the most powerful. If this is universally acknowledged, so is the fact that the source of that power is the extraordinarily vehement depth of feeling with which Trollope extended his previous sketch, in *Framley Parsonage*, of the Reverend Josiah Crawley. For many critics, the Crawley of *The Last Chronicle of Barset* is as near as Trollope ever came to absolute greatness. The portrait of the harassed, poverty-stricken and stiffly proud clergyman has even been likened to King Lear in the character's partly self-induced suffering and in the intensity with which his creator shares his mind.

In showing how the 'contrariety' of Mr Crawley contributes to the novel's sense of tragedy, Ruth ApRoberts is able to suggest (in her study included in Part Three) that Trollope employs this theme with disturbing frequency, and that its presence in the subplots of *The Last Chronicle* may fuse the work into a unity which is not normally accorded it. For it is the customary argument that, for all that this novel comes near to greatness, its subsidiary plotting and characters are inferior. Laurence Lerner, who provides the countervailing approach in our selection, holds that the Dobbs Broughton material, in particular, flaws the structure.

Yet, in a novel where Josiah Crawley normally holds pre-eminent attention, Lerner does well to remind us of the triumphant writing in the Proudie plot; and he shrewdly suggests that it is not the famous death of Mrs Proudie which provides the central strength of this part of the book, but the breaking of the Bishop's heart, which draws the Barsetshire sequel towards a close in a manner every whit as conclusive and moving as the Crawley material itself.

NOTES

1. Anthony Cockshut, *Anthony Trollope: A Critical Study* (London, 1955).

2. Quoted – by Michael Sadleir, *Trollope: A Commentary* (1927; revised edition, London, 1945), p. 197 – from Edmund Yates, *His Recollections and Experiences* (London, 1884).

3. Anthony Trollope, *An Autobiography* (1883); World Classics collection, ed. M. Sadleir (1947; reprinted, Oxford, 1961), pp. 313–14.

4. *The Letters of Anthony Trollope*, ed. Bradford A. Booth (1951; new edition, London, 1980).

5. Quoted from a contemporary review of *John Caldigate* (published 1879).

6. Lance Tingay, 'Trollope's Popularity: A Statistical Approach', *Nineteenth-Century Fiction*, 11 (1957).

7. Elizabeth Bowen, *Trollope: A New Judgement* (London, 1946).

8. Hugh Walpole, *Anthony Trollope* (London, 1929); C. P. Snow, *Trollope* (London and Basingstoke, 1975).

9. David Skilton, *Anthony Trollope and His Contemporaries* (London, 1972).

10. R. H. Hutton, in the *Spectator*, xxxv (Oct. 1862).

11. *Saturday Review* (19 May 1860).

12. *Athenaeum* (26 March 1859).

13. Donald Smalley, *Trollope: The Critical Heritage* (London, 1969), p. 568.

14. Ibid., pp. 11–13.

15. See particularly John Halperin, *Trollope and Politics* (London, 1970).

16. Bill Overton, *The Unofficial Trollope* (Brighton, 1982).

17. David Skilton, Introduction to *The Warden* (World Classics collection, revised edition, Oxford, 1980).

PART ONE

Trollope and His Contemporaries

1. TROLLOPE ON HIS ART AND PRACTICE

I From *The Letters*

. . . if you don't like it, do it again. It is a great profession, that of writing; but you must spoil much paper and undergo many doubting, weary, wretched hours . . .

> From a letter to Kate Field, 6 January 1862: quoted from Bradford A. Booth (ed.), *The Letters of Anthony Trollope* (1951; new edition London, 1980), p. 104.

. . . I believe that the profession requires much less of what is extraordinary either in genius or knowledge than most outsiders presume to be necessary. But it requires that which all other professions require – but which outsiders do not in general presume to be necessary . . . considerable training and much hard grinding industry.   (ibid., p. 57)

. . . I cannot believe the Old Testament because labour is spoken of as the *evil* consequence of the Fall of Man. My only doubt as to finding a heaven for myself at last arises from the fear that the disembodied and beatified spirits will not want novels.   (ibid., p. 286)

II From *An Autobiography*

Development of the Imagination
. . . As a boy . . . I was thrown much upon myself. . . . Thus it came to pass that I was always going about with some castle in

the air firmly built within my mind. . . . For weeks, for months,
. . . from year to year, I would carry on the same tale, binding
myself down to certain laws, to certain proportions, and
proprieties, and unities. . . . I myself was of course my own
hero. Such is a necessity of castle-building. But I never became
a king, or a duke, . . . I never was a learned man, nor even a
philosopher. But I was a very clever person, and beautiful
young women used to be fond of me. And I strove to be kind of
heart, and open of hand, and noble in thought, despising mean
things; . . . I learned in this way to maintain an interest in a
fictitious story, to dwell on a work created by my own
imagination, . . . In after years I have done the same, – with this
difference, that I have . . . been able to lay my own identity
aside.

From *An Autobiography*, modern edition (Oxford, 1980), pp.
117–42.

Plot and Character

. . . A novel should give a picture of common life enlivened by
humour and sweetened by pathos. To make that picture
worthy of attention, the canvas should be crowded with real
portraits, not of individuals known to the world or to the
author, but of created personages impregnated with traits of
character which are known. To my thinking, the plot is but the
vehicle for all this; and when you have the vehicle without the
passengers, a story of mystery in which the agents never spring
to life, you have but a wooden show. There must, however, be a
story. You must provide a vehicle of some sort.

  (ibid., p. 126)

Teaching and Entertaining

. . . The writer of stories must please, or he will be nothing. And
he must teach whether he wish to teach or no. How shall he
teach lessons of virtue and at the same time make himself a
delight to his readers? That sermons are not in themselves often
thought to be agreeable we all know. Nor are disquisitions on
moral philosophy supposed to be pleasant light reading for our
idle hours. But the novelist, if he have a conscience, must
preach his sermons with the same purpose as the clergyman,

and must have his own system of ethics . . . make virtue alluring and vice ugly, while he charms his reader instead of wearying him.   (ibid., p. 222)

. . . There are many who would laugh at the idea of a novelist teaching either virtue or nobility, – those, for instance, who regard the reading of novels as a sin, and those also who think it to be simply an idle pastime. . . . I have regarded my art from so different a point of view that I have ever thought of myself as a preacher of sermons, and my pulpit as one which I could make both salutary and agreeable to my audience. I do believe that no girl has risen from the reading of my pages less modest than she was before, and that some may have learned from them that modesty is a charm well worth preserving. I think that no youth has been taught that in falseness and flashness is to be found the road to manliness; but some may perhaps have learned from me that it is to be found in truth and a high but gentle spirit. Such are the lessons I have striven to teach; and I have thought that it might best be done by representing to my readers characters like themselves, – or to which they might liken themselves.   (ibid., p. 146)

Methods of Composition
. . . It was while I was engaged on *Barchester Towers* that I adopted a system of writing which, for some years afterwards, I found to be very serviceable to me. . . . I found that I passed in railway-carriages very many hours of my existence. Like others, I used to read . . . But if I intended to make a profitable business out of my writing, and, at the same time, to do my best for the Post Office, I must turn these hours to more account than I could do even by reading. I made for myself therefore a tablet, and found after a few days' exercise that I could write as quickly in a railway-carriage as I could at my desk. I worked with a pencil, and what I wrote my wife copied afterwards. In this way was composed the greater part of *Barchester Towers* and of the novel which succeeded it, and much also of others subsequent to them. My only objection to the practice came from the appearance of literary ostentation, to which I found

myself to be subject when going to work before four or five fellow-passengers. But I got used to it.   (ibid., pp. 102–3)

Early Hours

. . . Few men I think ever lived a fuller life, and I attribute the power of doing this altogether to the virtue of early hours. It was my practice to be at my table every morning at 5.30 a.m.; and it was also my practice to allow myself no mercy. An old groom, whose business it was to call me, and to whom I paid £5 a year extra for the duty, allowed himself no mercy. During all those years . . . he never was once late with the coffee which it was his duty to bring me. I do not know that I ought not to feel that I owe more to him than to any one else for the success I have had. By beginning at that hour I could complete my literary work before I dressed for breakfast.   (ibid., p. 271)

Work-Diaries

. . . When I have commenced a new book, I have always prepared a diary, divided into weeks, and carried on for the period which I have allowed myself for the completion of the work. In this I have entered, day by day, the number of pages I have written, so that if at any time I have slipped into idleness for a day or two, the record of that idleness has been there, staring me in the face, and demanding of me increased labour, so that the deficiency might be supplied. According to the circumstances of the time, – whether my other business might be then heavy or light, or whether the book which I was writing was or was not wanted with speed, – I have allotted myself so many pages a week. The average number has been about 40. It has been placed as low as 20, and has risen to 112. And as a page is an ambiguous term, my page has been made to contain 250 words; and as words, if not watched, will have a tendency to straggle, I have had every word counted as I went. . . . I have prided myself on completing my work exactly within the proposed dimensions. But I have prided myself especially on completing it within the proposed time, – and I have always done so. There has ever been the record before me, and a week passed with an insufficient number of pages has been a blister to my eye, and a month so disgraced would have been a sorrow to my heart.   (ibid., pp. 118–19)

Writing by the Clock

. . . three hours a day will produce as much as a man ought to write. But then, he should have so trained himself that he shall be able to work continuously during those three hours, – so have tutored his mind that it shall not be necessary for him to sit nibbling his pen, and gazing at the wall before him, till he shall have found the words with which he wants to express his ideas. It had become my custom, – and it still is . . . to write with my watch before me, and to require from myself 250 words every quarter of an hour. I have found that the 250 words have been forthcoming as regularly as my watch went. But my three hours were not devoted entirely to writing. I always began my task by reading the work of the day before . . . weighing with my ear the sound of the words and phrases. . . . By reading what he has last written, just before he recommences his task, the writer will catch the tone and spirit of what he is then saying.

     (ibid., pp. 272–3)

Imaginative Symbiosis

. . . When my work has been quickest done, . . . the rapidity has been achieved by hot pressure, not in the conception, but in the telling of the story. . . . I have trebled my usual average, and have done so in circumstances which have enabled me to give up all my thoughts for the time to the book I have been writing. This has generally been done at some quiet spot among the mountains, – where there has been no society, no hunting, no whist, no ordinary household duties. And I am sure that the work so done has had in it the best truth and the highest spirit that I have been able to produce. At such times I have been able to imbue myself thoroughly with the characters I have had in hand. I have wandered alone among the rocks and woods, crying at their grief, laughing at their absurdities, and thoroughly enjoying their joy. I have been impregnated with my own creations till it has been my only excitement to sit with the pen in my hand, and drive my team before me at as quick a pace as I could make them travel.   (ibid., pp. 175–6)

... I have never troubled myself much about the construction of plots. ... I am not sure that the construction of a perfected plot has been at any period within my power. But the novelist has other aims than the elucidation of his plot. He desires to make his readers so intimately acquainted with his characters that the creations of his brain should be to them speaking, moving, living, human creatures. This he can never do unless he know those fictitious personages himself, and he can never know them well unless he can live with them in the full reality of established intimacy. They must be with him as he lies down to sleep, and as he wakes from his dreams. He must learn to hate them and to love them. He must argue with them, quarrel with them, forgive them, and even submit to them. He must know of them whether they be cold-blooded or passionate, whether true or false, and how far true, and how far false. The depth and the breadth, and the narrowness and the shallowness of each should be clear to him. And as, here in our outer world, we know that men and women change, – become worse or better as temptation or conscience may guide them, – so should these creations of his change, and every change should be noted by him. On the last day of each month recorded, every person in his novel should be a month older than on the first. If the would-be novelist have aptitudes that way, all this will come to him without much struggling; – but if it do not come, I think he can only make novels of wood.

It is so that I have lived with my characters, and thence has come whatever success I have attained. There is a gallery of them, and of all in that gallery I may say that I know the tone of the voice, and the colour of the hair, every flame of the eye, and the very clothes they wear. Of each man I could assert whether he would have said these or the other words; of every woman, whether she would then have smiled or so have frowned.

(ibid., pp. 232–3)

Inspiration

... There are those who . . . think that the man who works with his imagination should allow himself to wait till – inspiration moves him. When I have heard such doctrine preached, I have hardly been able to repress my scorn. To me it would not be more absurd if the shoemaker were to wait for inspiration or the tallow-chandler for the divine moment of melting. . . . *Mens sana in corpore sano*! The author wants that as does every other workman, – that and a habit of industry. I was once told that the surest aid to the writing of a book was a piece of cobbler's wax on my chair. I certainly believe in the cobbler's wax more than the inspiration.

It will be said, perhaps, that a man whose work has risen to no higher pitch than mine has attained, has no right to speak of the strains and impulses to which real genius is exposed. I am ready to admit the great variations in brain power which are exhibited by the products of different men, and am not disposed to rank my own very high; but my experience tells me that a man can always do the work for which his brain is fitted if he will give himself the habit of regarding his work as a normal condition of his life. I therefore venture to advise young men who look forward to authorship as the business of their lives, even when they propose that that authorship be of the highest class known, to avoid enthusiastic rushes with their pens, and to seat themselves at their desks day by day as though they were lawyers' clerks, – and so let them sit till the allotted task shall be accomplished.   (ibid., pp. 120–22)

Money and Artistic Integrity
. . . I have certainly always had . . . before my eyes the charms of reputation. Over and above the money view of the question, I wished from the beginning to be something more than a clerk in the Post Office. To be known as somebody, – to be Anthony Trollope if it be no more, – is to me much. The feeling is a very general one, and I think beneficent. It is that which has been called the 'last infirmity of noble mind'. The infirmity is so human that the man who lacks it is either above or below humanity. I own to the infirmity. But I confess that my first object in taking to literature as a profession was that which is common to the barrister when he goes to the Bar, and to the baker when he sets up his oven. I wished to make an income on which I . . . might live in comfort.

If indeed a man writes his books badly, or paints his pictures badly, because he can make his money faster in that fashion than by doing them well, and at the same time proclaims them to be the best he can do . . . he is dishonest, as is any other fraudulent dealer. . . . No doubt the author or the artist may have a difficulty . . . in settling within himself what is good work and what bad, – when labour enough has been given, and when the task has been scamped. It is a danger as to which he is bound to be severe within himself – in which he should feel that his conscience should be set fairly in the balance against the natural bias of his interest. If he do not do so, sooner or later his dishonesty will be discovered, and he will be estimated accordingly. But in this he is to be bound only by the plain rules of honesty which should govern us all. Having said so much, I shall not scruple . . . to attribute to the pecuniary result of my labours all the importance which I felt them to have.

(pp. 107–8)

. . . I am well aware that there are many who think that an author in his authorship should not regard money. . . . I do not know that this unnatural self-sacrifice is supposed to extend itself further. A barrister, a clergyman, a doctor, an engineer, and even actors and architects, may without disgrace follow the bent of human nature, and endeavour to fill their bellies and clothe their backs . . . as comfortably as they can by the exercise of their abilities and their crafts. They may be as rationally realistic, as may the butchers and the bakers; but the artist and the author forget the high glories of their calling if they condescend to make a money return a first object. They who preach this doctrine will be much offended by my theory . . . . They require the practice of a so-called virtue which is contrary to nature, and which, in my eyes, would be no virtue if it were practised. They are like clergymen who preach sermons against the love of money, but who know that the love of money is so distinctive a characteristic of humanity that such sermons are mere platitudes called for by customary but unintelligent piety. All material progress has come from man's desire to do the best he can for himself and those about him, and civilisation and Christianity itself have been made possible by such progress.

(pp. 105–6)

On Barsetshire

. . . as I wrote . . . I have become more closely acquainted than ever with the new shire which I had added to the English counties. I had it all in my mind, – its roads and railroads, its towns and parishes, its members of Parliament, and the different hunts which rode over it. I knew all the great lords and their castles, the squires and their parks, the rectors and their churches. . . . and as I wrote . . . I made a map of the dear county. Throughout these stories there has been no name given to a fictitious site which does not represent to me a spot of which I know all the accessories, as though I had lived and wandered there.   (ibid., p. 154)

2. COMMENT BY TROLLOPE AND CONTEMPORARY REVIEWERS

The Warden   (publication 1855)

Comment by its Author

On the Genesis of the Novel   . . . I visited Salisbury, and whilst
wandering there on a midsummer evening round the purlieus
of the cathedral I conceived the story of *The Warden*, – from
whence came that series of novels of which Barchester, with its
bishops, deans, and archdeacons, was the central site. I may as
well declare at once that no one at their commencement could
have had less reason than myself to presume himself to be able
to write about clergymen. I have been often asked in what
period of my early life I had lived so long in a cathedral city as to
have become intimate with the ways of a Close. I never lived in
any cathedral city, – except London; never knew anything of
any Close, and at that time had enjoyed no peculiar intimacy
with any clergyman. . . . I had to pick up as I went whatever I
might know or pretend to know about them. But my first idea
had no reference to clergymen in general. I had been struck by
two opposite evils, – or what seemed to me to be evils, – and
with an absence of all art-judgement in such matters, I thought
that I might be able to expose them, or rather to describe them,
both in one and the same tale. The first evil was the possession
by the Church of certain funds and endowments which had
been intended for charitable purposes, but which had been
allowed to become incomes for idle Church dignitaries. There
had been more than one such case brought to public notice at
the time, in which there seemed to have been an egregious

malversation of charitable purposes. The second evil was its
very opposite. Though I had been much struck by the injustice
above described, I had also often been angered by the
undeserved severity of the newspapers towards the recipients of
such incomes, who could hardly be considered to be the chief
sinners in the matter . . . . I felt that there had been some
tearing to pieces which might have been spared. But I was
altogether wrong in supposing that the two things could be
combined . . . and I now know myself well enough to be aware
that I was not the man to have carried out either of them.

On the Characterisation　. . . I have already said of the work
that it failed altogether in the purport for which it was intended.
But it has a merit of its own, – a merit by my own perception of
which I was enabled to see wherein lay whatever strength I did
possess. The characters of the bishop, of the archdeacon, of the
archdeacon's wife, and especially of the warden, are all well
and clearly drawn. I had realised to myself a series of portraits,
and had been able so to put them on the canvas that my readers
should see that which I meant them to see. There is no gift
which an author can have more useful to him than this. And the
style of the English was good, though from most unpardonable
carelessness the grammar was not unfrequently faulty. With
such results I had no doubt but that I would at once begin
another novel.

On the Archdeacon　. . . My archdeacon, who has been said to
be life-like, and for whom I confess that I have all a parent's
fond affection, was, I think, the simple result of an effort of my
moral consciousness. It was such as that, in my opinion, that an
archdeacon should be, – or, at any rate, would be with such
advantages as an archdeacon might have; and lo! an
archdeacon was produced who has been declared by competent
authorities to be a real archdeacon down to the very ground.
And yet, as far as I can remember, I had not then ever spoken to
an archdeacon.

On the Remuneration　. . . The novel-reading world did not go

mad about *The Warden*; but I soon felt that it had not failed. . . .
There were notices of it in the press, and I could discover that
people around me knew that I had written a book. . . . At the
end of 1855 I received a cheque for £9 8s. 8d., which was the
first money I had ever earned by literary work . . . . At the end
of 1856 I received another sum of £10 15s. 1d. The pecuniary
success was not great. Indeed, as regarded remuneration for
the time, stone-breaking would have done better.

SOURCE: extracts from *An Autobiography*, pp. 92–5, 98, 93, 98.

'EXAMINER'   (6 January 1855)

The Warden is a clever novel, though we are not quite content
with it. . . . Mr Trollope has done well to paint his warden as a
worthy old gentleman, a player of the violoncello, a believer in
all goodness; generous, gentle, sensitive; accepting his position
without sense of wrong, where nobody had ever hinted that
wrong was; stung to the quick as soon as his eyes were opened to
the unworthy character of his position; throwing his office up at
last when none required that he should do so, and retiring into
noble poverty. Mr Trollope has done well in this, and he has
painted the warden's character with not a little skill. It is well,
also, to have shown how the old men of the charity suffered
from the vigour of the efforts made in their behalf. But at the
same time there is a half-mocking spirit put into the account of
John Bold's proceedings – a half-sneering at his 'Roman virtue'
– which will tend to confuse some readers as to Mr Trollope's
real meaning. The vigorous sketch of the Archdeacon, the pillar
of all clerical abuse – harsh, overbearing, worldly – will indeed
keep the reader's mind from wandering too far astray as to the
actual intention, but it is not, on the whole, so clearly put as it
should be, if the book be meant for a didactic novel.

There are a good many touches of satire pointed at
contemporaries scattered about the book. The addition to the

household of the Archdeacon, of three sons . . . whose
characters are taken from three bishops frequently before the
public, has an effect now and then amusing. But the
introduction of the *Times* newspaper into the novel is not
managed in good taste, and the imitations of *Times* leaders are
far from clever. The caricatures and burlesques of living writers
are also in very bad taste . . . . As to its main scheme it is well
invented, and much of it is well written, though the invention of
the scenes is often better than the composition of them. The vice
of the whole is that its matter is not at all times well felt, and
that it shows the author's need of a much stricter education of
his taste.

[Unsigned review, p. 5. Donald Smalley suggests the author
may be John Forster, the friend and biographer of Dickens;
cf. Smalley's *Trollope: The Critical Heritage* (London, 1969), p.
307 – Ed.]

'LEADER'   (17 February 1855)

. . . The defective part of the book is the conclusion, which
seems to us careless and unsatisfactory – as if the author had got
tired of his subject before he had done with it. The passing
introduction too of living authors, under farcically fictitious
names, for the sake of criticising their books is a mistake . . . .
[We] will venture to point out . . . two defects in his manner as a
writer which he may easily remedy . . . . The first of the defects
is, that Mr Trollope speaks far too much in his own person in
the course of his narrative. It is always the reader's business,
never the author's, to apostrophize characters. The 'illusion of
the scene' is invariably perilled, or lost altogether, when the
writer harangues in his own person on the behaviour of his
characters, or gives us, with an intrusive 'I', his own
experiences of the houses in which he describes those
characters as living. . . .

The second defect of manner . . . is a want of thorough
earnestness in the treatment of the more serious passages of his

story. The mocking tone is well enough where the clerical aristocracy, and the abuses on which they live, form the subject for treatment. But where the main interest touches on the domain of real feeling – as in the chapter which illustrates the filial affection of the Warden's daughter, and the struggle between love and duty in the heart of her reforming lover – it is vitally important to the true effect of the scene on the reader, that the author should at least appear to feel sincerely with his characters. This Mr Trollope, in the case of the young lady especially, seems to avoid. He exposes the womanly weakness of some of her motives with an easy satirical pleasantry which convinces us that he was himself not in the least affected by his love scene while he was writing it.

[Unsigned review, pp. 164–5 – Ed.]

'ECLECTIC REVIEW'   (March 1855)

There is considerable talent displayed in this volume. It is visible in the delineation of character rather than in the construction of the plot. The latter is meagre and unsatisfactory, wanting a moral, and failing to satisfy reasonable expectations; but the former is spirited and clever, frequently effecting by a few bold touches what a more elaborate description might fail to accomplish. . . . In the sketch of the Bishop of Barchester and of his son, Dr Grantly, as also in that of the feeble-minded but conscientious warden, much descriptive power is evinced. There is, however, one defect in the volume, which . . . mars the whole. A *moral* is wanting. To say nothing of the fact – in itself significant – that the views of the author on the subject of ecclesiastical revenue are not apparent, there is no fitting end attained by all which is done. The only result of the measures adopted by John Bold is to unsettle everything, and to make all parties miserable. The bishop, the dean, the warden, the bedesmen, John Bold himself and the queen of his idolatry, are all perplexed and rendered wretched. The impression left, so far as it assumes any definite form, is that of regret at the affairs of the hospital having been brought into question. The facts of the case are sufficiently indicative of the inequitable arrangement maintained. But there is no indication of the better things that might have been done with the property bequeathed. Everything is left in disorder and ruin, as though the design of the writer was to teach the folly of attempting to rectify abuses which have grown up under our charitable trusts. It would have been a better, a wiser, and certainly a more useful course, to have shown how such funds might have administered to the comfort and well-being of a much larger number of aged men.

[Unsigned review: new series, IX, pp. 359–61 – Ed.]

Barchester Towers (publication 1857)

COMMENT BY ITS AUTHOR

. . . In the writing of *Barchester Towers* I took great delight. The Bishop and Mrs Proudie were very real to me, as were also the troubles of the archdeacon and the loves of Mr Slope. When it was done, Mr W. Longman required that it should be subjected to his reader; and he returned the MS. to me, with a most laborious and voluminous criticism, – coming from whom I never knew.[1] This was accompanied by an offer to print the novel on the half-profit system, with a payment of £100 in advance out of my half-profits, – on condition that I would comply with the suggestions made by his critic. One of these suggestions required that I should cut the novel down to two volumes. In my reply, I went through the criticisms, rejecting one and accepting another, almost alternately, but declaring at last that no consideration should induce me to put out a third of my work. I am at a loss to know how such a task could be perfor%med. I could burn the MS., no doubt, and write another book on the same story; but how two words out of every six are to be withdrawn from a written novel, I cannot conceive. . . . Mr Longman was too gracious to insist on his critic's terms; the book was published, certainly none the worse, and I do not think much the better, for the care that had been taken with it.

The work succeeded just as *The Warden* had succeeded. It achieved no great reputation, but it was one of the novels which novel readers were called upon to read. Perhaps I may be assuming more to myself than I have a right to do in saying now that *Barchester Towers* has become one of those novels which do not die quite at once, which live and are read for perhaps a quarter of a century; but if that be so, its life has been so far prolonged by the vitality of some of its younger brothers. *Barchester Towers* would hardly be so well known as it is had there been no *Framley Parsonage* and no *Last Chronicle of Barset*.

SOURCE: extract from *An Autobiography*, pp. 103–4.

NOTE

1. [Ed.] This reader's report and the ensuing correspondence may be found in Michael Sadleir, *Trollope: A Commentary* (1927); revised edition (London, 1945), pp. 160–5.

'SATURDAY REVIEW'   (30 May 1857)

Barchester Towers is a very clever book. Indeed it is, if anything, too clever, and the whole story is rather too much a series of brilliant but disjointed sketches. It is a continuation of . . . *The Warden*, and it is written in the same vein, but with more power and finish. . . . Every chapter is full of fresh amusement; and although we know that poetical justice is sure ultimately to fall heavily on the chaplain, for a long time he has it all his own way, and treads on the necks of his foes. Such a conflict is a hard matter to describe. It is necessary to make it lively, and yet real

– to give characteristic touches, and yet escape vulgarity – to
handle theological disputes without bitterness, injustice, or
profanity. Considering the dangers he runs, Mr Trollope's
success is wonderfully great. The theologians, unlike most
theologians in novels, are thoroughly human, and retain the
mixed nature of ordinary men; and, what is more, they are
described impartially. The author is not a party writer, trying
to run down the wrong party by painting it all black and the
right party all white. He sees and paints the follies of either
extreme. Then, again, he has the merit of avoiding the excess of
exaggeration. He possesses an especial talent for drawing what
may be called the second-class of good people – characters not
noble, superior, or perfect, after the standard of human
perfection, but still good and honest, with a fundamental basis
of sincerity, kindliness, and religious principle, yet with a
considerable proneness to temptation, and a strong
consciousness that they live, and like to live, in a struggling,
party-giving, comfort-seeking world. Such people are so
common, and form so very large a proportion of the betterish
and more respectable classes, that it requires a keen perception
of the ludicrous, and some power of satire, to give distinctness
to the types taken from their ranks by the novelist. Mr Trollope
manages to do this admirably; and though his pudding may
have the fault of being all plums, yet we cannot deny it is
excellent eating.

[Unsigned review: III, pp. 503–4 – Ed.]

'Examiner'   (16 May 1857)

. . . it does not depend only on story for its interest; the careful
writing, the good humour with a tendency often to be Shandean
in its expression, and the sense and right feeling with which the
way is threaded among questions of high church and low
church, are very noticeable, and secure for it unquestionable
rank among the few really well-written tales that every season
furnishes.

[Unsigned review, p. 308 – Ed.]

'SPECTATOR'   (16 May 1857)

. . . In a technical sense, there is greater variety in *Barchester Towers* than in *The Warden*, and consequently more of the novel. From this very extension and complexity it is scarcely so complete or satisfactory a book. The first work was obviously a satire, in which caricature is allowable provided the features of the person or the points of the case are markedly presented. This licence does not extend to the more regular novel, and Mr Trollope has a peculiarity that lessens his power in this direction. His characters are frequently rather abstractions of qualities than actual persons. They are rather the *made* results of skill and thought than the spontaneous productions of genius operating instinctively.

[Unsigned review: xxx, pp. 525–6 – Ed.]

'WESTMINSTER REVIEW'   (October 1857)

. . . decidedly the cleverest novel of the season, and one of the most masculine delineations of modern life in a special class of society. . . . Mr Trollope has satisfactorily solved a problem in this production. He has, without resorting to politics, or setting out as a social reformer, given us a novel that men can enjoy, and a satire so cleverly interwoven with the story, that every incident and development renders it more pointed and telling. In general our modern prose satirists spread their canvas for a common tale, out of which they start when the occasion suits, to harangue, exhort, and scold the world in person. Mr Trollope entrusts all this to the individuals of his story . . . . Man's great ambition to become a Bishop, and woman's wonderful art in ruling one, cannot fail to interest us exceedingly, and we hurry on without a halt to the overthrow of Slope and the rare act of self-immolation whereby the Rev. Mr Harding refuses a deanery . . . and bestows it on his son-in-law. . . . Mr Slope is possessed of extraordinary powers. He cannot move without inspiring nausea . . . yet he contrives to make men jealous of him. We have all of us met somebody like Mr Slope, and wished that, if he indeed could lay claim to the odour of sanctity, it were pleasanter to the poor human sense of smell. . . .

Mr Trollope seems wanting in certain of the higher elements that make a great novelist. He does not exhibit much sway over the emotional part of our nature . . . .

[Unsigned review: LXVIII, pp. 594–6 – Ed.]

Doctor Thorne (publication 1858)

COMMENT BY ITS AUTHOR

. . . I had finished *The Three Clerks* just before I left England, and when in Florence was cudgelling my brain for a new plot. Being then with my brother, I asked him to sketch me a plot, and he drew out that of my next novel, called *Doctor Thorne*. I mention this particularly, because it was the only occasion in which I have had recourse to any other source than my own brains for the thread of a story. How far I may unconsciously have adopted incidents from what I have read, – either from history or from works of imagination, – I do not know. . . . But when doing it I have not been aware that I have done it. I have never taken another man's work, and deliberately framed my work upon it. . . . It might probably have been better for my readers if I had done so, as I am informed that *Doctor Thorne* . . . has a larger sale than any other book of mine.

SOURCE: extract from *An Autobiography*, pp. 115–16.

'LEADER'   (29 May 1858)

We are heartily disposed to place the author of *Doctor Thorne*
among the extremely select few . . . . Indeed, we are prepared
to name him among the illustrious living writers of fiction . . . .
Each of the works that he has yet produced has been stamped
with its own independent and original characteristics; each has
gained in strength on the preceeding; each has been an advance
towards a higher and more assured excellence. . . . In *The
Warden*, in *Barchester Towers* . . . he has manifested a real
inventive faculty and a real constructive ingenuity; above all, a
real insight into human character and into the complexities of
human motives. . . . Above all, there was in each and all of
these remarkable fictions a strong purpose, not obtruded . . .
with didactic dulness nor merely subsidiary . . . but piercing
through the story as a good or evil purpose pierces through an
individual life. Defects, of course, were obvious to the critical
eye: defects of craft, of style, and of humour. The conduct of the
story was a little careless, not marching straight on. . . . The
style was occasionally bald and lax; and the exaggeration of
character was apt to degenerate into caricature.

In *Doctor Thorne* we cannot fairly say that these defects have
entirely disappeared, but they are sensibly mitigated, and we
think amply compensated. Considering that he does not stake
his reputation and success on character-painting only, but
quite as much on his constructive ingenuity, Mr Anthony
Trollope is perhaps a little too fond of taking his readers into his
confidence, and, as we should say of an actor, gagging his
audience. . . . When an author has succeeded in making us feel
for his personages as if they were vital flesh and blood, we resent
his coming forward from the wings to assure us that they are
only puppets, and that he is pulling the strings. When an
author has anything very subtle to say we willingly allow him to
lose his way for a moment in a by-path of humour or of
sentiment, but even this liberty admits of very sparing
indulgence. Mr Anthony Trollope's style is decidedly
improved; it was always masculine, vigorous, and free from any
mincing affectations and foreign fripperies, but it was often

inelegant and incorrect: in *Doctor Thorne* it has lost none of its
vigour and clearness, and it is less often marred by wilfull
negligence or coarseness. In character-painting, however, the
author of *The Warden* has more unequivocally gained strength.
There is much less propensity to caricature in *Doctor Thorne*: the
handling is broad and powerful, but sure, and under strong
restraint; every touch tells, because every touch is the result of
thought and feeling subdued with rare technical skill. . . . We
cannot help commending . . . the selection of our everyday
English life for the groundwork of the tale . . . the scenery, the
personages, the incidents are pure English, and such as might
have occurred last year. . . . Several of the constituents of
modern English society are represented with striking force and
fidelity; the factitious aristocracy of birth and wealth, the
self-made aristocracy of brain and will, and the true aristocracy
of simple faith and honest worth are contrasted in no forced,
conventional manner, and in no grudging or envious spirit. We
are not quite sure that in making Scatcherd . . . die of *delirium
tremens* . . . Mr Trollope has not . . . traduced the noble and
energetic pioneers of the rising democracy of labour in our age
of steam.

   [Unsigned review, pp. 519–20 – Ed.]

'EXAMINER'   (29 May 1858)

   . . . Perhaps the county families are over-hardly dealt with, but
there is a good deal of shrewd and pleasant malice in the great
debates on questions of blood and treasure. . . . There is more
exaggeration also in the picture of the brandy-drinking man of
the day, Roger Scatcherd, than belongs fairly to one of the main
characters in the story, and his gin-drinking clerk is an
extravagant abortion. These objections we suggest to a novelist
who has already taken a high position in his art, and who is able
to confirm a very genuine success. The quiet touches of satire
blended with the careful character-painting in *The Warden* and
Barchester Towers gave promise of a success more permanent

than can be achieved by the more showy strokes of caricature, for which we hope that Mr Trollope has not been emboldened to exchange them. There is plenty of the old grace and of the old sterling quality in *Doctor Thorne*; . . . There is sense in it, humour in it, now and then a touch of pathos; it is interesting, and is written in good English. . . . We speak of Mr Trollope as of one from whom the public has it knows not what – but surely much – to hope.

[Unsigned review, p. 340 – Ed.]

'SATURDAY REVIEW'   (12 June 1858)

. . . The plot is obviously as slight as anything can be; but it affords opportunities for a great deal of description which no one but Mr Trollope could have written, but which he with proper pains might have written much better. . . .

The fault of the book throughout is its carelessness. The story is languid. Whenever a difficulty arises, Mr Trollope tries to cut it instead of solving it. He turns to his reader, points out the difficulty, and coolly passes it over. . . . [He] must know that nothing in this world is more provoking than a breach of duty urged by way of apology for another breach of duty. . . . The contract of the writer with the reader is to create and maintain a reasonably perfect illusion as to the reality of the events which he relates, and he breaks that contract if he wantonly points out the difficulties of his task, and says that there is a way out of them, but that he does not choose to take the trouble to find it.

Mr Trollope has too much sense to write with any very definite moral, but he does the next worse thing that is to be done. He invests his books – and has invested this one in particular – with a sort of atmosphere which is not incapable of being condensed into the moral that people ought to marry for love and not for money, and that wealth and station are in themselves somewhat contemptible. . . . Frank Gresham is much applauded for his heroism in determining to marry Mary Thorne, a lady by nature and education though a bastard by birth, at the expense, as he supposes, of forfeiting for ever the family estate. We will not dwell upon the trifling inconsistency of praising a man for being disinterested in the first place, and paying him 300,000 l. for his disinterested conduct immediately afterwards.

[Unsigned review: v, pp. 618–19. Donald Smalley (op. cit., p. 75) suggests that the reviewer may well have been Sir Henry Maine – Ed.]

Framley Parsonage

(serialisation 1860, book publication 1861)

COMMENT BY ITS AUTHOR

. . . I had got into my head an idea of what I meant to write, – a morsel of the biography of an English clergyman who should not be a bad man, but one led into temptation by his own youth and by the unclerical accidents of the life of those around him. The love of his sister for the young lord was an adjunct necessary, because there must be love in a novel. And then by placing Framley Parsonage near Barchester, I was able to fall back upon my old friends Mrs Proudie and the Archdeacon. Out of these slight elements I fabricated a hodge-podge in which the real plot consisted at last simply of a girl refusing to marry the man she loved till the man's friends agreed to accept her lovingly. Nothing could be less efficient or artistic. But the characters were so well handled, that the work from the first to the last was popular . . . . The story was thoroughly English. There was a little fox-hunting and a little tuft-hunting, some Christian virtue and some Christian cant. There was no heroism and no villainy. There was much Church, but more love-making. And it was downright honest love, – in which there was no pretence on the part of the lady that she was too etherial to be fond of a man, no half-and-half inclination on the part of the man to pay a certain price and no more for a pretty toy. Each of them longed for the other, and they were not ashamed to say so. Consequently they in England who were living, or had lived, the same sort of life, liked *Framley Parsonage*. I think myself that Lucy Robarts is perhaps the most natural English girl. I ever drew . . . . Indeed I doubt whether such a character could be made more lifelike than Lucy Robarts.

And I will say also that in this novel there is no very weak part, – no long succession of dull pages.

SOURCE: extract from *An Autobiography*, pp. 142–3.

'LONDON REVIEW'   (11 May 1861)

. . . There is not a character in this story about the tracing of which is any blur or raggedness; all is cleanly drawn, sharp cut; definitely cleared; and we have made so many more actual friends and acquaintances in every person of the tale. Perhaps this exceeding definiteness and sharpness of delineation is Mr Trollope's best quality as a mere workman. When a writer is able to make his characters live and breathe and move before us – when he lifts them out of mere names and endues them with personality – he has done the greatest thing that lies before him in that direction. . . .

We regard this work of Mr Trollope as matchless in its way, being so perfectly pure and yet so manly . . . . Mr Trollope has no special theory to enforce. He cares to paint the world as he sees it – weaknesses, virtues, shortcomings, villainies – just as they flash across the mirror among the ordinary virtuous and failing, and contents himself with delineating the everyday men and women, who move about the world without special notice. . . . *Framley Parsonage* is about the most healthy and most masculine book that has been published in these later

times, which, to our thinking, is the highest term of praise to be
awarded any work whatever.

[Unsigned review: II, pp. 544–5 – Ed.]

'EXAMINER'   (20 April 1861)

. . . The weakest parts of the book are those which affect
political satire. The meeting at Gatherum Castle; all that
relates to the immensity of Tom Towers, to the Jupiter, and to
Mr Harold Smith, who becomes Lord Petty Bag, or to the
Parliamentary struggle described as a contest between the gods
and giants, is feeble and confused. The blending of false names
of party leaders with the most recent dates, and the triviality of
the particular allusion sometimes blended with a clumsy and
exaggerated general satire, represents the defective side of Mr
Trollope's literalness.

[Unsigned review, pp. 244–5 – Ed.]

'WESTMINSTER REVIEW'   (July 1861)

It is a curious and not very satisfactory phenomenon that a
novel so trivial and purposeless as *Framley Parsonage* should
have acquired the popularity it undoubtedly did during its
appearance in the *Cornhill Magazine*.[1] This can be attributed to
no higher qualities than a certain facility, not to say glibness of
composition peculiar to the author. . . .

Mr Trollope gives way too in this and other of his novels to a
weakness now very common with our writers of fiction, we
mean in the return to characters which they have treated with
more or less success in former works. This can hardly ever be
accomplished successfully, and while it betrays a great poverty
of invention, most commonly does but vulgarise if not destroy,
what may have been originally a happy conception. Few, we

think, will be edified by the part which Doctor Thorne is made
to play in the present novel. It would seem impossible for Mr
Trollope to invent a story without adding to his sketches of the
clergy in their relations to general society. Mark Robarts and
Mr Crawley are new figures in this somewhat extensive gallery;
his sitters have but little to thank him for, and it may be pleaded
by them that there is a fundamental injustice in constantly
treating a particular class of men from a point of view which is
but accidental to their position.

In *Framley Parsonage* there is no evolution; the story
progresses by constant aggregation of details; in this way novels
may be manufactured like Manchester goods, and retailed at so
much per yard so long as the colour and design retain their
hold, or what after all is no better than a passing vogue.

[Unsigned review: LXXVI, pp. 282–4 – Ed.]

NOTE

1. [Ed.] Thackeray, the editor of the *Cornhill Magazine*, had specially
commissioned *Framley Parsonage* as the leading fiction feature for the first issue
of the new magazine, in January 1860.

The Small House at Allington

(publication 1864)

COMMENT BY ITS AUTHOR

. . . *The Small House at Allington* redeemed my reputation . . . .
In it appeared Lily Dale, one of the characters which readers of
my novels have liked the best. In the love with which she has
been greeted I have hardly joined with much enthusiasm,
feeling that she is somewhat of a female prig. She became first
engaged to a snob, who jilted her; and then, though in truth she

loved another man who was hardly good enough, she could not extricate herself sufficiently from the collapse of her first great misfortune to be able to make up her mind to be the wife of one whom, though she loved him, she did not altogether reverence. Prig as she was, she made her way into the hearts of many readers, both young and old; so that, from that time to this, I have been continually honoured with letters, the purport of which has always been to beg me to marry Lily Dale to Johnny Eames. Had I done so, however, Lily would never have so endeared herself to these people as to induce them to write letters to the author concerning her fate. It was because she could not get over her troubles that they loved her.[1]

SOURCE: extract from *An Autobiography*, pp. 178–9.

NOTE

1. [Ed.] Cf. Trollope's remark in a reply to one such correspondent: '. . . the object . . . was to show that a girl under such circumstances should bear the effects of her own imprudence, & not rid herself of her sorrow too easily' – see fuller excerpts from this letter in Bradford A. Booth's discussion of the novel in Part Three, below.

'ATHENAEUM'   (26 March 1864)

. . . Mr Trollope has shown great skill in the management of the character of Adolphus Crosbie. He has kept the reader in charity with him, in spite of all his sins; even his faithlessness to Lily is made so natural that the candid reader cannot feel himself a Pharisee, and hug himself with complacency that he is not even like Adolphus Crosbie. The temptation to which he yielded was so suited to his weakness, and the point of view from which he saw things is given so fairly, that it is impossible not to understand how he fell from his own steadfastness under the enchantments of De Courcy Castle. There is no false excuse made for him, no palliation offered, except the truth, which appeals to each: 'consider thyself, lest thou also be tempted'.

The whole of that passage of life in De Courcy Castle, under the high pressure got up for those distinguished visitors, Lady Dumbello and Mr Plantagenet Palliser, is admirably true, as a sketch of manners and customs in a great house of that class, and true to the human nature of the different characters concerned in the story.

The gradual development of Crosbie's mistake, the recoil upon himself, the retribution which arises from the nature of things, and not from any machinery of human justice, are very subtly and skilfully indicated; it shows, too, what one is glad to have shown – the genuine human conscience, that lives and moves under all the apparent selfish indifference of society to matters not immediately personal. . . . As for Johnny Eames . . . he is rather a bore; no woman could ever feel the smallest interest in him, unless it were a kind elderly woman like Lady Julia de Guest. His entanglement with Amelia Roper is fatal to all his pretensions as a hero, and he behaves as ill to her as he knows how. Mr Trollope feels it necessary to apologise for two kisses bestowed on that young lady; but they are the only redeeming traits in the whole affair. With all his faults, the reader's sympathy is with Crosbie; he goes through his bad business with Lady Alexandrina in a dignified manner, accepting the consequences of his own fault with patience, and a manly endeavour to make the best of things.

[Unsigned review, pp. 437–8 – Ed.]

'READER'   (2 April 1864)

. . . To call Mr Trollope's delineations photographic would be too high a compliment to his fidelity – too much of a slur upon his art. His fidelity is, indeed, marvellous, but not wholly infallible; his art appears chiefly in his singularly free, broad, and easy handling, the very reverse of photographic hardness and precision. Hence there is a life and colour about his pictures . . . and the interest is increased tenfold by Mr Trollope's admirable method of exposition; his seductive

frankness and irresistible vigour; the piquancy, no less than the
pertinence, of his shrewd reflections; the dexterity with which
everything is adapted to the standard of the great body of
readers; his inexhaustible affluence of invention and
illustration. The variety of his *dramatis personae* seems illimitable;
if, after the manner of Mr Thackeray, he brings an old
character again upon the stage, he takes care to vindicate his
fertility by the simultaneous introduction of two or three new
ones; he never repeats a situation without good reason, and
never crowds his canvas with unnecessary figures, merely
summoned up to relieve some flagging chapter by a trait of the
ludicrous. . . . Each of his novels is in some sense an epitome of
contemporary English life; nor is there any other novelist from
whom posterity will, on the whole, derive so true and vivid a
conception of the actual condition of our society. This might
hardly be the case were Mr Trollope a man of poetic genius, or
of a very original cast of thought. . . . Mr Trollope possesses no
troublesome imaginative power to interfere with the directness
of his vision; his gifts are in no wise celestial, but just such as
enable him to descry what is going on around him, and to
report it in the style of a thorough man of business, seasoned
with the most captivating pleasantry.

[Unsigned review: III, pp. 418–19 – Ed.]

'SPECTATOR'   (9 April 1864)

Mr Trollope has written nothing more true or entertaining
than this admirable representation of our modern social world,
with its special temptations, special vices, and special kinds of
retribution. It is not so much a story . . . as a fragment of
complicated social strategy that he describes in these pages –
and describes with a delicacy of observation and a moral
thoughtfulness which matters apparently so trifling probably
never before received. . . . There is scarcely a chapter in the
book which does not in some way illustrate the laws of success
and failure in what we may call social tactics – from the great

advantage given by perfect frigidity and utter heartlessness to the splendid strategy of Lady Dumbello, to the slight advantage gained by Lily in her little contest with Hopkins, the gardener. . . . And this subtle estimate of the strategical worth of a 'situation' . . . of the value of the less obvious elements in the strategy of social life is, after all, what gives the chief humour as well as charm to this amusing book.

Mr Trollope's intellectual grasp of his characters . . . is nearly perfect; but then he chooses to display that grasp almost exclusively in the hold they get or fail to get over other characters, and in the hold they yield to other characters over them. It is in his command of what we may call the moral 'hooks and eyes' of life that Mr Trollope's greatest power lies.

[Unsigned review: xxxvii, pp. 421–3 – Ed.]

'SATURDAY REVIEW'   (14 May 1864)

Mr Trollope has achieved another great success in his own peculiar line. It may not be the highest of all possible lines, but it is a very pleasant one, and suffices to show the great powers of the author. If the inner feelings of young ladies and young gentlemen are to be described as they display themselves in the bosom of comfortable and respectable English families, it would be impossible to describe them better than Mr Trollope does. . . . He can do, in fact, what Miss Austen did, only that he does it in the modern style, with far more detail and far more analysis of character, although, perhaps, with less lightness of touch and gentle pervading wit. In his new story he has hit on a happy idea. He has found a new subject. A girl jilted in a natural, easy way, with no worse result to herself than that she is not married, and with no worse result to the perfidious lover than that he is tied to a dreary stick of a wife . . . is, so far as we know, a new basis for the action of a novel. It is impossible to praise too highly the skill with which this sad history of jilting is told.

[Unsigned review: xvii, pp. 595–6 – Ed.]

The Last Chronicle of Barset

(serialisation 1866, book publication 1867)

COMMENT BY ITS AUTHOR

. . . Taking it as a whole, I regard this as the best novel I have written. I was never quite satisfied with the development of the plot. . . . I cannot quite make myself believe that even such a man as Mr Crawley could have forgotten how he got [the cheque]; nor would the generous friend who was anxious to supply his wants have supplied them by tendering the cheque to a third person. Such fault I acknowledge, – acknowledging at the same time that I have never been capable of constructing with complete success the intricacies of a plot that required to be unravelled. But while confessing so much, I claim to have portrayed the mind of the unfortunate man with great accuracy and great delicacy. The pride, the humility, the manliness, the weakness, the conscious rectitude and bitter prejudices of Mr Crawley were, I feel, true to nature and were well described. The surroundings too are good. Mrs Proudie at the palace is a real woman; and the poor old dean dying at the deanery is also real. The archdeacon at his rectory is very real. There is a true savour of English country life all through the book. It was with many misgivings that I killed my old friend Mrs Proudie. I could not, I think, have done it, but for a resolution taken and declared under circumstances of great momentary pressure.

It was thus that it came about. I was sitting one morning at work upon the novel at the end of the long drawing-room at the Athenaeum Club . . . . As I was there, two clergymen, each with a magazine in his hand, seated themselves, one on one side of the fire and one on the other, close to me. They soon began to abuse what they were reading, and each was reading some part of some novel of mine. The gravamen of their complaint lay in the fact that I re-introduced the same characters so often! . . . Then one of them fell foul of Mrs Proudie. It was impossible for me not to hear their words, and almost impossible to hear them and be quiet. I got up, and standing between them, I acknowledged myself to be the culprit. 'As to Mrs Proudie', I said, 'I will go home and kill her before the week is over.' And so I did. . . .

I have sometimes regretted the deed, so great was my delight in writing about Mrs Proudie, so thorough was my knowledge of all the little shades of her character. It was not only that she was a tyrant, a bully, a would-be priestess, a very vulgar woman, and one who would send headlong to the nethermost pit all who disagreed with her; but that at the same time she was conscientious, by no means a hypocrite, really believing in the brimstone which she threatened, and anxious to save the souls around her from its horrors. And as her tyranny increased so did the bitterness of the moments of her repentance increase, in that she knew herself to be a tyrant, – till that bitterness killed her. Since her time others have grown up equally dear to me, – Lady Glencora and her husband, for instance; but I have never dissevered myself from Mrs Proudie, and still live much in company with her ghost.

SOURCE: extract from *An Autobiography*, pp. 274–5.

'SPECTATOR'   (13 July 1867)

. . . Perhaps the most *delicate* piece of moral portraiture ever completed by Mr Trollope is the inimitable sketch of the old warden, Mr Septimus Harding, whose death in this story has drawn tears from many an eye to which tears are usually strangers. No more perfect delineation of high breeding, humility, self-forgetfulness, and faith was ever painted. That having painted two such pictures as those of Mr Crawley and Mr Harding, Mr Trollope should be charged with a chronic disposition to libel the English priesthood, and make them a mere set of wordings, is strange to us. No doubt Mr Trollope sketches men chiefly as he sees them, whether in the Church or otherwise, and he does not see apparently very many men – either in the Church or otherwise – quite 'unspotted from the world'. Nay, even those who are unspotted by the *world* are sometimes otherwise not unspotted, like Mr Crawley. But if such a man as Mr Harding is seldom met with twice in any man's life, why should he be met with twice in any man's works? Again, nothing in its way can be finer than the picture of the Archdeacon's thorough practical worldliness, and the way it collapses before his impressionable and kind heart, when he comes to see a really pretty girl of high breeding in distress. Mr Trollope has drawn nothing better than the Archdeacon's interview with old Lady Lufton, wherein he describes his worldly feelings about his son's proposed marriage in a very frank way indeed, and the immediately succeeding interview with the young lady, whom he visits in order to show her the wickedness of marrying his son, and to whom he has given, before the end of the interview, his hearty consent – almost unconditionally – in form even conditionally only on her father's proved innocence of the supposed theft – to that marriage.

[Unsigned review: XL, pp. 778–80 – Ed.]

'EXAMINER'   (20 July 1867)

... Nobody is more literal than Mr Anthony Trollope in his reproduction of manners and conversation of the day for which he writes. If he gave in his firm, clear, unexaggerated way only the outside of men's talking and doing, his books would be very dull indeed; well written, but altogether commonplace. They interest us all, because, simple as they look, there is a true sympathy underlying his perceptions of the characters of men and women. The delicate charm of many of his portraits of women would be evidence enough of this, but is there any

sentiment . . . so true as that which has dealt tenderly with
Septimus Harding . . . and given us in this 'Last Chronicle of
Barset' so exquisite a sense of the beauty of his innocent old
age?
   [Unsigned review, pp. 452–3 – Ed.]

'LONDON REVIEW'   (20 July 1867)

. . . The character of Mr Crawley is certainly one of the most
powerful of Mr Trollope's conceptions. There is a rugged
grandeur and a harsh nobility about the man, both of which
qualities are admirably brought out and rendered prominent in
the course of the story. The wonderful ease with which Mr
Trollope writes, and the simplicity of the means by which he
generally produces his effects, have induced some of his critics
to underrate his powers, and to speak of him at times as if he
were capable of doing little more than write excellent chit-chat,
or analyse the mental vagaries of a young lady oscillating
between two attachments. No one can rival him in investing
commonplace with a winning charm; no one else can render
airy nothings so acceptable as he succeeds in making them; but
he has higher claims to be praised than these, and to their
existence such a character as that of Mr Crawley bears ample
testimony. It cannot have been an easy one to depict, but the
portrait is admirably executed. From first to last he is
consistent with himself, and while his foibles are pointed out
with genial humour, his native dignity is maintained, without
any apparent difficulty, at a height to which in most cases it
would have required a desperate effort to attain. There is
something very grand about this ecclesiastical Titan, bowed
down by troubles, and bound hand and foot by debt, while the
vulture of poverty is ever gnawing at his side, but who yet defies
the whole world, sets threats and persuasion equally at nought,
and stubbornly maintains his own in spite alike of friends and
foes.
   [Unsigned review: xv, p. 81 – Ed.]

'ATHENAEUM'   (3 August 1867)

There is one advantage in writing a story as a serial[1] – the individual portions have an elaboration and finish which a novel written in the piece does not always obtain. . . . These 'Last Chronicles' [sic] are very carefully written, and the characters have remarkable substance and vitality. It is not given to everyone to create characters out of the work-a-day world – neither better nor worse than persons whom we all meet every day – and yet to be able so to lay bare their hearts and stories that the reader accepts them as friends and acquaintances, follows their fortunes through the volume specially devoted to them, remembers the subordinate persons, and is glad to hear their story at length as soon as Mr Trollope is pleased . . . to take up one of the threads of the old story and weave a new one from it. The series of Barsetshire Chronicles have all been singularly real in their interest, and veraciously like Nature in the living characters introduced. Each chronicle has a central history, with slighter sketches grouped round it. The story of the subordinate personages has each in their turn been worked out at length. The interest has been kept up, the electric current has gone without break through the circle, from the days of the dear old Warden . . . to these last Chronicles of Barset, wherein Mr Harding, full of years and goodness, drops into an honoured grave. In the meanwhile, all the personages of the town and country have, in their turn, appeared before the reader, and if the reader does not believe in Barsetshire and all who live therein . . . the fault is not in Mr Trollope, but in himself.

[Unsigned review, p. 141 – Ed.]

NOTE

1. [Ed.] See *An Autobiography*, pp. 273 ff., where Trollope discusses the rather unusual arrangement for the novel's first appearance. It came out in thirty-two weekly parts, price sixpence each. 'I do not know that it answered very well', writes Trollope.

MRS MARGARET OLIPHANT   (September 1867)

. . . To kill Mrs Proudie was murder, or manslaughter at the least. We do not believe she had any disease of the heart; she died not by natural causes, but by his hand in a fit of weariness or passion. . . . It was cruel to us; and it rather looks as if he did not know how to get through the crisis in a more natural way. Then as to Lily Dale. Mr Trollope's readers have been cheated about this young woman. It is a wilful abandonment of all her natural responsibilities when such a girl writes Old Maid after her name. She has no business to do it; and what is the good of being an author . . . if a man cannot provide more satisfactorily for his favourite characters? . . . On the other hand, though he has thus wounded us in our tenderest feelings, our author has in this book struck a higher note than he has yet attempted.

[Extract from review in *Blackwood's Magazine*, cii, pp. 277–8 – Ed.]

'BRITISH QUARTERLY REVIEW'   (October 1867)

. . . the whole of the London life, the painting of Jael and Sisera, the life and suicide of Dobbs Broughton, the preposterous love-making of Mdlle Desmoulins, and other uninteresting matter connected with Conway Dalrymple and Johnny Eames, might have been omitted wtih advantage. There does not seem to be anything more than a smart and lively reproduction of rather improbable circumstances in the life of a not very interesting set of people, to give them currency or popularity.

[Unsigned review: xlvi, pp. 557–60 – Ed.]

PART TWO

General Assessments

Victorian and Twentieth-Century Judgements

E. S. Dallas (1859)

'The prince of the circulating library'

If Mudie were asked who is the greatest of living men, he would without one moment's hesitation say – Mr Anthony Trollope; and Mudie's opinion is worth much. . . . The wide world of authors and the wide world of readers alike regard him with awe; nay, even the sacred race of publishers have been known to kiss the hem of his garments and to invoke his favour. He is the mighty monarch of books that are good enough to be read, but not good enough or not cheap enough to be bought. He is the Apollo of the circulating library. He is the tenth Muse – the Muse of the three-volume novel. He is the autocrat of literature. Week by week and month by month he announces in various journals and magazines all the books which ought to be read; and authors run over the list with trembling to see whether Mr Mudie esteems their volumes worth of mention, and has purchased 2,500 copies or only 200. . . .

To be unknown to Mudie is to be unknown to fame; to bask in the smiles of Mudie is to put on immortality, and feel all the future in the instant. This majestic personage, whom authors worship and whom readers court, knows that at the present moment one writer in England is paramount above all others, and his name is Trollope. He is at the top of the tree; he stands alone; there is nobody to be compared with him. He writes faster than we can read, and the more that the pensive public reads the more does it desire to read. Mr Anthony Trollope is, in fact, the most fertile, the most popular, the most successful author – that is to say, of the circulating library sort. We believe there are persons who would rather not receive such praise, and who hold a circulating library success in great contempt, but they labour under a misapprehension. It is true that books which circulate without being cherished, which we read once and do not care to read a second time, which people borrow but never think of buying, are not the best of all books, and certainly are not the product of that mysterious something we call genius. But genius is not everything in this world, and the presence of a few comets in the literary firmament need not make us blind to the existence of a good many stars. There are people who find Mr Thackeray too thoughtful and Mr Dickens too minute, who are tired of dainty fare and curious wines, who have had enough of the heavenly manna, and who long for the flesh-pots of Egypt. Mr Trollope is the very man for them. There is no pretence about him, no shamming, no effort. He is always clever, often amusing, sometimes even great, or very near being great, but his predominating faculty is good sense. . . .

. . . His style is the very opposite of melodramatic; it is plain and straightforward, utterly devoid of clap-trap. It is the style of a man who has a good deal to say, who can afford to say it simply, who does not attempt to astonish, and who is content to give his readers innocent and rational amusement. These novels are healthy and manly, and so long as Mr Anthony Trollope is the prince of the circulating library, our readers may rest assured that it is a very useful, very pleasant, and very honourable institution.

Perhaps Mr Trollope carries his aversion from everything melodramatic to an extreme, and though he errs on the right side, still he errs. The essence of melodrama is surprise. The situations are unexpected; the characters are doing things for which we were not prepared; passions are evoked which are not justified by the facts, and sentiments are expressed which have no relation to the circumstances. Everything, in short, is a surprise. Mr Trollope, on the other hand, has vowed that there shall be no surprises in his novels. The characters shall be naturally evolved; the incidents shall grow out of each other; the passion shall not be exaggerated, and the sentiment shall veritably belong to the event. But in determining thus to show cause for every effect, and a sufficient motive for every act and word, Mr Trollope seems at times to be too anxious to avoid startling results; afraid lest the reader should be taken unawares, he lets out his secret too soon, and long before he has laid down his lines of action he forewarns us of what is to happen – what is to be the joyous consummation or the dismal catastrophe which is the intended result of all his plans. At the first mention of his heroine's name he says, ostentatiously, 'Now, this is to be my *prima donna* – the lady you must all love, the lady I am going to pet, the lady whom fortune is to favour, the lady who is to get the prime husband at the end of the third volume'. Here the story is at once told, all suspense is removed, and when we see the heroine afterwards under a cloud we know that the cloud means nothing, or is intended but to make the sunshine which afterwards bursts forth more bright. So of another personage, we are informed that his character is unsound and must inevitably end in misery and ruin. This is a sure way to prevent our being surprised when misery and ruin overtake the poor wretch; but it is also a method apt to damp our interest in the event, and to destroy all the excitement of suspense. It is the expression of a manly aversion to melodramatic art with which we cordially sympathize, but it is also an appeal to sources of interest which are more welcome to the student of philosophy than to the reader of novels. Mr Trollope says virtually, 'I will do what novelists never yet have done; I will begin with the end of the story; I will have no secrets; I will sacrifice all the interest of cunningly devised situations and mysterious occurrences; I will, not perhaps formally, but virtually, give my readers the action of the piece as an accomplished fact, and if I cannot amuse them with what else remains – namely, with the rational pleasure of following the story in its details, tracing the gradual rise and progress of events, and describing the attendant circumstances – then I may as well throw aside my pen altogether.' In making this resolve Mr Trollope throws away, needlessly we think, some of the resources of his art; while, on the other hand, he wins our respect, and proves that a success which has not been purchased by vulgar methods must be due to merits of a sterling kind.

SOURCE: excerpted from article in *The Times* (23 May 1859), p. 12.

Henry James (1865)

Trollope's 'small manner'

... he has diminished the real elements of passion. This is apt
to be the case in Mr Trollope's stories. Passion has to await the
convenience of so many other claimants that in the end she is
but scantily served. As for action, we all know what we are to
expect of Mr Trollope in this direction. ... Literally, then, Mr
Trollope achieves his purpose of being true to common life. But
in reading his pages, we . . . [are] . . . constantly induced to ask
ourselves whether he is equally true to nature; that is, whether
in the midst of this multitude of real things, of
uncompromisingly real circumstances, the persons put before
us are equally real. Mr Trollope has proposed to himself to
describe those facts which are so close under everyone's nose
that no one notices them. Life is vulgar, but we know not how
vulgar it is till we see it set down in his pages. ... Mr Trollope
has, we conceive, simply wished to interest us in ordinary
mortals. ... It is possible that ... [the] ... result is Mr
Trollope's misfortune rather than his fault. He has encountered
it in trying to avoid an error which he doubtless considers more
pernicious still, that of overcharging nature. He has doubtless
done his best to give us the happy middle truth. But ah – if the
truth is not so black as she is sometimes painted, neither is she
so pale!

We do not expect from writers of Mr Trollope's school (and
this we esteem already to be a great concession) that they shall
contribute to the glory of human nature; but we may at least
exact that they do not wantonly detract from it. Mr Trollope's
offence is, after all, deliberate. He has deliberately selected
vulgar illustrations. His choice may indeed be explained by an
infirmity for which he is not responsible: we mean his lack of
imagination. But when a novelist's imagination is weak, his
judgement should be strong. ... Mr Trollope is of course wise,
in view of the infirmity in question, in devoting himself to those

subjects which least expose it. He is an excellent, an admirable observer; and such an one may accomplish much. But why does he not observe great things as well as little ones? . . . Mr Trollope's devotion to little things, inveterate, self-sufficient as it is, begets upon the reader the very disagreeable impression that not only no imagination was required for the work before him, but that a man of imagination could not possibly have written it. This impression is fostered by many of Mr Trollope's very excellences. A more richly-gifted writer would miss many of his small (that is, his great) effects. It must be admitted, however, that he would obtain on the other hand a number of truly great ones. Yet, as great effects are generally produced at present by small means, Mr Trollope is master of a wide field. He deals wholly in small effects. His manner, like most of the literary manners of the day, is a small manner. . . . It can generally be said of this small manner that it succeeds; cleverness is certain of success; it never has the vertigo; it is only genius and folly that fail. But in what does it succeed? That is the test question: the question which it behooves us to impose now-a-days with ever growing stringency upon works of art; for it is the answer to this question that should approve or condemn them. It is small praise to say of a novelist that he succeeds in mortifying the reader. Yet Mr Trollope is master of but two effects: he renders his reader comfortable or the reverse. As long as he restricts himself to this scale of emotion, of course he has not need of imagination, for imagination speaks to the heart. . . .

. . . we are perhaps ill-advised to expect sympathy for any harsh strictures upon a writer who renders such excellent service. Let us, however, plainly disavow a harsh intention. Let us, in the interest of our argument, heartily recognise his merits. His merits, indeed! – he has only too many. His manner is literally freckled with virtues. We use this term advisedly, because its virtues are all virtues of detail: the virtues of the photograph. The photograph lacks the supreme virtue of possessing a character. It is the detail alone that distinguishes one photograph from another. What but the details distinguishes one of Mr Trollope's novels from another, and . . . consigns it to itself? Of course the details are charming, some of them ineffably charming. The ingenuous loves, the innocent flirtations, of Young England, have been described by Mr Trollope in such a way as to secure him the universal public good-will; described minutely, sympathetically, accurately, if it were not that an indefinable instinct bade us keep the word in reserve, we should say truthfully.

SOURCE: excerpted from article in the *Nation* (New York), I (13 July 1865), pp. 51–2. [James's later assessment is given below in Part Two – Ed.]

Anonymous (1872)

'The most entirely modern of novelists'

... Mr Trollope is a thoroughly consistent workman. He sticks to his last. He never strays from the novel to the romance. ... He has none of the versatility, none of the vagaries so commonly imputed to artists; he is a first-rate plodder; he has never mistaken the order or range of his powers, or been led by the suggestion of vanity to believe that because he can do certain things immeasurably better than any one else can do them, he must necessarily do other and opposite things well. He is in one sense the most serious of writers; though in another, that of solemnity or tragicalness, he is not serious at all beyond that seriousness necessary to the life-likeness of his fictions. His seriousness consists in his air and tone of absolute belief in the personages and the circumstances of his own creation. This it is which lends such form and persuasion to his realism. ... There are no characters in fiction so real, as persons, to the world, as the creations of Mr Trollope. ...

He has given life, and speech, and motion to scores of portraits, has sent them to walk abroad and continue, and to have their names on men's lips when the actual every-day affairs and incidents of life are talked of, to rise up in one's memory in one's silent cogitations, to suggest themselves as matters of fact, the readiest, handiest, most suitable of comparisons and illustrations. They come from all sides of his many-sided pictures of life; they are not his caricatures, for he rarely employs caricatures; they are not his avowedly comic personages, for there is in all his stories no unmixed jester, no one who goes through life merely on the broad grin, or producing it: they are not his set, distinct types, for he has none. . . . He avoids all exaggeration, in either good or evil, with such care and success, that sometimes one is almost provoked with him, especially in his later works, for his perfect, undeviating reasonableness; but his people, life-sized and life-like, are all thoroughly real to his readers, as he forces his readers to feel they are to himself. . . .

There is the sound, detailed, substantial completeness of sculpture in Mr Trollope's workmanship; of modern sculpture, in modern dress, with no allegorical draperies or insignia, and with as careful an avoidance of the grotesque as of the colossal. So his men and women are real creatures to us, when he turns them out of the studio of his brain, as they are to him. He is more than the painter, more than the sculptor of his people; he is the biographer of them all. He does not merely imagine Archdeacon Grantly and Johnny Eames, and put them into certain stories to play their parts in certain incidents, as is mostly the whole utility and destiny of fictitious persons in novels; he looks at them and into them, he turns them about; observes them, lives with them; knows them so thoroughly well and intimately, that he makes us know them almost as fully, and in quite a separate way, from the actual set of circumstances in which he exhibits them. . . .

The leading novelist of the day is in this instance its accurate representative, its faithful mouthpiece – not as regards the vulgar aspects, the tumultuous attributes of society, which are, indeed, represented by him, who is neither a subversive nor a sensational writer; but as regards its real, permeating motives, its spirit, its aims and its manners. It is not a little indication of the character of the time that this should be so. The present is an age which takes a keen, pressing, sleepless interest in itself.

Mr Trollope meets, suits, gratifies this taste. He is the most entirely modern of novelists, for, though he must perforce use the materials of which human lives have been made from the beginning, he handles and combines them exactly according to the latest fashions, and tells 'the old, old story' with the newest notes, and, for all their shrewd ingenuity, with the most conventional comments. He may prove to be the founder of a school, but at present he stands alone. . . . Nothing is so difficult to imitate as moderation, as the exquisite justness of vision which sees everything as it is, and the correctness of touch which presents it in its exact proportions; the accurate insight which knows what will be the line on which a given mind will travel under given circumstances, and the good taste which will never purchase effect at the price of distortion. Mr Trollope's style is in harmony with the purport and nature of his novels; it is as modern, as equable, as uniform as they are. It is exceedingly easy, but never careless; it is not remarkably refined, though it is never coarse, rough, or abrupt; it is not grand, sonorous, or elevated, though it always is, when he means it to be so, downright, striking and impressive; and the permanent effect which it produces is that it is at once unmistakable and, not unpleasantly, monotonous. . . . Perhaps the chief cause of this unmistakability is the not unpleasant monotony just alluded to. . . .

He is the least disappointing, because the most even, of all great novelists. . . . His fertility does not surprise us any longer: we are accustomed to a perpetual publication of books by him, and it does not alarm us, because he never does slovenly or ill-considered work; never displays over-confidence in his vast popularity, or disdain of public criticism. His steadiness is equal to his speed; his work is never scamped, and it is always highly-finished. Many of his novels are not exciting . . . but they are interesting, and in each there is some one particular person who stamps himself or herself upon the memory, though in the greater number of instances this effect is produced by no adventitious means, but simply by the convincing truth and humorous lifelikeness of the portrait. With all this, he is not a deep writer; he would not be at once the product and the representative of the times if he were. He is

singularly acute, ready and fair-minded. He is not profound, or
philosophical, or speculative in any universal, or indeed wide,
sense. He is not cynical: there is no more than good-humoured
satire in his delineation of human littleness, meanness, spite,
folly, time-serving, self-seeking, and servility; but there is an
entire absence of spirituality about him, of even a discernment
of things supernatural. . . .

SOURCE: excerpted from unsigned article in the *Dublin Review*,
LXXI (October 1872), pp. 393–430.

R. H. Hutton   (1882)

A valedictory tribute

The death of Mr Anthony Trollope, without a familiar
knowledge of whose works no historian who emulated the style
of Macaulay would even attempt to delineate English society in
the third quarter of the present century, marks almost the close
of an era. We can never again recall the endless gallery of his
social pictures, without associating with them the thought that
he whose imaginative world they peopled – he whose offspring,
indeed, they in some sense were – has passed away, and that
more and more from the present date they will represent the
figures, not of the present, but of a former age. For some time
past, indeed, many of his best-known figures have been
assuming a slightly remote aspect, not only to the world as it is,
but even to the world as he himself more recently pictured it.
Even in his own pages, the old order has changed, giving place
to new. His second Duke of Omnium was a very different figure
from his first, and a much nobler one; while in the third
generation, Lord Silverbridge, with more, perhaps, of generous
impulse than his father, had far less of his dignity and of his
profound sense of public duty. Again, the clergymen who

abounded to the great delight of the reader, in Mr Trollope's earlier and middle period, have grown fewer and less interesting of late years – in *The Duke's Children*, if we remember rightly, there was not one. Probably the type of the modern clergyman had changed, and become less intelligible to Mr Trollope. Septimus Harding seems to have lived quite a long time ago, even Archdeacon Grantly has an old-fashioned air, and Dean Arabin himself must have gone, though Mr Trollope never told us of his decease. Natural selection had brought speculating stockbrokers, American senators, and American heiresses into the foreground of Mr Trollope's pictures before he left us, and the advance of both plutocratic and democratic ideas might have been steadily traced in the vivid social pictures with which he so liberally supplied us. We shall still, we imagine, have posthumous children of Mr Trollope's though the fancy which produced them has passed to other worlds than ours; for his was a wonderfully prolific mind, always beforehand with the world, and we believe that there is more than one complete story of his writing of which not a page has yet seen the light. Still, now that he himself is gone, the changes creeping rapidly over the outlines, lights, and shadows of the social diorama with which he presented us, will seem to be more conspicuous than usual as we gaze at his lively scenes; and before another generation passes away, Mr Trollope's works will rank with those of other great novelists rather as works helping us to revive the past, than as works of which it is the great merit to interpret the relations in which we actually live.

That Mr Trollope's name will live in English literature follows at once from the fact that his books are at once very agreeable to read, and contain a larger mass of evidence as to the character and aspects of English Society during Mr Trollope's maturity than any other writer of his day has left behind him. It is too soon, and would be a mistake at the present moment, when he has only just vanished from amongst us, to fix what his place in English literature is likely to be. But we cannot think of him at all without remembering the greater features of his literary work – the ardent admiration with which he always painted humility and unworldliness, like Mr

Harding's, or even Dean Arabin's, in the rare instances in which he represented them, and the sense of something like moral wonder with which he regarded them;—the profound respect which he entertained for public spirit like that of his second 'Duke of Omnium', and the charity with which he regarded the authority of family traditions, even when waging war against the sense of justice in a radically just mind;—the scorn which he felt for all the knavery of commercial Rings, and, at the same time, the keen insight with which he contemplated the snares and toils of the speculative commercial life;—the thorough appreciation which he evinced in such stories as *Phineas Finn*, for the ties of party, as well as for the obligations of individual honour, and the zest with which he analysed the conflicts which arise between them;—the strength of his impression that almost every young man of his day has a vacillating heart, and that almost every young woman is in danger of overruling, for some strategic reason or other, whether interested or disinterested, the strong instincts of her own heart;—the loathing with which he regarded the passion of jealousy in men, and the dread which he evidently entertained for the craftiness of women;—the deep study he had given to all the tactics of social life, and the little account which he made of the results of even the most skilful of these tactics, when matched against the stronger passions and interests of human nature. All these are features which appear and reappear for ever in his stories, representing evidently impressions which had been gaining ground with him, day by day, in his shrewd study of life.

On the other hand, it is clear that there was little or no disposition in Mr Trollope to pierce much deeper than the social surface of life. It is not often that he takes us into the world of solitary feeling at all, and of the power of the positive influence of their religion over men, you would hardly gain more knowledge from Mr Trollope's stories than from those of the old-fashioned *régime*, when religion was thought too sacred to be touched-on at all as a real part of human life. The nearest thing which we can recall to any touch of a deeper kind in Mr Trollope, is his pathetic picture of Bishop Proudie, after his wife's death, saying the little prayer which he thus describes: 'It

may be doubted whether he quite knew for what he was
praying. The idea of praying for her soul now that she was dead
would have scandalized him. He certainly was not praying for
his own soul. I think he was praying that God might save him
from being glad that his wife was dead.' But touches as deep as
that are very rare in Mr Trollope.

That Mr Trollope's humour has played a great part in the
popularity of his novels, is evident enough, and yet his humour
may be called rather a proper appreciation of the paradoxes of
social life, than any very original faculty of his own. Mr
Trollope did not heighten, as Miss Austen does, the ludicrous
elements in human life by those quaint turns of expression and
those delicate contrasts which only a great genius of satiric
touch could invent. Mr Trollope's humour lay in his keen
perception of the oddity of human motives, pursuits, and
purposes, and his absolute truthfulness in painting them to the
life. This humour is shown in such descriptions as that of the
sportsman, Reginald Dobbes, who, making it his ambition to
obtain the largest bags of game in the Highlands, regards Lord
Silverbridge's defection from his shooting party, when once he
had joined it, as a moral treachery. 'It is hardly honest, you
know', said Reginald Dobbes.[1] The humour there is not
inventive, but perceptive. Reginald Dobbeses really do exist,
and Mr Trollope saw with the keenest enjoyment the absurdity
of that view of sport, and yet its complete naturalness also in a
man who had once thrown his whole energy into an
amusement, so as to make it the business of his life. These really
existing paradoxes Mr Trollope was the first to see, and as keen
as possible to delineate. So, too, he makes Archdeacon Grantly
insist, when he wants to break off the engagement between his
son and Grace Crawley, that his son is dependent upon
himself for the greater part of his income, and that *therefore* he
feels 'the greatest possible concern in his future prospects'. 'The
Archdeacon', remarks the novelist, 'did not know how to
explain clearly why the fact of his making a son an annual
allowance should give him a warmer interest in his son's affairs
than he might have had, had the Major been altogether
independent of him; but he trusted that Grace would
understand this by her own natural lights.' That is a kind of

humour which comes wholly from the keen insight into the little unconscious hypocrisies of worldly men's feelings. Mr Trollope saw through all these little make-beliefs with the clearest vision, and his humour depended on the clearness of that vision. But he did not add to the humour of the facts, when seen, by any very unusual art in their presentation. What was absurd in the tactics of society, he seized and defined, but hardly ever heightened. Only there is so much that is absurd in the tactics of society, that to see and define all that is absurd therein makes a man a humorist of no common power. Perhaps Mr Trollope never showed this humour more effectually than when he delineated the romantic vein in very vulgar and very selfish people – like Mrs Greenow, in *Can You Forgive Her?* when she treats herself to a husband of a romantic kind, or when Miss Dunstable forces her aristocratic suitor to remember that her fortune is made out of the sale of a quack ointment. Mr Trollope's humour is thoroughly realistic. He sees the coarseness of human life in its close contrast with its ambitiousness, and simply shows us what he sees.

For a writer who dealt, and always professed to deal, chiefly with the surface of society, Mr Trollope has been singularly sincere, never seeking to hide from us that there are deeper places of human nature into which he does not venture; nor his impression that the world and the motives of the world also penetrate into those places, and have perhaps as much to say to the practical result in conduct, as the higher motives themselves. Still, he cannot be called a satirist. He paints only a part of human life, but he paints that part precisely as he sees it, extenuating nothing and exaggerating nothing, but letting us know that he does not profess to see all, and does not try to divine by imaginative power what he cannot see. Probably no English writer of his day has amused Englishmen so much as Mr Trollope, or has given them that amusement from sources so completely free from either morbid weaknesses or mischievous and dangerous taints. His name will live in our literature, and though it will certainly not represent the higher regions of imaginative life, it will picture the society of our day with a fidelity with which society has never been pictured before in the history of the world.

SOURCE: article in the *Spectator*, LV (9 December 1882), pp. 1573–4.

NOTE

1. [Ed.] See *The Duke's Children*, ch. 38.

Henry James   (1883)

A posthumous revaluation

When, a few months ago, Anthony Trollope laid down his pen for the last time, it was a sign of the complete extinction of that group of admirable writers who, in England, during the preceding half century had done so much to elevate the art of the novelist. The author of *The Warden*, of *Barchester Towers*, of *Framley Parsonage*, does not, to our mind, stand on the very same level as Dickens, Thackeray and George Eliot; for his talent was of a quality less fine than theirs. But he belonged to the same family – he had as much to tell us about English life; he was strong, genial and abundant. He published too much; the writing of novels had ended by becoming with him, a perceptibly mechanical process. Dickens was prolific, Thackeray produced with a freedom for which we are constantly grateful; but we feel that these writers had their periods of gestation. They took more time to look at their subject; relatively (for to-day there is not much leisure, at best, for those who undertake to entertain a hungry public), they were able to wait for inspiration. Trollope's fecundity was prodigious; there was no limit to the work he was ready to do. It is not unjust to say that he sacrificed quality to quantity. Abundance, certainly, is in itself a great merit; almost all the greatest writers have been abundant. But Trollope's fertility was gross, importunate; he himself contended, we believe, that he had given to the world a greater number of printed pages of

fiction than any of his literary contemporaries. Not only did his
novels follow each other without visible intermission,
overlapping and treading on each other's heels, but most of
these works are of extraordinary length. . . . The imagination
that Trollope possessed he had at least thoroughly at his
command. I speak of all this in order to explain (in part) why it
was that, with his extraordinary gift, there was always in him a
certain infusion of the common. He abused his gift, overworked
it, rode his horse too hard. As an artist he never took himself
seriously; many people will say this was why he was so
delightful. The people who take themselves seriously are prigs
and bores; and Trollope, with his perpetual 'story', which was
the only thing he cared about, his strong good sense, hearty
good nature, generous appreciation of life in all its varieties,
responds in perfection to a certain English ideal. According to
that ideal it is rather dangerous to be explicitly or consciously
an artist – to have a system, a doctrine, a form. Trollope, from
the first, went in, as they say, for having as little form as
possible; it is probably safe to affirm that he had no 'views'
whatever on the subject of novel-writing. His whole manner is
that of a man who regards the practice as one of the more
delicate industries, but has never troubled his head nor clogged
his pen with theories about the nature of his business.
Fortunately he was not obliged to do so, for he had an easy road
to success; and his honest, familiar, deliberate way of treating
his readers as if he were one of them, and shared their
indifference to a general view, their limitations of knowledge,
their love of a comfortable ending, endeared him to many
persons in England and America. It is in the name of some
chosen form that, of late years, things have been made most
disagreeable for the novel-reader, who has been treated by
several votaries of the new experiments in fiction to unwonted
and bewildering sensations. With Trollope we were always
safe; there were sure to be no new experiments.

His great, his inestimable merit was a complete appreciation
of the usual. This gift is not rare in the annals of English fiction;
it would naturally be found in a walk of literature in which the
feminine mind has laboured so fruitfully. Women are delicate
and patient observers; they hold their noses close, as it were, to

the texture of life. They feel and perceive the real with a kind of personal tact, and their observations are recorded in a thousand delightful volumes. Trollope, therefore, with his eyes comfortably fixed on the familiar, the actual, was far from having invented a new category; his great distinction is that in resting there his vision took in so much of the field. And then he *felt* all daily and immediate things as well as saw them; felt them in a simple, direct, salubrious way, with their sadness, their gladness, their charm, their comicality, all their obvious and measurable meanings. He never wearied of the pre-established round of English customs – never needed a respite or a change – was content to go on indefinitely watching the life that surrounded him, and holding up his mirror to it. Into this mirror the public, at first especially, grew very fond of looking – for it saw itself reflected in all the most credible and supposable ways, with that curiosity that people feel to know how they look when they are represented, 'just as they are', by a painter who does not desire to put them into an attitude, to drape them for an effect, to arrange his light and his accessories. This exact and on the whole becoming image, projected upon a surface without a strong intrinsic tone, constitutes mainly the entertainment that Trollope offered his readers. The striking thing to the critic was that his robust and patient mind had no particular bias, his imagination no light of its own. He saw things neither pictorially and grotesquely like Dickens; nor with that combined disposition to satire and to literary form which gives such 'body', as they say of wine, to the manner of Thackeray; nor with anything of the philosophic, the transcendental cast – the desire to follow them to their remote relations – which we associate with the name of George Eliot. Trollope had his elements of fancy, of satire, of irony; but these qualities were not very highly developed, and he walked mainly by the light of his good sense, his clear, direct vision of the things that lay nearest, and his great natural kindness. There is something remarkably tender and friendly in his feeling about all human perplexities; he takes the goodnatured, temperate conciliatory view – the humorous view, perhaps, for the most part, yet without a touch of pessimistic prejudice. As he grew older, and had sometimes to go farther afield for his subjects, he acquired a savour of bitterness and reconciled himself sturdily to treating of the disagreeable. A more copious record of disagreeable matters could scarcely be imagined, for instance, than *The Way We Live Now*. But, in general, he has a wholesome mistrust of morbid analysis, an aversion to inflicting pain. He has an infinite love of detail, but his details are, for the most part, the innumerable items of the expected. When the French are disposed to pay a compliment to the English mind they are so good as to say that there is in it something remarkably *honnête*. If I might borrow this epithet without seeming to be patronising, I should apply it to the genius of Anthony Trollope. He represents in an eminent degree this natural decorum of the English spirit, and represents it all the better that there is not in him a grain of the mawkish or the prudish. He writes, he feels, he judges like a man, talking plainly and frankly about many things, and is by no means destitute of a certain saving grace of coarseness. But he has kept the purity of his imagination and held fast to old-fashioned reverences and preferences. He thinks it a sufficient objection to several topics to say simply that they are unclean. There was nothing in his theory of the story-teller's art that tended to convert the reader's or the writer's mind into a vessel for polluting things. He recognised the right of the vessel to protest, and would have regarded such a protest as conclusive. With a considerable turn for satire, though this perhaps is more evident in his early novels than in his later ones, he had as little as possible of the quality of irony. He never played with a subject, never juggled with the sympathies or the credulity of his reader, was never in the least paradoxical or mystifying. He sat down to his theme in a serious, business-like way, with his elbows on the table and his eye occasionally wandering to the clock. . . . The source of his success in describing the life that lay nearest to him, and describing it without any of those artistic perversions that come, as we have said, from a powerful imagination, from a cynical humour or from a desire to look, as George Eliot expresses it, for the suppressed transitions that unite all contrasts, the essence of this love of reality was his extreme interest in character. This is the fine and admirable quality in Trollope, this is what will preserve his best works in spite of those flatnesses which keep him from standing on quite the same level as the masters. Indeed this quality is so much one of the finest (to my mind at least), that it makes me wonder the more that the writer who had it so abundantly and so naturally should not have just that distinction which Trollope lacks . . . . If he was in any degree a man of genius (and I hold that he was), it was in virtue of this happy, instinctive perception of human varieties. His knowledge of the stuff we are made of, his observation of the common behaviour of men and women, was not reasoned nor acquired, not even particularly studied. All human doings deeply interested him, human life, to his mind, was a perpetual story; but he never attempted to take the so-called scientific view. . . . He had no airs of being able to tell you *why* people in a given situation would conduct themselves in a particular way; it was enough for him that he felt their feelings and struck the right note, because he had, as it were, a good ear. If he was a knowing psychologist he was so by grace; he was just and true without apparatus and without effort. He must have had a great taste for the moral question; he evidently believed that this is the basis of the interest of fiction. We must be careful, of course, in attributing convictions and opinions to Trollope, who, as I have said, had as little as possible of the pedantry of his art, and whose occasional chance utterances in regard to the object of the novelist and his means of achieving it are of an almost startling simplicity. But we certainly do not go too far in saying that he gave his practical testimony in favour of the idea that the interest of a work of fiction is great in proportion as the people stand on their feet. His great effort was evidently to make them stand so; if he achieved this result with as little as possible of a flourish of the hand it was nevertheless the measure of his success. If he had taken sides on the droll, bemuddled opposition between novels of character and novels of plot, I can imagine him to have said (except that he never expressed himself in epigrams), that he preferred the former class, inasmuch as character in itself is plot, while plot is by no means character. It is more safe indeed to believe that his great good sense would have prevented him from taking an idle controversy seriously. Character, in any sense in which we can get at it, is action, and action is plot, and any plot which hangs together, even if it pretend to interest us only in the fashion of a Chinese puzzle, plays upon our emotion, our suspense, by means of personal references. We care what happens to people only in proportion as we know what people are. Trollope's great apprehension of the real, which was what made him so interesting, came to him through his desire to satisfy us on this point – to tell us what certain people were and what they did in consequence of being so. That is the purpose of each of his tales; and if these things produce an illusion it comes from the gradual abundance of his testimony as to the temper, the tone, the passions, the habits, the moral nature, of a certain number of contemporary Britons.

His stories, in spite of their great length, deal very little in the surprising, the exceptional, the complicated; as a general thing he has no great story to tell. The thing is not so much a story as a picture; if we hesitate to call it a picture it is because the idea of composition is not the controlling one and we feel that the author would regard the artistic, in general, as a kind of affectation. There is not even much description, in the sense which the present votaries of realism in France attach to that word. The painter lays his scene in a few deliberate, not especially pictorial strokes, and never dreams of finishing the piece for the sake of enabling the reader to hang it up. The finish, such as it is, comes later, from the slow and somewhat clumsy accumulation of small illustrations. These illustrations are sometimes of the commonest; Trollope turns them out inexhaustibly, repeats them freely, unfolds them without haste and without rest. But they are all of the most obvious sort, and they are none the worse for that. The point to be made is that they have no great spectacular interest (we beg pardon of the innumerable love-affairs that Trollope had described), like many of the incidents, say, of Walter Scott and of Alexandre Dumas: if we care to know about them (as repetitions of a usual case), it is because the writer has managed, in his candid, literal, somewhat lumbering way, to tell us that about the men and women concerned which has already excited on their behalf the impression of life. It is a marvel by what homely arts, by what imperturbable button-holing persistence, he contrives to excite this impression. . . .

Trollope has described again and again the ravages of love, and it is wonderful to see how well, in these delicate matters, his plain good sense and good taste serve him. His story is always primarily a love-story, and a love-story constructed on an inveterate system. There is a young lady who has two lovers, or a young man who has two sweethearts; we are treated to the innumerable forms in which this predicament may present itself and the consequences, sometimes pathetic, sometimes grotesque, which spring from such false situations. Trollope is not what is called a colourist; still less is he a poet: he is seated on the back of heavy-footed prose. But his account of those sentiments which the poets are supposed to have made their own is apt to be as touching as demonstrations more lyrical. . . . Trollope had no time to give his tales a classic roundness; yet there is (in spite of an extraordinary defect), something of that quality in the thing that first revealed him. *The Warden* was published in 1855. It made a great impression; and when, in 1857, *Barchester Towers* followed it, every one saw that English literature had a novelist the more. These were not the works of a young man, for Anthony Trollope had been born in 1815. It is remarkable to reflect by the way, that his prodigious fecundity (he had published before *The Warden* three or four novels which attracted little attention), was enclosed between his fortieth and his sixty-seventh years. Trollope had lived long enough in the world to learn a good deal about it; and his maturity of feeling and evidently large knowledge of English life went for much in the effect produced by the two clerical tales. It was easy to see that he would take up room. What he had picked up, to begin with, was a comprehensive, various impression of the clergy of the Church of England and the manners and feelings that prevail in cathedral towns. This, for a while, was his speciality, and, as always happens in such cases, the public was disposed to prescribe to him that path. He knew about bishops, archdeacons, prebendaries, precentors, and about their wives and daughters; he knew what these dignitaries say to each other when they are collected together, aloof from secular ears. He even knew what sort of talk goes on between a bishop and a bishop's lady when the august couple are enshrouded in the privacy of the episcopal bedroom. This knowledge, somehow, was rare and precious. No one, as yet, had been bold enough to snatch the illuminating torch from the very summit of the altar. Trollope enlarged his field very speedily – there is, as I remember that work, as little as possible of the ecclesiastical in the tale of *The Three Clerks*, which came after *Barchester Towers*. But he always retained traces of his early divination of the clergy; he introduced them frequently, and he always did them easily and well. There is no ecclesiastical figure, however, so good as the first – no creation of this sort so happy as the admirable Mr Harding. *The Warden* is a delightful tale, and a signal instance of Trollope's habit of offering us the spectacle of a character. A motive more delicate, more slender, as well as more charming, could scarcely be conceived. It is simply the history of an old man's conscience. . . .

The subject of *The Warden*, exactly viewed, is the opposition of the two natures of Archdeacon Grantly and Mr Harding, and there is nothing finer in all Trollope than the vividness with which this opposition is presented. The archdeacon is as happy a portrait as the precentor – an image of the full-fed, worldly churchman, taking his stand squarely upon his rich temporalities, and regarding the church frankly as a fat social pasturage. It required the greatest tact and temperance to make the picture of Archdeacon Grantly stop just where it does. The type, impartially considered, is detestable, but the individual may be full of amenity. Trollope allows his archdeacon all the virtues he was likely to possess, but he makes his spiritual grossness wonderfully natural. No charge of exaggeration is possible, for we are made to feel that he is conscientious as well as arrogant, and expansive as well as hard. He is one of those figures that spring into being all at once, solidifying in the author's grasp. These two capital portraits are what we carry away from *The Warden*, which some persons profess to regard as our writer's masterpiece. We remember, while it was still something of a novelty, to have heard a judicious critic say that it had much of the charm of *The Vicar of Wakefield*. Anthony Trollope would not have accepted the compliment, and would not have wished this little tale to pass before several of its successors. He would have said, very justly, that it gives too small a measure of his knowledge of life.

It has, however, a certain classic roundness, though, as we said a moment since, there is a blemish on its fair face. The chapter on Dr Pessimist Anticant and Mr Sentiment would be a mistake almost inconceivable if Trollope had not in other places taken pains to show us that for certain forms of satire (the more violent, doubtless), he had absolutely no gift. Dr Anticant is a parody of Carlyle, and Mr Sentiment is an exposure of Dickens: and both these little *jeux d'esprit* are as infelicitous as they are misplaced. It was no less luckless an inspiration to convert Archdeacon Grantly's three sons, denominated respectively Charles James, Henry and Samuel, into little effigies of three distinguished English bishops of that period, whose well-known peculiarities are reproduced in the description of these unnatural urchins. The whole passage, as we meet it, is a sudden disillusionment; we are transported from the mellow atmosphere of an assimilated Barchester to the air of ponderous allegory.

I may take occasion to remark here upon a very curious fact – the fact that there are certain precautions in the way of producing that illusion dear to the intending novelist which Trollope not only habitually scorned to take, but really, as we may say, asking pardon for the heat of the thing, delighted wantonly to violate. He took a suicidal satisfaction in reminding the reader that the story he was telling was only, after all, a make-believe. He habitually referred to the work in hand (in the course of that work) as a novel, and to himself as a novelist, and was fond of letting the reader know that this novelist could direct the course of events according to his pleasure. Already, in *Barchester Towers*, he falls into this pernicious trick. In describing the wooing of Eleanor Bold by Mr Arabin he has occasion to say that the lady might have acted in a much more direct and natural way than the way he attributes to her. But if she had, he adds, 'where would have been my novel?' The last chapter of the same story begins with the remark, 'The end of a novel, like the end of a children's dinner party, must be made up of sweetmeats and sugar-plums.' These little slaps at credulity (we might give many more specimens) are very discouraging, but they are even more inexplicable; for they are deliberately inartistic, even judged from the point of view of that rather vague consideration of form which is the only canon we have a right to impose upon Trollope. . . .

It is a part of this same ambiguity of mind as to what constitutes evidence that Trollope should sometimes endow his people with such fantastic names. Dr Pessimist Anticant and Mr Sentiment make, as we have seen, an awkward appearance in a modern novel; and Mr Neversay Die, Mr Stickatit, Mr Rerechild and Mr Fillgrave (the two last the family physicians), are scarcely more felicitous. It would be better to go back to Bunyan at once. There is a person mentioned in *The Warden* under the name of Mr Quiverful – a poor clergyman, with a dozen children, who holds the living of Puddingdale. This name is a humorous allusion to his overflowing nursery, and it matters little so long as he is not brought to the front. But in *Barchester Towers*, which carries on the history of Hiram's Hospital, Mr Quiverful becomes, as a candidate for Mr Harding's vacant place, an important element, and the reader is made proportionately unhappy by the primitive character of this satiric note. A Mr Quiverful with fourteen children (which is the number attained in *Barchester Towers*) is too difficult to believe in. . . .

His fund of acquaintance with his own country – and indeed with the world at large – was apparently inexhaustible, and it gives his novels a spacious, geographical quality which we should not know where to look for elsewhere in the same degree, and which is the sign of an extraordinary difference between such an horizon as his and the limited world-outlook, as the Germans would say, of the brilliant writers who practise the art of realistic fiction on the other side of the Channel. Trollope was familiar with all sorts and conditions of men, with the business of life, with affairs, with the great world of sport, with every component part of the ancient fabric of English society. He had travelled more than once all over the globe, and for him, therefore, the background of the human drama was a very extensive scene. He had none of the pedantry of the cosmopolite; he remained a sturdy and sensible middle-class Englishman. But his work is full of implied reference to the whole arena of modern vagrancy. He was for many years concerned in the management of the Post-Office; and we can imagine no experience more fitted to impress a man with the diversity of human relations. It is possibly from this source that he derived his fondness for transcribing the letters of his love-lorn maidens and other embarrassed persons. No contemporary story-teller deals so much in letters; the modern English epistle (very happily imitated, for the most part), is his unfailing resource. . . . In one respect *Barchester Towers* is (to the best of our recollection) unique, being the only one of Trollope's novels in which the interest does not centre more or less upon a simple maiden in her flower. The novel offers us nothing in the way of a girl; though we know that this attractive object was to lose nothing by waiting. Eleanor Bold is a charming and natural person, but Eleanor Bold is not in her flower. After this, however, Trollope settled down steadily to the English girl; he took possession of her, and turned her inside out. . . . he bestowed upon her the most serious, the most patient, the most tender, the most copious consideration. He is evidently always more or less in love with her, and it is a wonder how under these circumstances he should make her so objective, plant her so well on her feet. But, as I have said, if he was a lover, he was a paternal lover; as competent as a father who has had fifty daughters. He has presented the British maiden under innumerable names, in every station and in every emergency in life, and with every combination of moral and physical qualities. She is always definite and natural. She plays her part most properly. She has always health in her cheek and gratitude in her eye. She has not a touch of the morbid, and is delightfully tender, modest and fresh. Trollope's heroines have a strong family likeness, but it is a wonder how finely he discriminates between them. One feels, as one reads him, like a man with 'sets' of female cousins. Such a person is inclined at first to lump each group together; but presently he finds that even in the groups there are subtle differences. Trollope's girls, for that matter, would make delightful cousins. . . . Trollope's genius is not the genius of Shakespeare, but his heroines have something of the fragrance of Imogen and Desdemona. . . .

He always provided a sort of underplot to alternate with his main story – a strain of narrative of which the scene is usually laid in a humbler walk of life. It is to his underplot that he generally relegates his vulgar people, his disagreeable young women; and I have often admired the perseverence with which he recounts these less edifying items. Now and then, it may be said, as in *Ralph the Heir*, the story appears to be all underplot and all vulgar people. These, however, are details. As I have already intimated, it is difficult to specify in Trollope's work, on account of the immense quantity of it; and there is sadness in the thought that this enormous mass does not present itself in a very portable form to posterity.

Trollope did not write for posterity; he wrote for the day, the moment; but these are just the writers whom posterity is apt to put into its pocket. So much of the life of his time is reflected in his novels that we must believe a part of the record will be saved; and the best parts of them are so sound and true and genial, that readers with an eye to that sort of entertainment will always be sure, a certain proportion, to turn to them. Trollope will remain one of the most trustworthy, though not one of the most eloquent, of the writers who have helped the heart of man to know itself. The heart of man does not always desire this knowledge; it prefers sometimes to look at history in another way – to look at the manifestations without troubling about the motives. There are two kinds of taste in the appreciation of imaginative literature: the taste for emotions of surprise and the taste for emotions of recognition. It is the latter that Trollope gratifies, and he gratifies it the more that the medium of his own mind, through which we see what he shows us, gives a confident direction to our sympathy. His natural rightness and purity are so real that the good things he projects must be real. A race is fortunate when it has a good deal of the sort of imagination – of imaginative feeling – that had fallen to the share of Anthony Trollope; and in this possession our English race is not poor.

Source: excerpted from article in the *Century Magazine*, new series IV (July 1883), pp. 385–95.

Frederic Harrison   (1895)

Trollope's place in English Literature

. . . Even at his worst, he writes pure, bright, graceful English; he tells us about wholesome men and women in a manly tone, and if he becomes dull, he is neither ridiculous nor odious. He is very often dull: or rather utterly commonplace. It is the fashion with the present generation to assert that he is never anything but commonplace; but this is the judgment of a perverted taste. His besetting danger is certainly the commonplace. It is true that he is almost never dramatic, or powerful, or original. His plots are of obvious and simple construction; his characters are neither new, nor subtle, nor powerful; and his field is strictly limited to special aspects of the higher English society in town and country. But in his very best work, he has risen above commonplace and has painted certain types of English men and women with a really exquisite grace and consummate truth.

One of Trollope's strong points and one source of his popularity was a style almost perfect for his own limited purpose. It is limpid, flexible and melodious. It never rises into eloquence, poetry or power; but it is always easy, clear, simple and vigorous. Trollope was not capable of the sustained mastery over style in *Esmond*, nor had he the wit, passion and pathos at Thackeray's command. But of all contemporaries he comes nearest to Thackeray in easy conversations and in quiet narration of incidents and motives. Sometimes, but very rarely, Trollope is vulgar – for good old Anthony had a coarse vein – it was in the family. But as a rule his language is conspicuous for its ease, simplicity and unity of tone. This was one good result of his enormous rapidity of execution. His books read from cover to cover, as if they were spoken in one sitting by an *improvisatore* in one and the same mood, who never hesitated an instant for a word, and who never failed to seize the word he wanted. This ease and mastery over speech was the fruit of prodigious practice and industry both in office work and in literary work. It is a mastery which conceals itself, and appears to the reader the easiest thing in the world. How few of these millions have studied that subtle mechanism of ear and thought which created the melodious ripple of these fluent and pellucid words.

His work has one special quality that has not been sufficiently noticed. It has the most wonderful unity of texture and a perfect harmony of tone. From the first line to the last, there is never a sentence or a passage which strikes a discordant note; we are never worried by a spasmodic phrase, nor bored by fine writing that fails to 'come off'. . . . This uniform ease, of course, goes with the absence of all the greatest qualities of style; absence of any passion, poetry, mystery or subtlety. He never rises, it is true, to the level of the great masters of language. But, for the ordinary incidents of life amongst well-bred and well-to-do men and women of the world, the form of Trollope's tales is almost as well adapted as the form of Jane Austen.

In absolute realism of spoken words Trollope has hardly any equal. His characters utter quite literally the same words, and no more, that such persons utter in actual life. The characters, it is true, are the average men and women we meet in the educated world, and the situations, motives and feelings described are seldom above or below the ordinary incidents of modern life. But within this very limited range of incident, and for this very common average of person and character, the conversations are photographic or stenographic reproductions of actual speech. His letters, especially his young ladies' letters, are singularly real, life-like and characteristic. . . .

This photographic realism of conversation is common enough now: but it has too often the defects of photography; it is bleared, coarse and ill-favoured. As we all know, in the new realism a young woman and her lover talk thus: 'Old gal! why so glum?' said he – 'It's my luck!' says she, and flings her straw hat on the floor. That is the new photographic style, but it does not please us of an older generation. Now Trollope makes his people utter such phrases as the characters he presents to us actually use in real life – or rather such phrases as they did use thirty years ago. And yet, although he hardly ever rises into eloquence, wit, brilliancy, or sinks into any form of talk either unnaturally tall or unnaturally low – still, the conversations are just sufficiently pointed, humorous or characteristic, to amuse the reader and develop the speaker's character. Trollope in this exactly hits the happy mean. Like Mr Woodhouse's gruel, his conversations are 'thin – but not so very thin'. He never attempts grandiloquence; but then he never sinks into the fashionable bathos of – 'Sugar in your tea, dear?' – 'Another lump, if you please' – nor does he fall into the fashionable realism of – 'Dry up, old man!' No! Trollope's characters speak with literal nature; and yet with enough of point, humour, vigour to make it pleasant reading.

We may at once confess to his faults and limitations. They are plain enough, constant, and quite incapable of defence. Out of his sixty works, I should be sorry to pick more than ten as being worth a second reading, or twenty which are worth a first reading. It is a serious crime to have published some forty books which an admirer has to confess to be nearly worthless. Nor amongst the good books could I count any of the last ten years. The range of characters is limited to the clergy and professional men of a cathedral city, to the county families and the respectabilities of a quiet village, to the life of clubs, public offices and Parliament in London, and to the ways of 'society' as it existed in England in the third quarter of the present century. The plots are neither new nor ingenious; the incidents are rarely more than commonplace; the characters are seldom very powerful, or original or complex. There are very few 'psychologic problems', very few dramatic situations, very few revelations of a new world and unfamiliar natures. . . .

This is no doubt the cause of the revulsion of opinion by which in some English circles Trollope has suffered of late. If there are fashions, habits and tastes which the rising generation is certain to despise, it is what were current in the youth of their own parents about thirty or forty years before them. The collars, the bonnets, the furniture, the etiquette, the books of that age always seem to the young to be the last word of all that is awkward and 'bad form', although in two or three generations these very modes regain a certain quaint charm.

And for the moment poor Anthony represents to the emancipated youth of our time all that was 'banal' and prosy some thirty years ago. The taste of our youth sets hard for a new heaven, or at least a new earth, and if not that, it may be a new hell. Novels or poems without conundrums, without psychologic problems, with no sexual theorems to solve, with no unique idiosyncrasies to fathom, without anything unnatural, or sickening, without hospital nastiness – are all, we are assured, unworthy the notice of the youth of either sex who are really up to date. In the style of the new pornographic and clinical school of art, the sayings and doings of wholesome men and women who live in drawing-rooms and regularly dress before dinner are 'beastly rot', and fit for no one but children and old maids.

But we conservatives of an older school are grateful to Anthony that he produces for the last generation an immense collection of pleasant tales without a single foul spot or unclean incident. It was his boast that he had never written a line which a pure woman could not read without a blush. This is no doubt one of the grounds on which he is so often denounced as *passé*. His tales, of course, are full of love, and the love is not always discreet or virtuous. There are cases of guilty love, of mad love, of ungoverned and unreasoning passion. But there is not an impure or prurient passage in the whole library of tales. Much more than this: in the centre of almost every tale, we are taken to the heart of a spotless, loving, refined, brave English girl. In nothing does Anthony Trollope delight more than when he unveils to us the secret thoughts of a noble-hearted maiden who loves strongly but who has a spirit as strong as her love, a clear brain and a pure will. In nothing is he more successful; nowhere is he more subtle, more true, more interesting. In this fine gift, he surpasses all his contemporaries, and almost all other English novelists. Mary Thorne, Lily Dale, Lucy Robarts – I almost wish to add, Martha Dunstable – may not be heroines of romance, and are certainly not great creations. But they are pure, right-minded, delicate, brave women; and it does one good to be admitted to the sacred confessional of their hearts. . . .

All this is now said to be commonplace, goody-goody and

Philistine. There are no female acrobats, burglars, gutter-urchins, crapulous prostitutes, no pathological anatomy of diseased bodies and carious souls, hardly a single case of adultery in all Trollope. But they who can exist without these stimulants may find pleasant reading yet in his best work. . . .

Anthony Trollope was not a fraud, nor even a mere tradesman. His reputation may perhaps partially revive, and some of his best work may be read in the next century. His best work will of course be a mere residuum of his sixty books, as is the best of nearly all prolific writers. I am inclined to think the permanent survival may be limited to the 'Barchester' cycle, with *Orley Farm* and the two 'Phineas Finns'. In any case, his books will hereafter bear a certain historical interest, as the best record of actual manners in the higher English society between 1855 and 1875. That value nothing can take away, however dull, *connu*, and out of date the books may now seem to our new youth. It is a curious problem why our new youth persists in filling its stomach with the poorest trash that is 'new' – i.e., published in 1895, whilst it will not look at a book that is 'old' – i.e., published in 1865, though both are equally unknown to the young reader. If our new youth ever could bring itself to take up a book having 1865 on its title-page, it might find in the best of Anthony Trollope much subtle observation, many manly and womanly natures, unfailing purity of tone, and much wholesome enjoyment.

SOURCE: excerpted from article in the *Forum* (May 1895), pp. 324–37.

Sir Leslie Stephen   (1901)

'Sacrifice to the duty of fidelity'

. . . We can see plainly enough what we must renounce in order to enjoy Trollope. We must cease to bother ourselves about art. We must not ask for exquisite polish of style. We must be content with good homespun phrases which give up all their meaning on the first reading. We must not desire brilliant epigrams suggesting familiarity with aesthetic doctrines or theories of the universe. A brilliant modern novelist is not only clever, but writes for clever readers. He expects us to understand oblique references to esoteric theories, and to grasp a situation from a delicate hint. We are not to be bothered with matter-of-fact details, but to have facts sufficiently adumbrated to enable us to accept the aesthetic impression. Trollope writes like a thorough man of business or a lawyer stating a case. We must know exactly the birth, parentage and circumstances of all the people concerned, and have a precise statement of what afterwards happens to everybody mentioned in the course of the story. We must not care for artistic unity. Trollope admits that he could never construct an intricate plot to be gradually unravelled. That, in fact, takes time and thought. He got hold of some leading incident, set his characters to work, and followed out any series of events which happened to be involved. In one of his stories, if I remember rightly, the love affairs of four different couples get mixed up, and each of them has to be followed out to a conclusion. He simply looks on, and only takes care to make his report consistent and intelligible. To accept such writing in the corresponding spirit implies, no doubt, the confession that you are a bit of a Philistine, and can put up with the plainest of bread and butter, and dispense with all the finer literary essences. I think, however, that at times one's state is the more gracious for accepting the position. There is something so friendly and simple and shrewd about one's temporary guide that one is the better for taking a stroll with him and listening to gossiping family stories, even though they be rather rambling and never scandalous. One difficulty is suggested, indeed, by Trollope's sacrifice of all other aims to the duty of fidelity. We begin to ask whether it can be worth while to read a novel which is a mere reflection of the commonplace. Would it not be better to read genuine biographies and narratives of real events?

. . . Trollope's best achievement, I take it, was the series of Barsetshire novels. They certainly passed at the time for a marvel of fidelity. Trollope tells us that he was often asked when he had lived in a cathedral close and become intimate with archdeacons; and had been able to answer that he had never lived in a close and had never spoken to an archdeacon. He had evolved the character, he declares, 'out of his moral consciousness', and is pleasantly complacent over his creation. Though one would not like to disparage the merits of the performance, the wonder seems to be pretty simple. Trollope had been to Harrow and Winchester, and the headmaster of one had become a dean, and the headmaster of the other a bishop. He afterwards spent two years riding through English country, and a visit, during this period, to Salisbury close, had suggested the first Barchester novel. It is not wonderful that, after such experience, he should have been equal to the costume of archdeacons; and, apart from their costumes, archdeacons are not essentially different, I fancy, from bishops or headmasters, or from the average adult male of the upper classes. Archdeacon Grantly is certainly an excellent and life-like person; an honourable, narrow-minded English gentleman with just the necessary tinge of ecclesiastical dignity. Still, if our hypothetical descendants asked us, Were English archdeacons like that? we should be a little puzzled. If Miss Yonge could be called as a witness to character, she would certainly demonstrate. Archdeacons, she would say, in her time, high-church archdeacons at least, were generally saints. They could be spiritual guides; they had listened to Newman or been misled by *Essays and Reviews*; but had, at least, been interested in the religious movements of the day. Trollope's archdeacon is as indifferent to all such matters as were the much-reviled dignitaries of an older generation. He is supposed to do his official duties, and he carefully says, 'Good Heavens!' where a layman would use another phrase; but he never gives the slightest indication of having any religious views whatever beyond a dislike to dissenters. He has a landed estate, and is as zealous as any squire to keep up the breed of foxes, and he threatens to disinherit his son for making an unworldly marriage as if he were the great Barchester magnate – the Duke of Omnium himself.

I do not presume to inquire how far such a man represents the prevalent type more accurately than the more ethereal divine of pious lady novelists. The Trollope theory of the archdeacons might be held to confirm Matthew Arnold's description of the Church as an 'appendage of the barbarian'; and the philosophical historian might infer that in the nineteenth century the normal country farmer was a very slightly modified squire. Perhaps Trollope's view may be a useful corrective to the study of the ordinary lives in which the saintliness of respectable clergymen tends to be a little over-emphasised; still, it omits or attenuates one element – the religious, namely – which must have had some importance in the character of contemporary divines. And what can we say for the young women who charmed his readers so thoroughly? Vulgar satire in those days was denouncing the 'girl of the period' – the young lady who was chafing against established conventions of all kinds. The young women of Barchester seem to have been entirely innocent of such extravagance. Trollope's heroines are as domestic as Clarissa Harlowe. They haven't a thought beyond housekeeping or making a respectable marriage. We could hardly expect such delineations of the fair feminine qualities as could be given by feminine novelists alone. We could not ask him for a Jane Eyre or still less for a Maggie Tulliver. But were the average girls of forty years back made of such very solid flesh and blood with so small an allowance of the romantic? His are so good-natured, sensible, and commonplace that he has the greatest difficulty in preventing them from at once marrying their lovers. He has to make them excessively punctilious on some point of their little code of propriety. One is loved by a lord, whose mother objects to a *mésalliance*; another is of doubtful legitimacy, and a third is the daughter of an excellent man whose character is for a moment under a cloud. They have to hold out till their lovers and their lovers' families have got over such scruples, or the cause has been removed. The most popular of all was Miss Lily Dale, whom Trollope himself unkindly describes as 'somewhat of a French prig'. She will not marry the man whom she loves because she has been cruelly jilted by a thorough snob, and makes it a point of honour not to accept consolation or admit that she can love twice. Readers, it seems, fell in love with her, and used to write to Trollope entreating him to reconcile her to making her lover happy. Posterity, I think, will make a mistake if it infers that English girls were generally of this type; but it must admit, though with a certain wonder, that the type commended itself to a sturdy, sensible Briton of the period, as the very ideal of Womanhood, and delighted a large circle of readers.

The prosaic person, it must remember, has a faculty for ignoring all the elements of life and character which are not prosaic, and if Trollope's picture is accurate it is not exhaustive. The weakness thus indicated is significant. Trollope made it a first principle to keep rigorously to the realities of life. He inferred that nothing strange or improbable should ever be admitted. That is not the way to be life-like. Life, as we all find out, is full of the strange and improbable. Every character has its idiosyncrasies: its points of divergence from the ordinary. If the average man whose qualities are just at the mean between the extremes, who is half-way between genius and idiot, villain and saint, must be allowed to exist, it may be doubted whether he is not, on the whole, more exceptional than the so-called exceptions. Trollope inclines to make everybody an average specimen, and in his desire to avoid exaggeration inevitably exaggerates the commonplaceness of life. He is afraid of admitting any one into his world who will startle us by exhibiting any strength of character. His lovers, for example, have to win the heroine by showing superiority to the worldly scruples of their relations. The archdeacon's son proposes to marry a beautiful and specially-virtuous and clever girl, although her father had been accused of stealing. He endangers his prospects of inheriting an estate, but he had, in any case, enough to live upon. Surely some men would be up to such heroism, even though the girl herself hesitates to accept the sacrifice. But, to make things probable, we are carefully told that the hero has great difficulty in rising to the occasion; he has to be screwed up to the effort by the advice of a sensible lady; and even her encouragement would scarcely carry the point, had not the accusation been disproved. In this, and other cases, the heroes have all the vigour taken out of them, that they may not shock us by diverging from the most commonplace standard. When a hero does something energetic, gives a thrashing, for example, to the man who has jilted a girl, we are carefully informed that he does it in a blundering and unsatisfactory way.

By the excision of all that is energetic, or eccentric, or impulsive, or romantic, you do not really become more lifelike; you only limit yourself to the common and uninteresting. That misconception inspires Trollope's work and accounts, I suspect, for the decline of our interest. An artist who systematically excludes all lurid colours or strong lights, shows a dingy, whitey-brown universe, and is not more true to nature.

SOURCE: excerpted from article in the *National Review*, XXXVIII (1901), pp. 69–84.

Sir Arthur Quiller-Couch (1925)

'Wise and unerringly right every time'

... no man ever wrote himself down at a more delicately ill-chosen time than did Trollope by the publication (posthumous) of his *Autobiography* in 1883. It was a brave – if unconsciously brave – and candid book. But it fell on a generation of young men fired in literature by Flaubert, in painting (say) by Whistler; on a generation just beginning to be flamboyant over 'art for art's sake', the *mot juste*, and the rest. It all seems vain enough at this distance, and the bigots of each successive iron time will always be arraigning their fathers' harmless art, no doubt to the ultimate advancement of letters. But by young men quite honestly and frenetically devoted to chiselling out English as though (God rest them!) in devotion to a Higher Power, it may be allowed that such a confession as the following would be felt as an irritant: 'All those, I think, who have lived as literary men – working daily as literary labourers – will agree with me that three hours a day will produce as much as a man ought to write. . . .'[1]

The reader may easily imagine the maddening effect of that upon any ambitious young writer, indolent by habit yet conscientious in his craft, reminiscent of hours spent in gazing at a wall for words with which he wanted to express his ideas. How many times did Plato alter the opening sentence of *The Republic*? How many times did Gray recast the *Elegy*?

But time, which should bring the philosophic mind, will lead most critics who follow criticism sincerely to the happy conviction that there are no rules for the operation of genius; a conviction born to save a vast amount of explanation – and whitewash. Literary genius may be devoted, as with Milton; nonchalant, as with Congreve; elaborately draped, as with Tennyson. Catullus or Burns may splash your face and run on; but always the unmistakable god has passed your way. In reading Trollope one's sense of trafficking with genius arises more and more evidently out of his large sincerity – a sincerity in bulk, so to speak; wherefore, to appraise him, you must read him in bulk, taking the good with the bad, even as you must with Shakespeare. (This comparison is not so foolish as it looks at first sight: since, while no two authors can ever have been more differently gifted, it would be difficult to name a third in competition as typically English.) The very mass of Trollope commands a real respect; its prodigious quantity is felt to be a quality, as one searches in it and finds that – good or bad – better or very much worse – there is not a dishonest inch in the whole. He practised among novelists of genius: Dickens, Thackeray, Disraeli, the Brontës, George Eliot, Ouida were his contemporaries; he lived through the era of 'sensational novels', *Lady Audley's Secret* and the rest; and he wrote, as he confesses, with an eye on the publisher's cheque. But no success of genius tempted him to do more than admire it from a distance; no success of 'sensation' seduced him from his loom of honest tweed. He criticises the Gods and Titans of his time. He had personal reasons for loving Thackeray, who gave him his great lift into fame by commissioning him to write the serial novel that opened the *Cornhill* upon a highly expectant public. Trollope played up nobly to the compliment and the responsibility. *Framley Parsonage* belongs to his very best: it took the public accurately (and deservedly) between wind and water. Thackeray was grateful for the good and timely service; Trollope for the good and timely opportunity. . . .

Again, honest though he was, he accepted and used false tricks and conventions calculated, in the 'eighties and 'nineties, to awake frenzy in any young practitioner who, however incompetent, was trying to learn how a novel should be written. The worst 'stage aside' of an old drama was as nothing in comparison with Trollope's easy-going remark, dropped anywhere in the story, and anyhow, that 'This is a novel, and I am writing it to amuse you. I might just as easily make my heroine do *this* as do *that*. Which shall it be? . . . Well, I am going to make her do *that*; for if she did *this*, what would become of my novel?' One can imagine Henry James wincing physically at such a question posed in cold print by an artist; as in a most catholic and charitable paper – written in 1883, when the young dogs were assembling to insult Trollope's carcase – he reveals himself as wincing over the first sentence in the last chapter of *Barchester Towers*: 'The end of a novel, like the end of a children's dinner-party, must be made up of sweetmeats and sugar plums.' James laments:

These little slaps at credulity . . . are very discouraging, but they are even more inexplicable; for they are deliberately inartistic, even judged from the point of view of that rather vague consideration of form which is the only canon we have a right to impose upon Trollope. . . .[2]

Yes; but on further acquaintance with Trollope one discovers that this trick (annoying always) of asking, 'Now what shall we make Mrs Bold do? – accept Mr Arabin, or reject him?' is no worse than 'uncle's fun', as I may put it. Uncle is just playing with us, though we wish he wouldn't. In fact, Trollope never chooses the wrong answer to the infelicitous question. He is wise and unerringly right every time. You will (I think) search his novels in vain for a good man or a good woman untrue to duty as weighed out between heart and conscience.

Another offence in Trollope is his distressing employment of facetious names – 'Mr Quiverful' for a philoprogenitive clergyman, 'Dr Fillgrave' for a family physician, etc. 'It would be better,' murmurs Henry James pathetically, 'to go back to Bunyan at once.' (Trollope, in fact, goes back farther – to the abominable tradition of Ben Jonson; and it is the less excusable because he could invent perfect names when he tried – Archdeacon Grantly, Johnny Eames, Algernon [sic – Ed.] Crosbie, Mrs Proudie, the Dales of Allington, the Thornes of Ullathorne, Barchester, Framley – names, families, places fitting like gloves.) And still worse was he advised when he introduced caricature, for which he had small gift, into his stories; 'taking off' eminent bishops in the disguise of objectionable small boys, or poking laborious fun at Dickens and Carlyle under the titles of Mr Sentiment and Dr Pessimist Anticant. *The Warden* is in conception, and largely in execution, a beautiful story of an old man's conscience. It is a short story, too. I know of none that could be more easily shortened to an absolute masterpiece by a pair of scissors.

With Trollope, as with Byron, in these days a critic finds himself at first insensibly forced, as though by shouldering of a crowd, upon apology for the man's reputation. . . .

. . . He arose regularly at 5.30 a.m., had his coffee brought him by a groom, had completed his 'literary work' before he dressed for breakfast; then on four working days a week he toiled for the General Post Office, and on the other two rode to hounds. In all kinds of spare time – in railway-carriages or crossing to America – he had always a pen in his hand, a pad of paper on his knee, or on a cabin table specially constructed.

As he sets it all down, with parenthetical advice to the literary tyro, it is all as simple, apparently, as a cash account. But don't you believe it! The man who created the Barsetshire novels lived quite as intimately with his theme as Dickens did in *David Copperfield*; nay, more intimately. To begin with, his imaginary Barsetshire is as definitely an actual piece of England as Mr Hardy's Wessex. . . .

He not only carried all Barsetshire in his brain as a map, with every cross-road, by-lane, and footpath noted – Trollope was great at cross-roads, having as an official reorganised, simplified and speeded-up the postal service over a great part of rural England – but knew all the country-houses, small or great, of that shire, with their families, pedigrees, intermarriages, political interests, monetary anxieties, the rise and fall of interdependent squires, parsons, tenants; how a mortgage, for example, will influence a character, a bank-book set going a matrimonial intrigue, a transferred bill operate on a man's sense of honour. You seem to see him moving about the Cathedral Close in 'very serviceable suit of black', or passing the gates and lodge of a grand house in old hunting-pink like a very wise solicitor on a holiday: garrulous, to be sure, but to be trusted with any secret – to be trusted most of all, perhaps, with that secret of a maiden's love which as yet she hardly dares to avow to herself. . . .

The fortunes and misfortunes of Trollope's comfortable England have always this element of the universal, that they are not brought about by any devastating external calamity, but always by process of inward rectitude or inward folly, reasonably operating on the ordinary business of life. In this business he can win and keep our affection for an entirely good man – for Mr Harding, for Doctor Thorne. In all his treatment of women, even of the *jeune fille* of the Victorian Age, this lumbering, myopic rider-to-hounds always (as they say) 'has hands' – and to 'have hands' is a gift of God. He was, as Henry James noted, 'by no means destitute of a certain saving grace of coarseness', but it is forgotten on the instant he touches a woman's pulse. Over that, to interpret it, he never bends but delicately. No one challenges his portraits of the maturer ladies. Mrs Proudie is a masterpiece, of course, heroically consistent to the moment of her death – nay, living afterwards consistently in her husband's qualified regrets (can anything be truer than the tragedy told with complete restraint in chapters 66 and 67 of

The Last Chronicle?). Lady Lufton's portrait, while less majestic, seems to me equally flawless, equably flawless. Trollope's women can all show claws on occasion; can all summon 'that sort of ill-nature which is not uncommon when one woman speaks of another'; and the most, even of his maidens, betray sooner or later some glance of that *malice* upon the priestly calling, or rather upon its pretensions, which Trollope made them share with him:

'Ah! yes: but Lady Lufton is not a clergyman, Miss Robarts.'
It was on Lucy's tongue to say that her ladyship was pretty nearly as bad, but she stopped herself.

Difference of time and convention and pruderies allowed for, Trollope will give you in a page or so of discourse between two Victorian maidens – the whole of it delicately understood, chivalrously handled, tenderly yet firmly revealed – the secret as no novelist has quite revealed it before or since. At any moment one may be surprised by a sudden Jane Austen touch; and this will come with the more startling surprise, being dropped by a plain, presumably blunt, man. For Trollope adds to his strain of coarseness, already mentioned, a strain – or at least an intimate understanding – of cheapness. His gentle breeding and his upbringing (poverty-stricken though it had been) ever checked him on the threshold of the holies. But he had tholed too many years in the GPO to have missed intimate acquaintance with

The noisy chaff
And ill-bred laugh
Of clerks on omnibuses.

Those who understand this will understand why he could not bring himself to mate his 'dear Lily Dale' with that faithful, most helpful, little bounder Johnny Eames. He knew his Johnny Eames too well to introduce him upon the Cathedral Close of Barchester, though he could successfully dare to introduce the Stanhope family. He walks among rogues, too, and wastrels, with a Mr Sowerby or a Bertie Stanhope, as sympathetically as among bishops, deans, archdeacons, canons. His picture of Sowerby and the ruin he has brought on an ancient family, all through his own sins, is no less and no more truthful than his picture of Mrs Proudie in altercation with Mr Slope; while they both are inferior in imaginative power to the scene of Mr Crawley's call on the Bishop. In the invention of Crawley, in his perfect handling of that strong and insane mind, I protest that I am astonished almost as though he had suddenly shown himself capable of inventing a King Lear. In this Trollope, with whom one has been jogging along under a slowly growing conviction that he is by miles a greater artist than he knows or has ever been reckoned, there explodes this character – and out of the kindliest intentions to preach him up, one is awakened in a fright and to a sense of shame at never having recognised the man's originality or taken the great measure of his power.

SOURCE: excerpted from *Charles Dickens and Other Victorian Novelists* (Cambridge, 1925), pp. 219–34.

NOTES

1. [Ed.] *An Autobiography* (1883; reprinted Oxford, 1980), pp. 271–2. 'Q' continues in the original to quote the passage reproduced – as 'Writing by the Clock' – in section 1 of Part One, above.

2. [Ed.] James's 'catholic and charitable paper' of 1883 and also his denigratory assessment of 1865 are excerpted, above, in this Part Two selection.

Frank O'Connor (1957)

Trollope the realist

Trollope's reputation has suffered so much from the results of his own senile fatuity that it is now almost impossible to define his proper place in English fiction with reasonable accuracy. He left behind him a posthumous autobiography in which he described his method of work and attempted to decry the element of inspiration in literature. Although he merely showed that he was incapable of recognising it in himself, he has been taken at his word. His reputation collapsed and has never been restored. When his admirers praise the 'honesty' of the *Autobiography*, they do him little service; there is a difference between honesty and uncouthness, and as far as the business of literature is concerned, one paragraph of Flaubert's letters is worth everything that Trollope wrote.

Yet it was discovered that young men in England, leaving for the Second World War, were leaving with some novel of Trollope's in their pockets. Though a writer of no great reputation, he was, as Lord David Cecil remarks, 'almost the only Victorian novelist whom our sensitive intelligentsia appear to be able to read without experiencing an intolerable sense of jar'.[1] Elizabeth Bowen traced the young people's interest to the stability of the world he wrote of – and, being a natural Tory, Trollope certainly wrote of the most stable part of his world and paid small attention to its firebrands and crackpots. Lord David traces his popularity to a 'realism' that has kept his work fresh while the less realistic work of his great contemporaries, filled with the burning questions and great ideals of their day, has dated. For those few kind words in favour of realism, one can forgive Lord David much, but even he will not admit Trollope among the greatest of the Victorians. He argues that Trollope's creative imagination is weak; that his characters have not the 'preternatural vitality' of Dickens's; that his style is bad by comparison with Hardy's, whose words 'at their worst ... manage to convey their author's temperament; at their best convey it with supreme force and beauty'; and that his power of visualising a scene – witness Johnny Eames's attack on Crosbie – is slight when we compare it with Troy's exhibition of swordplay in *Far from the Madding Crowd*.[2]

All this is so very convincing that I almost convince myself in recording it, but there is another side to the story. Hugh Walpole, too, uses the illustration of Troy's swordplay, but it seems to me a most unfortunate example. It is a remarkable and beautiful bit of writing, which might well have strayed into Hardy's novel from some romance of Stevenson's, and might equally well have strayed out again without anyone's noticing its absence. Nor do I desire characters to have the 'preternatural vitality' of Mr Pecksniff or Mr Punch, for this seems to me to degrade them to the level of puppets. The only thing I am sure of is that Trollope's style is weak compared with Hardy's or Dickens's. He had little or no feeling for poetry, and, what is considerably worse from my point of view, he also had little feeling for prose; his writing at its best never rises to the level of Stendhal's or Tolstoy's, which is Continental prose without benefit of poetry. Yet I think Trollope was as great a novelist as either, and a far greater novelist than Hardy.

This is something difficult to establish because there is no one novel of his which is outstanding. *The Last Chronicle of Barset* is, to my mind, a masterpiece as great as *The Red and the Black* or *Anna Karenina*, but it is disgracefully and inconsequentially padded, and I find it necessary to ask my students to make a rough reconstruction of it before making a final judgement. But Trollope's enduring popularity is evidence that needs to be examined. Lord David, as I say, ascribes this to Trollope's 'realism', but, in spite of his careful definition, it still seems to me a vague term in this particular context. For Jane Austen is likewise a 'realist', but her popularity is of a very different kind.

If one compares the realism of the two writers, one finds, I think, the quality that has kept Trollope so popular. She writes from a preconceived idea of conduct, where he does not. She is a moralist; Trollope is whatever the opposite of a moralist may be. Though Cecil declares that his standards were those of 'the

typical mid-Victorian gentleman', and though the statement
could be liberally documented from the pages of the
Autobiography, I do not for an instant think it is true.

If there is one phrase more than another which identifies a
novel by Trollope it is a phrase like 'With such censures I
cannot profess that I completely agree'. His favourite device is
to lead his reader very gently up the garden path of his own
conventions and prejudices and then to point out that the
reader is wrong. This is not very like the behaviour of a typical
mid-Victorian gentleman. On the contrary, it is an original and
personal approach to conduct, and I think that it is Trollope's
approach, rather than his treatment, which pleases intelligent
people in our time.

I do not mean that Trollope was a revolutionary figure. In
fact, he was a pernickety and crusty conservative who
distrusted all new views and methods. But, unlike most English
novelists, he did not start out with a cut-and-dried system of
morals and try to make his characters fit it. Instead, he made
the system fit the characters.

For instance, to take a slight example, one of the conventions
of the English novel is that of 'one man, one girl', and such is the
power of artistic convention that, whatever our own experience
may have taught us, we never question this as we read. We
could not conceive of Mr Knightly in love with Harriet Smith
as well as with Emma. We certainly could not believe that,
having been rejected by Emma, Mr Knightly would ever
immediately propose to Harriet. But Trollope's characters
usually behave in that way. One of his principal characters is
an Irish politician, Phineas Finn, who is engaged to a very nice
County Clare girl called Mary Flood-Jones. But when Phineas
comes to London, he immediately forgets all about Mary and
falls in love with a society woman, Lady Laura Standish. When
Lady Laura rejects him for a dreary Scottish fanatic named
Kennedy, Phineas at once transfers his affections to an heiress
called Violet Effingham, and when she, in turn, marries a mad
nobleman named Chiltern, he toys with the affections of a
Jewish widow, Madame Max Goesler. Her he finally does
marry, but not until he has become the widower of Mary
Flood-Jones. And if the reader, forgetting his own errors,

denounces Finn as a heartless rogue, Trollope, in that maddening way of his, chimes in with his pet phrase: 'With such censures I cannot profess that I completely agree.' Literature is one thing, life another.

If it were to be asserted here that a young man may be perfectly true to a first young woman while he is falling in love with a second, the readers of this story would probably be offended. But undoubtedly many men believe themselves to be true while undergoing this process, and many young women expect nothing else from their lovers.

Not only is Trollope not a moralist in Jane Austen's sense; he even loathes the sort of moral consistency she admires. This, I feel sure, goes back to something in his own youth and early manhood. His childhood was gloomy with the desperate gloom that poverty imposes on people of gentle birth. He grew up ignorant and a bit of a waster, and was pushed into a Civil Service job for which he was not qualified. It is probably significant that he could never reconcile himself to the principle of competitive examination, for had there been such a thing in his own youth, he might never have made good. 'I was always in trouble', he says mournfully. The dun who haunts Phineas Finn's lodgings with his perpetual 'I wish you would be punctual' was the same who haunted Trollope at his office. It was in despair of his own future that the poor wretch decided to become a novelist at all, for it was the only career his miserable education seemed to have left open to him. There is something almost heartbreaking in his admission that he became a writer only in default of something better, and a novelist because the 'higher' branches of literature were closed to him.

Poetry I did not believe to be within my grasp. The drama, too, which I would fain have chosen, I believed to be above me. For history, biography or essay writing, I had not sufficient erudition. But I thought it possible that I might write a novel.[3]

'*Only* a novel!' one can hear Jane Austen retort. 'Only some work in which the greatest powers of the mind are displayed, in which the most thorough knowledge of human nature, the happiest delineations of its varieties, the liveliest effusions of wit and humour are conveyed to the world in the best chosen language.'

It was only after Trollope's transfer to a miserable job in Ireland – perhaps by contrast with people worse off than himself – that he acquired command of himself and finally became the model of steadiness and probity we meet in the *Autobiography*. It is more than probable that when he diverts criticism from his characters, he is really diverting it from himself. He had endured more than his share, and proved its hollowness by his ultimate success.

But, whatever the reason, he expresses again and again his dislike for men of strong character. 'The man who holds out', he says in *The Duke's Children*, 'is not the man of the firmest opinions but the man of the hardest heart.' ('Heart', incidentally, is a key word with him.) 'He has probably found himself so placed that he cannot marry without money', explains an old lady in *The Eustace Diamonds*, 'and has wanted the firmness, or perhaps you will say the hardness of heart to say so openly.' And here is the same thing in an even more striking passage:

In social life we hardly stop to consider how much of that daring spirit which gives mastery comes from hardness of heart rather than from high purpose or true courage. The man who succumbs to his wife, the mother who succumbs to her daughter, the master who succumbs to his servant, is as often brought to servility by the continual aversion to the giving of pain, by a softness which causes the fretfulness of others to be an agony to himself as by any actual fear which the firmness of the imperious one may have produced. There is an inner softness, a thinness of the mind's skin, an incapability of seeing or even of thinking of the troubles of others with equanimity which produces a feeling akin to fear; but which is compatible not only with courage but with absolute firmness of purpose when the demand for firmness arises so strongly as to assert itself.[4]

There, in a paragraph, is the essential Trollope, the message of Trollope, if such a writer can be said to have a message; and there, unless I am grievously mistaken, speaks a man who had himself been badly mauled by life and who experienced an almost physical terror of doing the same to others. I suspect that this, too, is the real key to his conservatism in religion and politics. He detested reformers like Carlyle, Dickens and Ruskin because they were men of strong principles, and strong principles were things that he associated with hard hearts.

It is not merely that Trollope sympathised with so-called 'weak' people in situations that were merely ambiguous. Though he wrote within very strict taboos and his love stories are usually as conventionalised as the plots of seventeenth-century French comedies, he had the same sort of understanding of irregular relationships. One of the most delightful characters in English fiction is Lady Glencora Palliser, yet we find her in *Can You Forgive Her?* on the point of eloping with a penniless adventurer, Burgo Fitzgerald, and hindered only by the arrival of her husband to bring her home. The two lovers are at a dance, where they are being closely watched, and the whole episode is so characteristic of Trollope that one cannot ignore it. Here, better than anywhere else, one can see what importance he attaches to what he calls the 'heart'.

> The Duchess of St Bungay saw it and shook her head sorrowing – for the Duchess was good at heart. . . . Mrs Conway Sparkes saw it and drank it down with keen appetite . . . for Mrs Conway Sparkes was not good at heart. Lady Hartletop saw it and just raised her eyebrows. It was nothing to her. She liked to know what was going on as such knowledge was sometimes useful; but as for her heart – what she had in such matters was neither good nor bad.[5]

This, then, rather than realism, represents Trollope's true quality as a novelist. Not merely loyalty to the facts, but loyalty to a certain attitude to the facts, to a humility and passivity in the face of life. I do not wish to suggest that artistically this is an unmixed blessing. When Trollope is not inspired by his subject, it gives his work a flabbiness and lack of energy that leave the reader feeling very flat indeed. Even on the trivial plane of 'one man, one girl', it results in a lack of incisiveness; Phineas Finn would have been as happy with Lady Laura as with Madame Max; Lord Silverbridge would have done as well with Lady Mabel as with the American girl, Isabel Boncassen. Stendhal would have been inspired by these things to some sweeping generalisations about men and women, but Trollope merely notes that they are so and that to pretend otherwise would mean being false to one's experience.

But it is important to remember that this very humility gives Trollope a quality not possessed to a similar degree by any other English novelist. That quality is range, and by range I do not mean merely the ability he shares with Tolstoy of handling great masses of material while keeping its elements distinct. I mean primarily the power of exploring his characters fully, of so understanding their interior perspective that by a simple change of lighting he can suddenly reveal them to us in a different way; as, for instance, in the scene in *Can You Forgive Her?* where Burgo Fitzgerald, the penniless and desperate adventurer whose only hope is to seduce Lady Glencora for her money, buys a meal for a prostitute. It is a most remarkable scene. In any other novelist of the period it would prove that Fitzgerald had a heart of gold, or, alternatively, that the prostitute had a heart of gold, or that both had hearts of gold. In Trollope it is merely one of those minor shocks by which he reminds us that life is not simple; it indicates to us that Lady Glencora is not altogether a fool, and that Fitzgerald, for all his faults, retains a capacity for spontaneous behaviour which endears him to women.

But the best illustration is the wonderful scene of the death of Mrs Proudie in *The Last Chronicle of Barset*. It is also the best example of the fatuous attitude adopted by Trollope to his own work. In the *Autobiography* he tells us that one day, sitting in the Athenaeum Club, he overheard two clergymen denounce his work, particularly the character of Mrs Proudie. . . . Trollope fails to tell us what he could have done with Mrs Proudie if the two clergymen had not spoken. Of course, intuitively, if not intellectually, he had already known that Mrs Proudie had to die because Mr Crawley, the central figure of the novel, is drawn on such a scale that she and her henpecked husband could no longer be treated as figures of fun. You cannot be merely funny at the expense of Lear, and from the opening of the book we know that Mrs Proudie has at last met her match and that sooner or later she will be broken. She is broken, and leaves the room, knowing that her husband hates her. And then –

In spite of all her roughness and temper, Mrs Proudie was in this like other women – that she would fain have been loved had it been possible. She had always meant to serve him. She was conscious of that: conscious also in a way that although she had been industrious, although she had been faithful, although she was clever, yet she had failed. At the bottom of her heart she knew that she had been a bad wife.[6]

'Industrious, faithful, clever' – how subtly the woman's character has been deepened before she goes upstairs to die. Perhaps only a story-teller can realise the miracle that takes place in those chapters; the miracle of elevating two characters of low comedy to the plane of high tragedy without a single false note. Only one who understood his characters completely even in their absurdities could have changed the lighting so impressively and revealed the real perspective of their souls. The lines about Mrs Proudie, like the passage in Jane Austen's *Emma* where the heroine denounces Mrs Elton's vulgarity, are written on three different levels. On the conscious level, Mrs Proudie knows that she had always meant to be a good wife. On the semi-conscious level (notice the phrasing, 'conscious also *in a way*') she knows that she has failed. But in her feelings, in her 'heart', the only ultimate tribunal that Trollope recognises, there exists the knowledge, not yet permitted to reach consciousness, that she has been a bad wife.

But there is another sort of range which Trollope also had, and that is the power of describing extreme psychological types, types that are pathological or bordering on it. The principal character in *He Knew He Was Right* – a bad novel by Trollope's own standard – is a masterly presentation of pathological jealousy. Now, Proust can describe pathological jealousy with similar mastery, but Proust was the victim of what he described, and the fact that he described it so well meant that there were scores of other psychological states that he could not describe at all. Balzac could describe a variety of extreme psychological states, but his romantic imagination made it impossible for him to treat them from the point of view of simple normality, so that ultimately they fail to impress us. Trollope, because his capacity came from the passiveness and humility with which he contemplated people, could describe scores of such types, but each one rises simple and sheer from a flat plain of normality. Mr Kennedy, the Scotch puritan in *Phineas Finn*, is an example, as is 'the mad lord', Chiltern. But Mr Crawley of *The Last Chronicle* is the supreme example. He rises out of the commonplace and placid plane of the story, a giant figure who, even when we are looking elsewhere, still magnetises us like some mountain peak. And of all these characters it is almost impossible to say when they pass the limits of sanity, so closely have they been observed, so carefully has each step been recorded.

The Last Chronicle is the final volume in the Barchester series, and I do not think anyone has ever analysed the strange development in the works. This is the timetable:

1855	*The Warden*
1857	*Barchester Towers*
1858	*Doctor Thorne*
1861	*Framley Parsonage*
1864	*The Small House at Allington*
1867	*The Last Chronicle of Barset*[7]

In the manuscript of the *Autobiography*, Trollope deliberately deleted *The Small House at Allington*. This leaves us with five novels, of which four deal almost entirely with clerical life. The fifth, *Doctor Thorne*, is a book I find extremely dull. It was written to a plot of Thomas Trollope's, and even Trollope himself thought badly of it. Leave it in, and you have a panorama of English provincial life, centred on a cathedral city; take it out, and you have a saga of clerical life, all sections of it dealing in different ways with the same problem, the problem that in Mr Crawley is presented to us in its most complex and tragic form.

The saga begins in a very interesting way. *The Warden* deals with a contemporary controversy – that of clerical sinecures. English liberals, aiming at the abolition of feudal privileges, had exposed a succession of scandals concerning sinecures, and Trollope took advantage of this in an astute journalistic way. Trollope took a strong High Church line and satirised very cruelly and cleverly both Carlyle and Dickens, whom he disliked as reformers. He pokes fun at his own reformer, John Bold, who was so mad on the subject that he took up the cause of an old woman who had been overcharged at a turnpike by another old woman, 'rode through the gate himself, paying the toll, then brought an action against the gate-keeper and proved that all people coming up a certain by-lane and going down a certain other by-lane were toll-free'. John Bold was, in fact, another of those moralists whom Trollope disliked because their firmness of principle seemed to him to express a hardness of heart.

But Grantley [*sic* – Ed.], Bold's clerical opponent, is equally unfeeling. It is interesting to watch Grantley's development through the series. In this book he is very harshly handled. Though the son of a saintly bishop, he is a money-grubbing, success-worshipping man who reads Rabelais when he is supposed to be attending to his religious duties.

The Warden is a charming book. It has the quality of the best English novels, of entertaining in a civilised way, but it has no other outstanding quality, and I suspect that if it stood alone, it would be read only by fanatic admirers of Trollope like myself. The important thing is that it does not stand alone. For some reason, Trollope's imagination continued to linger about the cathedral close – as it was later to linger about the British House of Commons – and to ponder the problem of worldliness and sanctity in the Anglican Church. The result was *Barchester Towers*, an infinitely better book, and one that would have been outstanding, whoever had written it, even if it had had no successor. Once again, it has a background of newspaper controversy. For the cruel Whigs, who had attacked clerical sinecures, were attacking High Church bishops and replacing them by nominees of their own who would work with the Low Church and dissenting groups that were the backbone of the Liberal party. Trollope had as great a dislike for Low Church clergymen as he had for reformers. The book opens with the death of old Bishop Grantley, and after his son the Archdeacon has failed of his hopes, there arrive a Liberal, Low Church bishop, Proudie, his preposterous wife, and his greasy chaplain, Mr Slope. The book is a lament for the good old days when the church was the preserve of English gentlemen.

Few things are more interesting than the sudden change of attitude we feel toward the Archdeacon in those first brilliant chapters. He is as worldly as ever; all his hopes are centred on getting the see for himself; we feel that there is little to be said in his favour, even as opposed to the Proudies and the Slopes, but suddenly Trollope pulls us up with that phrase which I have already quoted, 'With such censures I cannot profess that I completely agree.'

> Our archdeacon was worldly – who among us is not so? He was ambitious – who among us is ashamed to own that 'last infirmity of noble minds'? He was avaricious, my readers will say. No – it was for love of lucre that he wished to be bishop of Barchester. He was his father's only child, and his father had left him great wealth. . . . He would be a richer man as archdeacon than he could be as bishop. But he certainly did desire to play first fiddle; he did desire to sit in full lawn sleeves among the peers of the realm; and he did desire, if the truth must out, to be called 'My Lord' by his reverend brethren.[8]

Even more interesting is the character of Grantley's friend, the scholar-priest Arabin, whom Grantley introduces into the diocese to gain an ally against the Low Church faction. Arabin is one of Newman's colleagues, so steeped in church history that he has already been tempted in the direction of Rome and saved from it only by the counsel of a half-crazy parson in a remote West Country village. This is the first hint we get of the character we later learn to know as Crawley, an extraordinary example of the way in which Trollope brooded over his creations. [We retain F.O'C.'s mis-spelling of Grantly – Ed.]

Barchester Towers is a fine book, spoiled, as Longman's reader pointed out,[9] by the introduction of the Stanhope family, who are an alien and jarring note. The intention is right, as showing the queer fish High Church discipline introduced into English religious life, but Trollope failed to allow for the fact that they tempt one to take a Low Church view of the whole situation. There is no such fault in *Framley Parsonage*. Once more the conflict is between piety and worldliness, but though Mark Robarts has led an irregular life and got himself badly into debt, Trollope comes out on his side in a much more outspoken way. It is all to the same tune: 'We are all the same. Life is like that. Don't be too censorious.'

It is no doubt very wrong to long after a naughty thing. But nevertheless we all do so. One may say that hankering after naughty things is the very essence of the evil into which we have been precipitated by Adam's fall. When we confess that we are all sinners, we confess that we all long after naughty things. And ambition is a great vice – as Mark Antony told us a long time ago – a great vice no doubt if the ambition of the man be with reference to his own advancement and not to the advancement of others. But then how many of us are there who are not ambitious in this vicious manner?[10]

Sanctity in this book is represented by Mr Crawley, whom his friend Arabin has brought to the neighbourhood, but even in him the issue of worldliness is not left out. Far from it; for, whether or not he realised it, Trollope had at last found the perfect character through whom he could express the essence of the conflict. Crawley is a saint, but a saint with a wife and family and only a hundred and thirty pounds a year to keep them on. Crawley's sanctity has had to take a terrible beating from his vanity.

He had always at his heart a feeling that he and his had been ill-used, and too often solaced himself at the devil's bidding with the conviction that eternity would make equal that which life in this world had made so unequal; the last bait that with which the devil angles after those who are struggling to elude his rod and line.[11]

There is one very curious thing about the character of Crawley on which no one has, I think, commented. His vanity is a writer's vanity, the same that Trollope described in the *Autobiography*, apparently unaware that every word he wrote could be applied with equal force to his greatest figure.

The author's poverty is, I think, harder to be borne than any other poverty. The man, whether rightly or wrongly, feels that the world is using him with extreme injustice. The more absolutely he fails, the higher, it is probable, he will reckon his own merits; and the keener will be the sense of injury in that he whose work is of so high a nature cannot get bread, while they whose tasks are mean are wrapped in luxury. 'I with my well-filled mind, with my clear intellect, with all my gifts, cannot earn a poor crown a day, while that fool, who simpers in a little room behind a shop, makes his thousands every year.' The very charity to which he too often is driven, is bitterer to him than to others. While he takes it he almost spurns the hand that gives it to him, and every fibre of his heart within him is bleeding with a sense of injury.[12]

It is Lord David Cecil who lumps Mr Crawley with the Archdeacon, Miss Dunstable, and Mrs Proudie as 'simple and positive, absorbed in the avocations of average human beings, devoid alike of psychological complexities and abstruse spiritual yearnings, made up of a few strongly marked qualities and idiosyncrasies'. I do not think this describes Trollope's characters very well, and I certainly do not think it describes Mr Crawley at all. He is one of the subtlest figures in all literature, and even between *Framley Parsonage* and *The Last Chronicle* Trollope continued to make discoveries about his character, and they still continue to astonish us. All the manifestations of his stern and ill-regulated piety we are familiar with, but who would suspect the sly and brutal humour or the childish pleasures of the true scholar?

And there was at times a lightness of heart about the man. In the course of the last winter he had translated into Greek irregular verse the very noble ballad of Lord Bateman, maintaining the rhythms and the rhyme, and had repeated it with uncouth glee till his daughter knew it by heart.[13]

How good that 'uncouth glee' is! It is like the playfulness of a rhinoceros.

But the problem for the critic remains – why the Church? The answer should be in that dull *Autobiography*, but it isn't, at least on the surface. Why is Trollope so obsessed by the conflict between sanctity and worldliness? Why does he come down again and again on the side of worldliness? Is it perhaps a personal conflict that he never consciously dealt with, a relic of those bitter early days of his?

In some way, the Church in these four novels represents vocation, and Trollope seems to be fighting off the admission of his own vocation and the responsibilities it imposes. His character remains something of a mystery. He had the dual character of the perfect Civil Servant and the author, and he must frequently have wondered which was the true Anthony Trollope. The thing that hindered him from being a great writer and that makes the *Autobiography* so unrevealing was the same thing that made him the great novelist he certainly was: lack of self-consciousness. The only character this patient and humble observer could never observe was his own, and one element in that character was certainly the Reverend Josiah Crawley.

SOURCE: excerpted from *The Mirror in the Roadway* (London, 1957), pp. 165–83.

NOTES

1. [Ed.] See Lord David Cecil, *Early Victorian Novelists* (London, 1934), pp. 245–79 passim.
2. [Ed.] See *Far From the Madding Crowd*, ch. 28.
3. [Ed.] *An Autobiography* (1883; new edn Oxford, 1980), pp. 52–3.
4. [Ed.] *The Way We Live Now*, ch. 47.
5. [Ed.] *Can You Forgive Her?*, ch. 50.
6. [Ed.] *The Last Chronicle of Barset*, ch. 66.
7. [Ed.] In considering O'Connor's timetable, we need to bear in mind that the Barsetshire novels were interspersed by others: see the discussion in the Introduction, above.
8. [Ed.] *Barchester Towers*, ch. 1.
9. [Ed.] See Trollope's comment on *Barchester Towers* in section 2 of Part One, above.
10. *Framley Parsonage*, ch. 4.
11. Ibid., ch. 15.
12. [Ed.] *An Autobiography*, p. 214.
13. [Ed.] *The Last Chronicle of Barset*, ch. 4.

Ronald Knox (1958)

'The secret of Barsetshire'

Those of us who can boast that we loved Trollope a generation ago, long before his almost unprecedented return to public favour, usually mean, if we will be honest with ourselves, that we loved Barsetshire. Not that you can write him off as *homo sex librorum*; but it is by a single group of his works that he stands or falls – if a man 'does not see anything' in *Framley Parsonage*, there is no more to be said. It was the publication of *The Warden* in 1855 that first brought Trollope fame; within two years after the publication of *The Last Chronicle* in 1867, his fame began to decline. And during the long years of occultation, you would meet a hundred people who had heard of Mrs Proudie for every one who had heard of Burgo Fitzgerald. Refuse, if you will, to put the Barsetshire novels on a separate pedestal; you must still put them in a separate category.

Trollope's 'clerical' novels have a principle of unity to which his political novels make no claim – unity of place. The world of *Phineas Finn* is real to us only because it is inhabited by the same set of people, and they are all interested in the same kind of thing. But *Doctor Thorne* does not reintroduce us to any of the characters we met in *Barchester Towers*, except the De Courcy lot; nor does the tentative sacerdotalism of Mr Oriel amount to anything more than a whiff of incense. It is the medical, not the clerical world of Barchester that comes and goes. Yet we know where we are, because there are familiar names on every sign-post. By an extraordinary piece of magic Trollope, alone among our novelists, has enriched England with a forty-first county. Nothing could be more unexpected; Trollope had no eye for scenery, and did not begin to notice things till he was inside your front gate. A carpet-bagger, if ever there was one, Trollope is for ever carrying off his readers to Scotland or Ireland, or even taking them for a Mediterranean cruise – it was in the Near East, actually, that he wrote *Doctor Thorne*.

Only in Barsetshire did he find a home wicket; for his readers, as for himself, it acquires the same kind of objectivity which belongs to Sherlock Holmes or Mr Pickwick. Even in *The Small House at Allington*, though we are in a different county, it is the next county, and Courcy Castle lies in fatal proximity.

He had stumbled on fairyland by accident. Notoriously, he himself claimed that Barchester was Winchester, not Salisbury or Wells, although he was prepared to admit (as if it were a thing of no consequence) that the county lay farther west. Ullathorne Court could only be appreciated by those who 'know something of the glories of Wiltshire, Dorsetshire and Somersetshire',[1] and Lady de Courcy, in what is plainly a catalogue of local *mésalliances*, draws attention to the fate of 'young Mr Everbeery, near Taunton'.[2] But in *The Warden* he had no intention of creating a county. The only place visited, outside Barchester and London, is the Archdeacon's rectory at Plumstead; the name is perhaps an echo from Somerset, from Huish Episcopi, but the description given is deliberately unfriendly. There is nothing to show that greater things are in the germ, Ullathorne, and Greshamsbury, and Framley, and Courcy, and Chaldicotes.

Indeed, *The Warden* gives promise of nothing beyond itself. It was conceived as a satire, by an author whom nature had not designed for a satirist. Trollope had a robust dislike of shams and abuses, an equally robust dislike of the glib reformer; and he admits that in *The Warden* he attempted the impossible feat of satirising both parties to a dispute at once. The funds of St Cross Hospital at Winchester had, so the newspapers said, been maladministered; and Trollope did not know whether to be more angry with the Church for having maladministered them, or with the newspapers for having said so. He attacked, simultaneously, the Church and the Press; the second part of his moral was the more noticeable, since it is common form in novels to attack the Church. People complained that the burlesque of Carlyle and of Dickens was a poor affair; the idols of a day are not easily dethroned. Actually, the parody of Carlyle is not bad, and the criticism of Dickens not undeserved. What really upsets the balance of the book is its anti-clericalism; there was no reason why the Archdeacon should keep a copy of Rabelais in a locked drawer, why one of his sons should have been nicknamed 'Soapy', in undisguised allusion to a well-known bishop. Either attack might have proved successful, but not both. You cannot horsewhip two people at the same time.

Two things redeem the book from failure – the melodramatic but moving role assigned to Eleanor, and the character of Mr Harding. Designed, perhaps, merely as a foil to show up the arrogance of the clergy by contrast, Mr Harding became a favourite with his author, and it was perhaps a reluctance to leave his story unfinished that gave the world *Barchester Towers*. Trollope, more than most authors, was a bad judge of his own works, but he could not fail to realise that Mr Harding was a creation. So sensitive a conscience, impressed by the world's judgments not from any tinge of worldliness, but because the world's judgements were its own mirror; so much mild obstinacy, that could hold its own in defiance of arguments which it could not meet, of dominant characters whom it was powerless to face – all *that* was a human being, real as Barsetshire is real, and deserved, no less than Barsetshire, an encore. If Mr Harding was capable of resigning the hospital, he was capable of refusing the deanery; he had not said his last word yet.

By a fortunate chance, a craftsman may be able to fashion something worth while out of his own waste material, as when the arms of an ivory crucifix take shape for themselves out of the parings left over from the tusk. And, in something the same way, authors have been able before now to produce a living character out of what was meant to be a mere accessory, a mere foil. Pinkerton in *The Wrecker* was perhaps invented as a foil to the amiable *fainéance* of Loudon Dodd, and it was only a desire to set off the inhuman cleverness of Sherlock Holmes that produced Dr Watson. Mr Harding – himself, as has been suggested, a foil for certain unamiable clerical characteristics – had to be set off by contrast with another clergyman; and he, Archdeacon Grantly, became a living figure in his turn, though not, take him for all in all, unamiable. There is, to be sure, no subtlety about him; no psychology to be compared with the psychology of his father-in-law. But he has become an institution; we long for his appearance because we know exactly what to expect of him. We know that he is always destined to be a spoke in the wheel, but a friendly, a well-meaning spoke. Do not be deceived by his portrait in *The Warden*; by the secret volume of Rabelais, by the ungracious triumph over a repentant John Bold; all that was but the raw material of the Archdeacon. In the first chapter of *Barchester Towers*, when he sat by the death-bed of his father the Bishop, wondering whether death would come before the ministry went out, he won Trollope over. The two shook hands, and he was a changed man thenceforward. An ogre, to be sure; an ogre to his sister-in-law and to Grace Crawley (not to mention Lord Dumbello), but an ogre with his heart in the right place. That is part of his creator's genius; by the same right as Lady Lufton, the Archdeadon is an ogre all the more effective because he is so companionable.

By now, Trollope had found fresh enemies to do his work for him. The two Proudies, bishop and bishopess, and their chaplain, Mr Slope, belong to a school of worldly, place-hunting Low Churchmen who can no longer claim the honoured name of 'Evangelical'. For the Proudies, Trollope has no good word till you reach the *Last Chronicle*; for Mr Slope, none at all. If he had weakened towards them, they would not have been such admirable figures of fun. Yet, with all his dislike of these, the new brooms, he is fair-minded enough to admit that there were abuses in the old order of things – witness Dr Vesey Stanhope, and the extraordinary family which he brought up in his villa on Lake Como. Their introduction into the atmosphere of a Cathedral close is the making of the book; they were so useful to its author that he cannot help rather liking them, for all his deep disapproval. With Mr Arabin, it is the other way round; Trollope loves him dearly, but as usual makes his hero something of a stick.

After such a resounding achievement, he must have been tempted to let well alone; the Barchester situation had now really worked itself out. But, to the comfort of posterity, Trollope found himself suffering from a nostalgia for Barsetshire. When he wrote *Doctor Thorne* he was on his travels, away from books; he could not remember that there was no 'e' in Grantly, and only one 'p' in Plumstead; it must be added that he fell into fatal errors about Barsetshire geography. But he was now committed to a series; the thing had become a habit with him. *Doctor Thorne* is probably his best book, certainly his best plot – though in a sense it was not his; he tells us that it was presented to him by his brother.[3] Its chief contribution to the saga of the county is, beyond doubt, Miss Dunstable. Trollope hated vulgarity, distrusted the *arriviste*, more than most authors. But Miss Dunstable, with her extraordinary faculty for making herself at home everywhere, sailed straight into Trollope's heart, with her companion, her pert doctor, her parrot and her poodle complete. She was too good to be dropped; and so we got *Framley Parsonage*.

But Miss Dunstable and the Greshams are not the only link which binds *Framley Parsonage* to *Doctor Thorne*. In a sense, it is the same story retold. This also is characteristic of Barsetshire, that the same patterns recur in it, almost as familiar as the sign-posts themselves. When Mr Crawley is tricked into accepting a lift from Farmer Mangle, on his famous visit to the palace, we get that curious clairvoyant feeling that all this has happened before. The memory which is really disturbing us is that of Mrs Quiverful, also bound for the palace, invoking the aid of Farmer Subsoil. When Johnny Eames attacks Mr Crosbie at Paddington, there is another echo from the past; Frank Gresham had horsewhipped Mr Moffat for the same offence – by some trick of unconscious memory, Trollope has called Mr Moffat Gustavus, and Mr Crosbie Adolphus. Bertie Stanhope proposing to Eleanor so as to please Charlotte, Frank Gresham proposing to Miss Dunstable to please his mother, Nat Sowerby proposing, again to Miss Dunstable, by way of Mrs Harold Smith – it is all the same pattern, somehow unspoiled for us by repetition. On a larger scale, it is no new thing when Lord Lufton succumbs to the bright eyes of Lucy Robarts, and she behaves perfectly, and the powers that rule at Framley are with difficulty overcome; it is the old story of Frank Gresham, and Mary Thorne, and Lady Arabella. Only, this time, it is more like Trollope; the melodrama has faded out, and you have a human situation instead. Lady Lufton is so infinitely more sympathetic than Lady Arabella; Lucy suffers from no disabilities of income or of blood. It all turns on the penetrating question, 'Is she not insignificant?' Nor, I think, if Lucy had suddenly become a great heiress would the *châtelaine* of Framley have made the same vulgar *volte-face* as Lady Arabella. It was because Lucy nursed Mrs Crawley through her illness that at last, unobtrusively but unmistakably, she signified.

With *Framley Parsonage*, Trollope climbs back into the pulpit which he had abandoned since *The Warden*. The ostentatious contrast between Mr Crawley and Mark Robarts is not accidental; the book is meant to be a tract about a subject which always haunted Trollope's mind, the unequal distribution of clerical incomes. But he does not succeed in writing a tract; his absorbing interest in human nature betrays him. Mr Crawley, who was perhaps only invented as a set-off to Mark Robarts's wealth, comes to dominate his author's mind, just as Mr Harding did. He is splendidly alive; a heroic figure, but with all the defects of his qualities, proud, obstinate, inconsiderate. For that very reason, he does not enforce the author's moral so cogently as poor Mr Quiverful. If Trollope is felicitous in portraying the clergy, he is still more so in portraying the wives of the clergy. It is to Mrs Crawley, as to Mrs Robarts, that our sympathies go out.

Framley Parsonage came three years after *Doctor Thorne*, *The Small House at Allington* three years later, *The Last Chronicle* three years later again – so admirably was Trollope a creature of routine. It almost looks as if *The Small House* had been forced into the series *malgré lui*, merely because Trollope said to himself 'It's time we gave 'em another Barchester'. To be sure, we spend an uncomfortable week at Courcy; we sample, for a moment, the cheerful loquacity of Mr Harding, the ominous silence of his granddaughter. But Allington is in a different county; in a different diocese, we may suspect, and a different hunt – if there was one. But there is worse than that; the general character of the book does not quite conform to type. The story is slow-moving, the plot thin, the interest concentrated on a very few persons, the pathos too sustained; Lord de Guest is the only quite convincing figure. Authentic Trollope it may be, but it has not the *élan* of Barsetshire.

It may have been some consciousness of this which induced

Trollope, most regrettably, to make the next novel of his series the last. By general admission *The Last Chronicle of Barset* is one of his very best books; but what most endears it to us is a kind of sunset glory – it reflects, at a hundred angles, those other chronicles which preceded it. The mystification about the cheque is a breath of wind which keeps the story moving, but hardly an end in itself; Grace Crawley, the heroine, repeats the experience of Mary Thorne and Lucy Robarts, but in a less spirited way; the sub-plot, up in London, is frankly unreadable. What delights us is to see all the characters we loved come on to the stage, make their bows, and take their applause. Mr Harding's death is worthy of his life; the Archdeacon is still impotently repressive, his wife still patiently critical of him; Mrs Proudie vulgarly obtrusive, her husband a forlorn puppet; Eleanor Arabin, to the last, does the wrong thing from the right motives. Miss Dunstable, now Mrs Thorne, is at her old tricks, impelling the hero to defy family opposition. Mr Crawley is still unmanageable, his wife still labouring to manage him; Lady Lufton so kind, but so heavy-handed, the Robartses so helpful, but so ineffective; Griselda as beautiful as ever, and as boring. Johnny Eames is a little older, but still a fool, Crosbie still irreclaimably a cad, Lily Dale still unreasonably a spinster. Even the minor characters are true to type; Mr Harding must not die without Dr Filgrave (though to be sure he has lost an 'l') to pronounce his medical epitaph, and what better piece of dialogue did Trollope ever write than Mr Robarts and Mr Oriel discussing Grace Crawley? 'We think her a great beauty', says the Rector of Framley; 'as for manners, I never saw a girl with a prettier way of her own.' 'Dear me', said Mr Oriel. 'I wish she had come to breakfast.' Poor Mr Oriel, so excellent and so comfortably off, yet always somehow missing the higher experiences!

Thus our author reassembles his characters, their destinies intertwined at last; a perfect mosaic, made up out of what we thought were brilliant chips from the master's workshop. So well trained are they by now, these Barsetshire folk, that each reacts effortlessly to the situation at a mere crack of the whip. Doubtless the question will always be debated, whether Mrs Proudie was artistically killable. But, once her death-warrant was out, who else could have described the repercussions of it with such courageous realism? Nor can we be certain, on merely artistic grounds, that the stroke which fell on Mrs Proudie was unpremeditated. We have all been brought up on the story of Trollope going home and finishing her off out of mere bravado, as the result of a chance remark made at the Club. But it is arguable that he 'had it in for her' already. The story was designed to have a happy ending – a happy ending, not simply for Grace Crawley and her father, not only for Plumstead Rectory, but for a whole countryside. Barsetshire was to be left at peace, and what peace could there be, so long as – we must leave it to the Archdeacon to finish up the quotation. The Whig principle which first reared its head when John Bold took up the wrongs of Hiram's bedesmen has worked itself out. Mr Slope has disappeared, and the Scatcherds, and Chaldicotes has been rescued from falling into the hands of the Duke. One focus of Whiggery remains, there in the palace. Let Mrs Proudie be liquidated, and Barchester can return to the immemorial peace which it enjoyed at the beginning of *The Warden*; the epic cycle is complete.

That, after all, is the secret of Barsetshire; that is why it appeals to a nostalgic age like our own. It symbolises the twilight of an *ancien régime*; a twilight which seemed to its contemporaries as though it might, perhaps, be only cloud. The reforms which belong to the first half of the nineteenth century had left their mark on English society, but as yet only an uncertain one, like ripples on the surface of a clear pool. Outwardly, the governing forces of English life seemed to remain what they were – the landed gentry, the Established Church, the two ancient universities; and yet that world of privilege was threatened. For a moment, when he sketched out the plot of *The Warden*, Trollope half believed that he was on the side of the reformers. But when, in the first chapter of *Barchester Towers*, the Government went out just in time to secure the appointment of a Whig bishop, the die was cast; from that point onwards the series is an epic of reaction; all Trollope's heroes are Conservatives, all his villains are Whigs. In the political novels, politics are only a game; in the 'clerical' novels all is in deadly earnest – every contested election, every vacant prebend, begins to matter. He could not save the old order of things, the world of privilege he so intimately loved, but his sympathies have embalmed the unavailing conflict.

Not that he will ever allow his characters to develop into a set of types, mere champions of the thing they stand for. And indeed, of all his clerical characters the one he loves best is the one he invented first, no champion at all, but a laggard, a skulker from the battle – that same Mr Harding who made the *gran rifiuto* over Hiram's Hospital, and could even reconcile himself to the thought of having Mr Slope for a son-in-law. All through the series the apologetic figure of the Precentor flits in and out, a man whose unaffected holiness acts as a kind of spirit-level by which the motives of other men can be gauged, even if they be as crooked as the motives of Adolphus Crosbie. Trollope seems more reluctant to make an end of his favourite than even of Mrs Proudie – would not have done so, perhaps, if he had not wanted to create a vacancy and install Mr Crawley as rector of St Ewold's. (As a matter of fact, Mr Harding never had been rector of St Ewold's; but he had been so patient and contented ever since he lost the wardenship that Trollope quite thought he was.)[4] Of all the Barsetshire novels, *The Warden* is perhaps the least conclusive and the least characteristic. But it is a fitting preface to the series, just because its hero is a man who contrives to stand outside all that epic of conflict; a man so essentially Christian that, if the world in general were like him, there would be no conflict at all.

SOURCE: excerpted from *Literary Distractions* (London, 1958), pp. 134–44.

NOTES

1. *Barchester Towers*, ch. 22.
2. *Doctor Thorne*, ch. 6.
3. [Ed.] See Trollope's comment on *Doctor Thorne* in section 2 of Part One, above.
4. *Barchester Towers*, last paragraph; cf. *The Last Chronicle of Barset*, ch. 36.

Arthur Pollard (1978)

The background to Barsetshire

. . . The clerical community of the mid-nineteenth century was a brilliant choice for a novelist to make, for it was not only of central concern in the eyes of the nation – it is difficult for a reader nowadays to realise how much the Church mattered then – but it was also at that particular period beset by enemies without and within. Wesley had done his work in the eighteenth century, and that work had bequeathed to the Church of England a revitalised section of Evangelicals and a schismatic split of Methodist dissenters. These latter with other nonconformist sects became ever more influential throughout the nineteenth century, but though this happened, and happened the more evidently at every widening of the parliamentary franchise in the successive Reform Acts, giving more power to the lower and urban classes, for all practical purposes the Dissenters made no significant impact on English society until after the Act of 1867. Their influence was not only limited; it was, as Matthew Arnold pointed out in *Culture and Anarchy* (1869), essentially provincial and lacking in standards.

The ecclesiastical world, then, that Trollope portrays, between the Reform Acts of 1832 and 1867, manifests the late flowering glories of the Church of England, but it is one also in which the shape of things to come is both evident and unwelcome. It was a world envisaged at a precise turning-point in its history, and Trollope was enough of a romantic to view with sorrow the world that was passing, even though there was much in it of which he could not approve. It is just such an environment that leads him into nostalgic raptures and sad regrets as he describes a typical cathedral close with its 'modest, comfortable clerical residents':

On one side there is an arched gate, – a gate that may possibly be capable of being locked, which gives to the spot a sweet savour of monastic privacy and ecclesiastical reserve; while on the other side the close opens itself freely to the city by paths leading, probably, under the dear old towers of the cathedral, by the graves of those who have been thought worthy of a resting-place so near the shrine. . . . It is true, indeed, that much of their glory has now departed from these hallowed places. The dean still keeps his deanery, but the number of resident canons has been terribly diminished. Houses intended for church dignitaries are let to prosperous tallow-chandlers, and in the window of a mansion in a close can, at this moment in which I am writing, be seen a notice that lodgings can be had there by a private gentleman – with a reference.

Clergymen of the Church of England (1866), pp. 38–9.

That had not happened to Archdeacon Grantly's Barchester, but it is the imminence of change – and its unwelcome distastefulness – that gives so much vigour to *Barchester Towers*. In old Bishop Grantly's time Barchester was a city of easy-going decorum: the archdeacon was *de facto* ruler of the diocese; the prebendaries and minor canons did their job – or didn't, as they chose. There were fashionable and not over-zealous clergy, as Mark Robarts is shown to be in *Framley Parsonage*; there were underpaid and overworked clergy like Crawley at Hogglestock; and there was Mr Harding in his leisured but innocent ease at Hiram's Hospital. Each had his place, and peace, even if it was of lethargy, spread, comfortably for the most part, over the diocese.

The change comes with the arrival of a new bishop, a friend of Evangelicals, if not an Evangelical himself. Those Anglicans who had been filled with the new spirituality which had inspired Wesley came mainly from Cambridge, where Charles Simeon exercised a lengthy and remarkable influence from 1782 to his death in 1836. Evangelicalism emphasised the need for deep personal commitment, and its earnestness resulted in vast new missionary endeavour abroad and social concern at home. Saintliness, however, was easily imitated by sanctimoniousness, and the enemies of the Evangelicals were not slow, nor disinclined, to confuse the one with the other. Mrs Trollope herself did this in what can only be regarded as a libellous portrait of J.W. Cunningham, Vicar of Harrow, in her novel, *The Vicar of Wrexhill*. Trollope himself confessed that he might 'have inherited some of [his] good mother's antipathies towards a certain clerical school'.[1] He possessed, however, somewhat greater self-control than she did in expressing them.

By the 1850s the Evangelicals were at the zenith of their power in the Church of England, and by their influence the whole tenor of English social life had been transformed. Inevitably, there was hypocrisy masquerading as piety; Thackeray in *The Newcomes* and Charlotte Brontë's Mr Brocklehurst both remind us of this. There was also the tremendously dynamic urge to social reform which is associated with the names of men like Shaftesbury. The novelists either did not see or else had no use for this. For Trollope, Shaftesbury merely recalled 'the last decade of years in which bishops are popularly supposed to have been selected in accordance with the advice of a religious Whig nobleman' (*Clergymen of the Church of England*, p. 18). Hence the power which he derives in the opening pages of *Barchester Towers* from the suspense as to which will die first, the bishop or the ministry.

The earlier dissolution of the latter brings Bishop Proudie to Barchester, and with him Mrs Proudie. The bishop is a liberal. His wife, however, in this, as in other ways, is made of sterner stuff. She is probably in Trollope's eyes an Evangelical: she is certainly a Sabbatarian. In other words, Trollope shrewdly took one aspect of Evangelical profession and chose to emphasise that alone. The attack on Mr Slope, the bishop's chaplain, is mounted from other angles (*Barchester Towers*, ch. 4). He is personally repulsive with red hair and clammy hands, Trollope probably remembering Uriah Heep in *David Copperfield*. Slope 'had been a sizar (i.e., a poor scholar) at Cambridge'; and one remembers Samuel Butler's jibe in *The Way of All Flesh* about the sizars of St John's, 'unprepossessing in features, gait and manners, unkempt and ill-dressed beyond what can be easily described'. He too is a Sabbatarian, but he is also more recognisably a Protestant with his dislike of Puseyites and their practices, preaching in the cathedral, for example, tactlessly indeed but with sentiments widely shared at the time, against the intoning of the service. Trollope's sympathies lie elsewhere, as can be seen when he speaks of the energy he attributes to the Tractarian Movement, which between 1833

and 1845 flourished in Oxford and from which the
Anglo-Catholic element in the Church of England traces its
origins:

> Dr Newman has gone to Rome, and Dr Pusey has perhaps helped to send
> many thither; but these men, and their brethren of the Tracts, stirred up
> throughout the country so strong a feeling of religion, gave rise by their works
> to so much thought on a matter which had been allowed for years to go on
> almost without any thought that it may be said of them that they made
> episcopal idleness impossible, and clerical idleness rare.
>
> *Clergymen of the Church of England* (1866), p. 25.

Yet in *Barchester Towers* it was the other party that was active,
and that Trollope portrays, with some animosity, in part for
being so.

The dangerous activities of Mr Slope have to be countered by
importation of Mr Arabin from Oxford. By contrast with Slope,
Arabin has the right background – son of a country gentleman,
Winchester and New College; not a double first because he had
been involved in the politics of Puseyism, 'but he revenged
himself on the university by putting firsts and double firsts out
of fashion for the year' (*Barchester Towers*, ch. 20); Fellow of
Lazarus, 'richest and most comfortable abode of Oxford dons'
(surely Christ Church, whose Dean at the time, Gaisford,
receiving a note from the Dean of Oriel, is said to have
commented: 'Alexander the coppersmith sendeth greeting to
Alexander the Great'!). He retreated (as Newman did to
Littlemore) to a remote Cornish parish to battle in agony of
soul with his inclinations towards Rome. Unlike Newman, he
returned 'a confirmed Protestant' and an established Oxford
man, 'ready at a moment's notice to take up the cudgels in
opposition to anything that savoured of an evangelical
bearing'. The Oxford Movement stressed the spiritual
integrity of the Church against what it saw as the dangerous
liberal Erastianism of the period after 1832. It exalted the office
of the priest and sought to dignify the externals of worship.
Trollope, however, is not concerned with these; he would have
claimed an inability to be so. For him it is High Church against
Low, Arabin against Slope.

Arabin, moreover, represents the establishment against the *parvenu*. Trollope may deplore the poverty of curates (*Clergymen of the Church of England*, p. 103; and cf. the portrait of Mr Saul in *The Claverings*), but he can still look with approval upon the wealth of the upper clergy:

A poor archdeacon, an archdeacon who did not keep a curate or two, an archdeacon who could not give a dinner and put a special bottle of wine upon the table, an archdeacon who did not keep a carriage or at least a one-horse chaise, an archdeacon without a man servant or a banker's account, would be no where, – if I may so speak, – in an English diocese. (ibid., p. 44)

One reason for deploring the poverty of curates is that it brings into the Church 'men of a lower class in life, who have come from harder antecedents ... all modern Churchmen will understand what must be the effect on the Church if such be the recruits to which the Church must trust' (ibid., p. 104). Such men will probably be mere 'literates' from theological colleges, and the result – 'an altered man, and as a man less attractive, less urbane, less genial, – in one significant word, less of a gentleman' (ibid., p. 60). Such was Thumble of Barchester, who could so brusquely attempt to intrude himself into Mr Crawley's duties at Hogglestock; by contrast, poor as he was, Crawley was learned and a gentleman.

Trollope's Church was a church of gentlemen within an established and recognised order. As Ronald Knox put it in his introduction to the Oxford edition of *The Warden* (1855), Trollope 'could not save the old order of things, the world of privilege he so intimately loved, but his sympathies have embalmed the unavailing conflict'.

SOURCE: excerpted from *Anthony Trollope* (London, 1978), pp. 49–53.

NOTE

1. T. H. Sweet Escott, *Trollope: His Public Services, Private Friends and Literary Originals* (London, 1913), p. 11.

PART THREE

Modern Studies on the Individual Novels

1. *THE WARDEN*

Anthony Cockshut   'Nothing is Sentimentalised'   (1955)

I

The Warden is the story of a clergyman who gave up his preferment because the newspapers attacked him. It may seem, at first sight, a meagre subject for a novel, and the emotions of the characters may seem excessive. The setting is parochial, the action limited. Gradually though, as we read, we find that the story has its wider implications, but that the author is leaving us to discover them for ourselves. The familiar theme of a clash between conscience and an established order is given unusual variations. For here conscience is halting, and the established order, though it may not be altogether lovable, has a good case; while the reformers are apt to be mixed in their motives and inaccurate in their facts. A delicate balance is maintained between the need to preserve and the need to change. Each party in the conflict seems, on his own ground, unanswerable.

Even in the material sense, of course, much more is at stake than one minor piece of preferment. Trollope distrusted prophecy, but he provided his readers with the materials for prophecy. If the imposing structure of the temporalities of Church and State shows a crack at one point, there will soon be other cracks. Iconoclasts are not satisfied with a single success. The archdeacon and the attorney-general were right to be seriously disturbed.

It is sometimes supposed that the Barchester world is perennially sunny and carefree. The late Sir Edward Marsh was expressing a very general view when he ascribed Trollope's appeal largely to the fact that 'it is pleasant to live for a space in a legendary era of peace and plenty, of solidity and stability'. No doubt it is pleasant, but no such era is to be found in *The Warden* or indeed in Trollope's work as a whole. Mr Harding has seen with humility and resignation, Dr Grantly has seen with baffled rage, the writing on the wall. The era of peace and plenty (did it ever exist?) is, for the characters in this book, already passing. The regrets which the more nostalgic modern readers feel for the calm of Barchester Close have already begun in Mr Harding's own heart. Our vision of that legendary calm is like the echo of an echo.

II

Mr Harding himself has proved to be one of the most appealing of Victorian heroes. Though he gives up nearly all his possessions for conscience, he is free from the self-confidence and condescension which so often prevent the noble heroes of fiction from being sympathetic. He does not lecture or generalise. He does not lay down the law for anyone else. He has seen a disturbing vision of himself as an exploiter of the poor, and it concerns himself alone. Modestly, persistently, and quite unsuccessfully, he tries to explain his vision to others. Its rational content eludes him, but we are made to feel its compelling imaginative force.

Most fictional accounts of a great renunciation fail because they deal only with the great gesture and overlook its practical effects. Trollope does not make this mistake. In chapter sixteen we see the great gesture as it appears to the man who makes it, complicated by miserable financial calculations, marred by the vain balance of imponderable possibilities for the future. We see too the sense of emptiness which follows when a great moral act has drained the soul of all its energy. Nothing is sentimentalised; indeed timidity plays its part with charity and gentleness in forming Harding's decision. And because it is all so realistic in detail, so unsentimental in conception, we feel the moral grandeur of the act more keenly than any rhetoric could make us do.

The same chapter also gives us a sample of one of Trollope's greatest gifts. He can convey, as well as anyone, a sense of the passage of time. Mr Harding's twelve weary hours in London all contain their full sixty minutes. What he can do for a day, Trollope can do also with the years. The Barchester cycle covers a long period and it makes us conscious of each drop in an ocean of time. Many things which are mentioned casually in *The Warden* (such as John Bold's ownership of 'The Dragon of Wantley') will become important in later Barchester stories. *The Warden* can be enjoyed by itself, but it can only be fully appreciated with its companions.

Mr Harding's mildness is slightly deceptive. He allows himself to be hectored and badgered for a long time, but in the end he will turn and stand at bay. Without perhaps being aware of it, the reader has been waiting for this. It is a great moment when the old man defies the attorney-general. The imaginary 'cello which has played so many mournful muted strains now has a different message: 'He was standing up, gallantly fronting Sir Abraham, and his right arm passed with bold and rapid sweeps before him, as though he were embracing some huge instrument, which allowed him to stand thus erect, and with the fingers of his left hand, he stopped, with preternatural velocity, a multitude of strings, which ranged from the top of his collar to the bottom of the lappet of his coat. Sir Abraham listened and looked in wonder.'

The long day in London has something of the excitement of the chase. All the time we are listening for the archdeacon's avenging step behind the fugitive. We hardly pause to ask ourselves why Mr Harding needed to go to London. He did not really want the attorney-general's advice; he knew in advance what it would be and had already decided to reject it. No, he was driven on by a deep need to signalise the momentous decision with a memorable and unprecedented act. Trollope does not tell us this. It is not his way to draw attention to his own subtleties.

III

It has been suggested that Trollope's grasp of character stops short at the upper and middle classes of society. To dispose of this charge it is merely necessary to turn to chapters four and twenty, where the old pensioners reveal their wisdom and their folly. The instinctive wisdom of Bunce, the vanity of Skulpit, afraid to lose his reputation as a scholar if he shows that he cannot sign his name, the pitiful avarice of the dying Bell, all these are unanswerably genuine. Trollope knew the peculiarities of every class, but he saw the same human weaknesses in them all. And the chief of these, in his eyes, was self-deception, which he detected in the most unlikely corners. The archdeacon, John Bold, Eleanor Harding, are all honest people, but all, like the ambitious bedesmen, are deceived about their own motives.

To say this may give the impression that Trollope was a bitterly satirical author. Satirical he was, but never bitter. Weakness and folly seemed to him too universal to be worth any large indignation. Indeed, he reserves his most severe attacks precisely for those satirists and reformers who ignore the natural frailty of mankind, divide everything into black and white, and thunder tediously on, drunk with their own rectitude. Thus John Bold, who has just a touch of this failing, is perhaps the least sympathetic of the book's leading characters. Mr Popular Sentiment, Mr Pessimist Anticant and *The Jupiter* receive no mercy at all.

Under these three aliases, Trollope was attacking Dickens, Carlyle and *The Times* newspaper respectively. Two objections might be made to these pieces of caricature – that they are unfair, and that, in a novel, they are irrelevant. There is some truth in each charge. Of the irrelevance we may perhaps say as Johnson said of certain passages in *Paradise Lost*, 'superfluities so beautiful, who would take away?' It should be remembered, too, that the novel of the 1850s was a much less specialised performance than the novel of to-day. The Jamesian concept of the novel as a pure work of art was unknown. Lively comments on topical questions interspersed in a good story were considered normal and even desirable.

The charge of unfairness is not so easy to deal with judicially. Of course there was much more in that genius Dickens, *The Times*, perhaps even in Carlyle, than appears in *The Warden*. Yet the tone of each is most amusingly caught, and the serious criticisms underlying the parody are not groundless. *The Times* was pontifical in 1855; Dickens was hasty in his judgements and inclined to wallow in his feelings of pity and indignation. Above all, Carlyle did thoroughly enjoy being gloomy and prophetic, and indeed made a very good thing out of it.

A more interesting question, perhaps, is why did Trollope find Dickens and Carlyle distasteful, when most of his contemporaries admired them so much. Primarily he was distrustful of all exaggeration, and did not recognise its important function in Dickens's art. His generation, as a whole, expected and welcomed exaggeration in literature. He felt that facts were sacred, motives were devious, even in the best of men. Writers who ignored these considerations he thought superficial.

IV

In some ways *The Warden* reads like a young man's book. The attack on Dickens is a little intemperate; the mock heroics and occasional archaisms are a little clumsy; the technical grasp is not yet quite certain. It is surprising to learn that Trollope was verging on forty when he wrote it. His boyhood and early manhood had been unhappy, and though his intelligence was good, its development was unusually slow. He had written several books before *The Warden*, with Irish or French settings, and none of them had been a success. *The Warden* was a new start, and it inaugurated a series of masterpieces. If Trollope at forty felt uncertain of himself, young for his age, and almost a failure, the vein commenced in *The Warden* was to make him, at fifty, a writer of great achievements.

As we finish reading, we feel we know Barchester and its inhabitants, and the London hotels and streets, and we know a good deal about the England of a hundred years ago. One thing we do not know – the author's own attitude to church reform. Trollope was a Liberal in politics, and intellectually convinced of the need for reform in church and state. But his deepest feelings were always more conservative than his thoughts. In the book's treatment of reform, there is a deep ambiguity, which springs partly indeed from the author's wish to be fair to all parties, but partly also from a division within himself. The character and history of Archdeacon Grantly provide an apt illustration of this. He appears first as a loud and somewhat shallow voice of church authority, and a secret and hypocritical reader of Rabelais. Even before the end of *The Warden* he has softened and improved. By the time we reach *The Last Chronicle of Barset* he has become a character of endless interest and intricacy, one of the most dear both to author and readers of Trollope's numerous creations. In the development of Dr Grantly we can read something of Trollope's own inconsistencies. On the whole these inconsistencies were a gain to him as a writer. What he lost in consistency he more than made up in subtlety and comprehensiveness.

Many people, of whom the present writer was one, begin their reading of Trollope with *The Warden*, the first book in his most celebrated series. If the Barsetshire books have a little unfairly crowded out his brilliant novels of the 'seventies and early 'eighties, that is not their fault. The rest of Trollope is usually underrated, but the Barsetshire books are fully worthy of their high reputation. In reading *The Warden* one is taking the first step into one of the most fascinatingly varied and satisfying territories of the English novel. Everyone should read Trollope. He appeals to the highly intellectual, and can be enjoyed by the lowbrow. *The Warden* is the best of all places to begin.

SOURCE: 'Introduction' to Collins New Classics edition (London, 1955), pp. 11–18.

M. A. Goldberg   A Commentary on the 'Age of Equipoise'   (1963)

Anthony Trollope, like his contemporary, Walter Bagehot, has frequently been viewed as the perfect exponent of the Victorian era. References to an 'age of Trollope' or an 'age of Bagehot' are numerous. Yet, almost invariably, historians have turned to Trollope's later political novels – *The Way We Live Now*, *Phineas*

Redux, The Prime Minister – rather than to the earlier works, *The Warden* or *Barchester Towers*, the two books on which Trollope's literary reputation seems to rest today. *The Warden*, especially, seems so non-political, that critics appear to have limited themselves to discussing the charm of Trollope's characterisation or to echoing Hawthorne's appraisal that, like all of Trollope's volumes, this is 'just as English as beef-steak'.

Early in *The Warden*, the author describes the position assumed by the Reverend Septimus Harding, precentor of Barchester Cathedral, toward the controversy raging about him. As warden of Hiram's Hospital, Mr Harding is the recipient of funds attendant to his position. When distribution of the funds is challenged, Mr Harding appears as the passive and innocent victim, caught between the battles of conservative church dignitaries (represented by his son-in-law, Archdeacon Grantly) and the radicals (represented by his prospective son-in-law, John Bold). In his analysis of the warden's situation, Trollope writes:

. . . Different feelings kept him silent; he was as yet afraid of differing from his son-in-law – he was anxious beyond measure to avoid even a semblance of rupture with any of his order, and was painfully fearful of having to come to an open quarrel with any person on any subject. His life had hitherto been so quiet, so free from strife; his little early troubles had required nothing but passive fortitude: his subsequent prosperity had never forced upon him any active cares – had never brought him into disagreeable contact with any one. He felt that he would give almost anything . . . could he by so doing have quietly dispelled the clouds that were gathering over him – could he have thus compromised the matter between the reformer and the conservative, between his possible son-in-law, Bold, and his positive son-in-law, the archdeacon.[1]

This is not just a problem of characterisation which we encounter here with the kindly old warden; nor is it wholly a matter of Trollope's political conservatism or his desire for ecclesiastical reform. True, we can interpret Mr Harding's passivity, his anxiety to avoid quarrels, his desire for peace and quiet, as essential characteristics of his personality; or, like Bradford A. Booth, who views this as a social drama which anticipates Ibsen by several decades, we can examine that personality in relation to the ethical problems posed, the larger

moral dilemma.[2] But another and larger dimension is added to
the novel if we grasp the characterisation and the ethical
problem within the framework of the age – in particular, the
1850s, when the novel first appeared, and which historians
increasingly have called the 'age of compromise' or the 'age of
equipoise'.

These were the middle Victorian years, the calm that
followed the bitter dissensions of the 1840s with open talk of
imminent revolution and class war, and the hostilities of the
1880s when English history was being molded by Irish
nationalism and Victorian radicalism was merging into
twentieth-century socialism. It is in this middle period, with
the Great Exhibition of 1851 at one pole and the Second Reform
Bill of 1867 at the other, that Asa Briggs discerns a
'superficially secure and comfortable England', preaching its
gospel of work and peace, while rallying round a banner
marked 'Rest and be thankful'.[3] G.M. Young perceives 'the
great peace of the fifties' by contrasting the starkness of James
Mill's earlier political dogmas with Bagehot's humorous
wisdom in the *English Constitution*, where large allowances were
made for stupidity, idleness and the good nature of mankind.
Life was too secure and too leisurely for agitation at this point,
the reforms of the prior decades having temporarily satisfied
both the conscience of the rich and the aspirations of the
impoverished, according to Young. Following the surges of an
impetuous and demanding youth, Victorianism was preparing
to settle down to a comfortable middle-age, one that was to
reach fulfillment with the Education Act of 1870, the Public
Health Act of 1874, the Municipal Conference summoned in
1875, or the Factory Acts of 1878.[4]

It is understandable why the tide of Trollope's literary affairs
turned with the publication of *The Warden* in 1855. Here, for the
first time, Trollope managed to capture the spirit of his age:
peace, quietude, equipoise, stability, compromise. We see this
spirit most clearly in the warden himself. Throughout the novel
he prefers compromise to strife, quietude to upheaval. Early in
the text, for example, when the first murmurs of discontent are
heard, that hospital funds have not been fairly divided between
the warden and his twelve bedesmen, Mr Harding declares his

intention of adding to each man's pittance twopence a day from his own pocket, thus raising the daily stipend to one shilling and sixpence. This appears as a munificent gesture, but it is aimed more at quelling dissension than at removing an evil, as the author himself insists:

> . . . That he himself was overpaid with his modest eight hundred pounds; – he who, out of that, voluntarily gave up sixty-two pounds eleven shillings and fourpence a year to his twelve old neighbours; – he who, for the money, does his precentor's work as no precentor has done it before, since Barchester Cathedral was built; – such an idea has never sullied his quiet, or disturbed his conscience (p. 12).

Though later the archdeacon urges him to dissuade the bedesmen from petitioning for a larger share of funds available, the warden prefers to 'remain quiet in the matter' (p. 62). He is 'in quiet possession of the good things he had' and would willingly have 'compromised the matter' out of his 'sheer love of quiet' (p. 70).

The situation demands some kind of change in the peace-loving warden, yet he remains adamant to the close – reinforced by Eleanor, his unmarried daughter who hopes her father 'would escape all this dreadful turmoil' (p. 177); and also by his friend, the old bishop, who 'wanted peace on the subject' (p. 112). To capitulate to the conservatives – the Archdeacon and Mrs Grantly, Sir Abraham Haphazard, Mr Chadwick, and Messrs Cox and Cumming – demands that Mr Harding deny the allegations of the newspapers, reject the petition of the bedesmen, and affirm the supremacy of the church militant. To accede to the reformers – John Bold, Tom Towers, the *Jupiter*, Dr Anticant and Mr Sentiment – demands that Mr Harding involve himself with the problem of justice, deny the supremacy of his order, and initiate some plan to distribute the funds more equitably. Mr Harding does neither. Instead, he slips quietly out of the dilemma by resigning. True, he speaks of an awakened conscience, but this is a conscience more nudged than aroused, for his resignation is aimed at removing himself from attack, not at alleviating wrongs. When he returns to his hotel, following his resignation, it is with no great moral exaltation, but 'quietly, and with a palpitating heart; he almost longed to escape round the corner, and delay the coming storm'. Chastised by his son-in-law, he feels small need to defend his stand; instead, we are told, his mind is chiefly engaged in reflecting 'how he could escape to bed'. His formal resignation, casting no aspersion upon the position being vacated, concedes that he will regard his successor 'as enjoying a clerical situation of the highest respectability'. And in his last farewell, urging his bedesmen 'to raise no further questions among yourselves as to the amount of his [the new warden's] income', he admits, 'I cannot say what should be the disposition of these moneys, or how they should be managed, and I have therefore thought it best to go' (pp. 238–72).

The quiet passivity of Mr Harding is somewhat determined by his worship of St Cecilia, who provides him with 'the divine source of all his melodious joy' (p. 47). As editor of *Harding's Church Music* and director of the Barchester choir, the warden, affectionately named 'old Catgut' by several of his bedesmen, is known to play the violoncello daily, honoring his friends with 'strains which were to him so full of almost ecstatic joy; and he used to boast that such was the air of the hospital, as to make it a precinct specially fit for the worship of St Cecilia' (p. 28).

Significantly, this is not the St Cecilia of Dryden, the saint who has the power to draw an angel down to earth with music that can 'untune the sky'. Nor is this Pope's Cecilia, whose powers can 'lift the soul to heaven'.[5] For Pope and Dryden, the dynamic harmony between the temporal and the eternal, a balance between the terrestrial and the celestial is embodied in the music of St Cecilia. The resultant order is cosmic – but for Mr Harding, music is an escape from the demands of both the mortal and the divine. For Mr Harding, Cecilia is the embodiment of personal peace, quiet and passivity. When John Bold comes to explain his projected attack upon the wardenship, Mr Harding removes himself from the troublesome matter by playing rapidly on his imaginary violoncello (p. 33). When the archdeacon arrives to counsel him on his role in the ensuing battle, the warden creates 'an ecstatic strain of perfect music, audible to himself and to St Cecilia' (p. 60). Forced to hear the legal equivocations of Sir

Abraham Haphazard, he escapes by 'playing sad dirges on invisible stringed instruments in all manner of positions' (p. 115). In London, while awaiting an audience with Sir Abraham, his dreams turn the coffee-house clock 'into a violoncello, with piano accompaniments'; and throughout his interview with the eminent barrister, to whom he first announces his resignation, the warden consistently plays 'a slow tune on an imaginary violoncello' (pp. 224–33).

Throughout, Trollope certainly handles the warden with a sympathy and a gentleness of satire, much as Fielding handles Parson Adams or as Goldsmith treats his benevolent Vicar. Both Parson Adams and Dr Primrose, however, are representative of the excesses of simple benevolence; they are Shaftesburian extremists who fail to recognise the prevalence of deceit and artifice in the world around them. For all his kindness and gentleness, though, Mr Harding is no advocate of Shaftesburian principle. At his advanced age, he can only advocate snugness and security. Clearly, his world is far removed from the doubts and affirmations of Mill and Carlyle, Newman and Hardy, Arnold and Ruskin.

In his *Autobiography*, Trollope outlines his initial intentions for the novel. At first glance, these appear more consonant with the political and ecclesiastical reforms of the thirties and forties. 'I had been struck by two opposite evils, – or what seemed to me to be evils, and . . . I thought that I might be able to expose them, or rather to describe them both in one and the same tale', Trollope announces . . . [Goldberg quotes 'the two evils' passage excerpted, as 'Genesis of the Novel', in the section on *The Warden* in Part One, above.] Though this may represent a polemical statement of the author's original intentions, we are told almost immediately of the novel that 'it failed altogether in the purport for which it was intended'.[6]

This disparity between thematic intent and artistic fulfilment is made all the more clear when we examine Trollope's satiric techniques in exposing the 'two opposite evils' with which he was initially concerned:

In former times great objects were attained by great work. When evils were to be reformed, reformers set about their heavy task with grave decorum and laborious argument. . . . We get on now with a lighter step, and quicker: ridicule is found to be more convincing than argument, imaginary agonies touch more than true sorrows, and monthly novels convince, when learned quartos fail to do so (pp. 205–6).

By elevating Mr Harding's two antagonists to the nobility and grandeur of epic heroes, while proportionately diminishing the value of their attendant actions, Trollope succeeds in mounting his ridicule of Archdeacon Grantly whose 'great fault is an overbearing assurance of the virtues and claims of his order' and whose 'great foible is an equally strong confidence in the dignity of his own manner and the eloquence of his own words'; and of John Bold who is 'too much imbued with the idea that he has a special mission for reforming' (pp. 15–21). The satire is made all the more propitious by providing the antagonists with the non-heroic, cello-playing warden as the object of their struggles.

Trollope's satiric techniques are clearly suggestive of Pope's *Rape of the Lock*, and certainly within the tradition of Boileau's *Le Lutrin* and Dryden's *MacFlecknoe*. This is not to suggest that Trollope is offering here a mock-epic, or even that the mock-epic devices are sustained throughout the text. Within a limited degree, however, the novelist develops his ridicule of the 'two opposite evils' through a series of epic allusions scattered throughout the book. These are especially concentrated in four significant chapters: 'The Warden's Tea Party' (ch. vi), 'The Jupiter' (ch. vii), 'Iphigenia' (ch. xi), and 'Mount Olympus' (ch. xiv).

Archdeacon Theophilus Grantly, whose praenomen satirises his temporal concerns, is very vigilant to the slightest attack upon the power and wealth of the church. A Virgilian simile describes the archdeacon girding himself for battle against the petitioning bedesmen: 'As the indomitable cock preparing for the combat, sharpens his spurs, shakes his feathers, and erects his comb, so did the archdeacon arrange his weapons for the coming war, without misgiving and without fear' (p. 55). Similarly, when the archdeacon indulges in a short game of whist during the warden's tea party, the scene is presented in the same mock-heroic manner. From one side of the room, to the sound of music, a black-coated corps engaged in terpsichorean skirmishes with the muslin ranks:

One by one they creep forth, and fire off little guns timidly, and without precision. Ah, my men, efforts such as these will take no cities, even though the enemy should be never so open to assault. At length a more deadly artillery is brought to bear; slowly, but with effect, the advance is made; the muslin ranks are broken, and fall into confusion; the formidable array of chairs gives way; the battle is no longer between opposing regiments, but hand to hand, and foot to foot with single combatants, as in the glorious day of old, when fighting was really noble (pp. 80–1).

Simultaneously, at the other side of the room arises another combat, more serious and more sober, for Archdeacon Grantly is engaged in the perils and enjoyments of whist against two prebendaries. Parallels with the famous card game in *The Rape of the Lock* are obvious:

See how the archdeacon, speechless in his agony, deposits on the board his cards, and looks to heaven or to the ceiling for support. . . . With care precise he places every card, weighs well the value of each mighty ace, each guarded king, and comfort-giving queen; speculates on knave and ten, counts all his suits, and sets his price upon the whole. . . . Thrice has constant fortune favoured the brace of prebendaries, ere the archdeacon rouses himself to the battle; but at the fourth assault he pins to the earth a prostrate king, laying low his crown and sceptre, bushy beard, and lowering brow, with a poor deuce (p. 81).

Precisely the same transvaluating techniques are perceptible in Trollope's handling of John Bold and his reforming friends. Recognisably 'the Barchester Brutus', Bold has initiated the attack upon the guardians of Hiram's Hospital. Confident that the warden's daughter, whom he loves, will not condemn him for doing what he thinks to be his duty, he bolsters himself 'with the consolations of a Roman'. The daily *Jupiter* has taken up the cause, and from its seat at Mount Olympus brought the affair under public notice 'in one of its leading thunderbolts' (pp. 76–90).

At Mount Olympus, 'the workshop of the gods', labors Tom

Towers, a 'heaven-sent messenger' who has been intimate with
Bold and often discussed with him the affairs of the hospital.

Who has not heard of Mount Olympus, – that high abode of all the powers of
type, that favoured seat of the great goddess Pica, that wondrous habitation of
gods and devils, from whence, with ceaseless hum of steam and never-ending
flow of Castalian ink, issue forth fifty thousand nightly edicts for the
governance of a subject nation?

Here, 'Tom Towers compounded thunderbolts for the
destruction of all that is evil and for the furtherance of all that is
good, in this and other hemispheres'. Tom Towers, who
appears 'as though he were a mortal man, and not a god
dispensing thunderbolts from Mount Olympus', is to be found
every morning, not far from the 'favoured abode of Themis',
where he can be seen 'inhaling ambrosia and sipping nectar in
the shape of toast and tea', striving studiously 'to look a man,
but knowing within his breast that he was a god' (p. 184).

When other characters enter the fray, they are also included
in Trollope's mock-epic. Thus, Mr Quiverful, the curate of
Puddingdale, whom the archdeacon suggests as the new
warden, is presented as a 'wretched clerical Priam, who was
endeavouring to feed his poor Hecuba and a dozen of Hectors
on the small proceeds of his ecclesiastical kingdom' (p. 264).
And Eleanor, who, unlike her father, is 'not at all addicted to
the Lydian school of romance', appears in the role of Iphigenia,
once she determines on self-sacrifice in extricating her father
from his miseries – though ultimately 'the altar on the shore of
the modern Aulis' reeks with no sacrifice, for John Bold agrees
readily to abandon his attack (pp. 138–55).

Although Trollope's initial intent was to expose the 'two
opposite evils', the Bolds and the Grantlys, the radicals and the
conservatives, obviously his own satiric techniques have
blunted the lance of his polemical battle. The satire is
humorous and sympathetic, more like Jane Austen's than
Swift's or Pope's. It lacks the clarity of aim and virulence of
manner so central to the great eighteenth-century satirists. In
the final analysis, Trollope is just as sympathetic to Bold and
Grantly, for all their excess, as he is toward the warden with his

moral evasions. Clearly at work with Trollope, mitigating his efforts as exposing the two evils, is his own desire for quietude and decorum. This is what made it impossible to take up one side and cling to it, cudgeling the *Jupiter*, say, or the warden – 'neither of these programmes recommended itself to my honesty', the novelist concedes in his autobiography.

Thus, satiric images surrounding John Bold are cushioned by Trollope's appraisal of Bold as 'brave, eager, and amusing; well-made and good-looking; young and enterprising; his character is in all respects good' (pp. 16–17). In addition, Bold's impending marriage with Eleanor necessarily diminishes from the effectiveness of Trollope's original goal, for this demands a sympathetic portrayal of the reformer.

Similarly, the archdeacon, presented throughout as an object of ridicule, is described in the closing pages as 'a gentleman and a man of conscience', one who 'improves the tone of society of those among whom he lives', whose 'aspirations are of a healthy, if not of the highest kind'. The novelist continues with this apologetic for Grantly:

We fear that he is represented in these pages as being worse than he is; but we have had to do with his foibles, and not with his virtues. We have seen only the weak side of the man, and have lacked the opportunity of bringing him forward on his strong ground. . . . On the whole, the Archdeacon of Barchester is a man doing more good than harm – a man to be furthered and supported, though perhaps also to be controlled; and it is a matter of regret to us that the course of our narrative has required that we should see more of his weakness than his strength (p. 266).

It is almost as if Trollope, anxious to avoid any semblance of political or ecclesiastical dissension, is carefully establishing his own system of checks and balances to enhance the peace and stability of the moment. Like the reigning political party, the novelist has as his responsibility securing and maintaining the peace within the microcosm of his art.

Professor Booth, viewing Mr Harding as the center of the novel, projects the warden as the embodiment of integrity, incorruptibility and virtue. Still, we must recognise that 'virtue' for the 1850s is to be distinguished from Shaftesburian benevolence, Paine's radicalism, or Mill's utilitarianism. For the warden, ethical principle is rather the essence of tranquillity, quietude and compromise. Trollope's gentle satire of the warden is no less apparent than his mock-heroics with Bold and Grantly. The whole situation is for Trollope a source of sympathetic humor. As with Bagehot's portrayal of the English constitution, large allowances must be made for stupidity, excessive zeal, and misplaced honor. What begins as ecclesiastical reform ends as a commentary on this whole 'age of equipoise'.

SOURCE: excerpted from *Nineteenth Century Fiction*, XVII (1963) pp. 381–90.

NOTES

1. *The Warden* (Oxford, 1980), p. 69. [The page-references in the text are to this edition – Ed.]
2. Bradford A. Booth, *Anthony Trollope: Aspects of His Life and Art*, (Bloomington, Indiana, 1958), pp. 34–9.
3. Asa Briggs, *Victorian People: A Reassessment of Persons and Themes*, 1857–67 (Chicago, 1954), pp. 1–14, 87–115.
4. G.M. Young, *Victorian England: Portrait of an Age* (1936; rev. ed., London and New York, 1954), pp. 131–8, 152–5.
5. For a fuller appraisal of shifting eighteenth-century standards toward St Cecilia in particular and toward music in general, see Norman Maclean, 'From Action to Image: Theories of the Lyric in the Eighteenth Century', in *Critics and Criticism*, ed. Ronald Crane (Chicago, 1952), pp. 408–60. Also Jean H. Hagstrum, *The Sister Arts: The Tradition of Literary Pictorialism and English Poetry from Dryden to Gray* (Chicago, 1958), pp. 203–5.
6. *An Autobiography* (Oxford, 1980), pp. 93–4.

Geoffrey Tillotson 'The Conscience of the Warden' (1964)

... To feel that he was in the wrongful receipt of money brought the warden into conflict with more than Mr Bold and England at large. It brought him into conflict with the archdeacon. His chief trouble is that he has an enemy within the camp, who is worse than the enemy outside it. The warden's resignation would have been easy, when once he was convinced that his position was justly questioned, if those around him had all been like his daughter and his friend the bishop. Having settled his conscience, the warden has still to settle his son-in-law.

Trollope is not a novelist to condemn any human being. He certainly does not condemn the archdeacon. At the end of the book comes a great plea for him. But he does not like the bully in him.

It is because of this presence of bullying that the story of *The Warden* is a variant of the David and Goliath story. It recounts the overthrow of the strong by the weak, of the noisy by the quiet, of the confident by the fearful, of the proud by the meek. It recounts a battle begun by Bold but, after his withdrawal, continued as a battle between two men who at the outset had both been on the same side. Because of this it is a story that is also a fable, that is, a story with a twofold interest: we are interested in the typical as well as in the specific, in the opposition of the weak and the strong as well as in the opposition of two clerics related by marriage and profession but otherwise sharply contrasted. In his farewell summary, Trollope speaks of the 'weak side' of the archdeacon, the side that made for his defeat. But that weak side, as the archdeacon reckoned it, was his strength:

... That he is a man somewhat too fond of his own way, and not sufficiently scrupulous in his manner of achieving it, his best friends cannot deny. That he is bigoted in favour not so much of his doctrines as of his cloth is also true; and it is true that the possession of a large income is a desire that sits near his heart. Nevertheless, the archdeacon is a gentleman and a man of conscience; he spends his money liberally and does the work he has to do with the best of his ability; he improves the tone of society of those among whom he lives. His aspirations are of a healthy, if not of the highest, kind. Though never an austere man, he upholds propriety of conduct both by example and precept. He is generous to the poor and hospitable to the rich; in matters of religion he is sincere and yet no Pharisee; he is in earnest and yet no fanatic. On the whole, the archdeacon of Barchester is a man doing more good than harm – a man to be furthered and supported, though perhaps also to be controlled; and it is matter of regret to us that the course of our narrative has required that we should see more of his weakness than his strength.

This summary does not take enough account of a trait of character that the story had made prominent – the archdeacon's secret indulgence in 'the witty mischief' of Rabelais. Because his reading of Rabelais was strictly secret, he was a hypocrite.

All told, the archdeacon was decidedly not a priest on the pattern that had been advocated by the great churchmen of the time. In one of the sermons preached just before he left the English church – twelve years before *The Warden* was published – Newman had asked:

Did our Saviour come on earth suddenly . . . in whom would He see the features of the Christians He and His Apostles left behind them?

And the answer had been that he would have seen those features in 'the humble monk, and the holy nun', for

. . . Who but these give up home and friends, wealth and ease, good name and liberty of will, for the kingdom of heaven? Where shall we find the image of St Paul, or St Peter, or St John, or of Mary the mother of Mark, or of Philip's daughters, but in those who, whether they remain in seclusion, or are sent over the earth, have calm faces, and sweet plaintive voices, and spare frames, and gentle manners, and hearts weaned from the world, and wills subdued; and for their meekness meet with insult, and for their purity with slander, and for their gravity with suspicion, and for their courage with cruelty; yet meet with Christ every where – Christ, their all-sufficient, everlasting portion, to make up to them, both here and hereafter, all they suffer, all they dare, for His Name's sake?

Now decidedly the archdeacon has nothing in common with
such people. He has more in common with the other clerical
ideal that in the mid-nineteenth century was championed by
Charles Kingsley, the ideal of the 'muscular Christian'.
Trollope suggests that he is of Kingsley's brand. When he is on
top of his world, as he thinks, the archdeacon assumes the
stance of a prizefighter: on one occasion 'he stood with his back
to the fire-place . . . stretching out vastly his huge arms, and
opening his burly chest'. On the other hand, Mr Harding has
much in common with the 'humble monk'. And in the sermon
placed next to that I have quoted is a sermon called 'Wisdom
and Innocence', which was given prominence when Kingsley
attacked Newman, nine years after the publication of *The
Warden*, in the famous quarrel that led Newman to write his
autobiography, *Apologia Pro Vita Sua*. Indeed we may read *The
Warden* as an illustration of that sermon, which took for text
Matthew x,16: 'Behold, I send you forth as sheep in the midst of
wolves; be ye therefore wise as serpents, and harmless as
doves.' Newman's argument was that the purer the church –
the more it had men like his humble monks, and in his way Mr
Harding, as its priests – the more it has been defenceless; 'the
more it has invited oppression, the more it has irritated the
proud and powerful'. Being forbidden to take up arms, humble
Christians when attacked, resort to subterfuge. By instinct men
avoid pain and trouble, and when Christians cannot do so they
are counselled by Jesus to find ways around their difficulties,
just as other weak persons would. And the way they get around
them is by practising 'the arts of the defenceless':

Even the inferior animals will teach us how wonderfully the Creator has
compensated to the weak their want of strength, by giving them other
qualities which may avail in their struggle with the strong. They have the gift
of fleetness; or they have a certain make and colour; or certain habits of living;
or some natural cunning, which enables them either to elude or even to
destroy their enemies. Brute force is countervailed by flight, brute passion by
prudence and artifice. Instances of a similar kind occur in our own race.
Those nations which are destitute of material force have recourse to the arts of
the unwarlike; they are fraudulent and crafty; they dissemble, negociate,
procrastinate, evading what they cannot resist, and wearing out what they
cannot crush. Thus is it with a captive, effeminate race, under the rule of the

strong and haughty. So is it with slaves; so is it with ill-used and oppressed children, who learn to be cowardly and deceitful towards their tyrants. So is it with the subjects of a despot, who encounter his axe or bowstring with the secret influence of intrigue and conspiracy, the dagger and the poisoned cup. They exercise the unalienable right of self-defence in such methods as they best may; only, since human nature is unscrupulous, guilt or innocence is all the same to them, if it works their purpose.

No wonder this sermon stuck in Kingsley's throat – Kingsley, who saw the Christian as a match for all comers, because of the openness of his nature and the courage to meet blows with blows. In *The Warden* the archdeacon is the muscular Christian and the warden the defenceless weakling who is put to deceitful shifts so as to get the better of his opponent. He contrives his escape from Barchester to London by underhand trickery:

> The warden had to make use of all his very moderate powers of intrigue to give his son-in-law the slip and get out of Barchester without being stopped on his road. No schoolboy ever ran away from school with more precaution and more dread of detection; no convict slipping down from a prison wall ever feared to see the jailer more entirely than Mr Harding did to see his son-in-law as he drove up in the pony-carriage to the railway station on the morning of his escape to London.

And when in London, with time on his hands before his interview with the attorney-general, his one concern is to evade discovery by the archdeacon, who he knows will be on his track. He puts holy places to use: he skulks in Westminster Abbey because – brilliant stroke! – he knows that that is one of the last places the archdeacon will think of visiting. Is not this exactly how the weak do act? Trollope is a profound psychologist, as Newman is. . . .

Source: excerpted from 'Afterword' to Signet Classics edition (New York 1964), pp. 206–12.

R. M. Polhemus   Changing England: Problems, Compromise and Comic Possibilities   (1968)

Returning home from Ireland in 1851, Trollope looked around him at the great transformation that was taking place in English life. Change brought difficulties to England, but unlike the change in Ireland, it was also bringing prosperity and hope. Exactly how, where, and why was the Victorian world moving, and what was all this sweeping social change likely to mean for typical Englishmen? Barsetshire gives us Trollope's answer.

In *The Warden*, *Barchester Towers*, and *Doctor Thorne*, he realised the comic potential of his world. Barset, where he set these three of his first four complete novels of English life, may be, as Hawthorne put it, 'just as real as if some giant had hewn a great lump out of the earth and put it under a glass case, with all its inhabitants going about their daily business';[1] but it is also a miniature England being hurled forward by the gigantic forces of history. The changing times of the fifties provided wonderful opportunities for social comedy. There is something inherently funny in the clash of newfangledness with old fashions, in a meeting, for example, between a freethinking bohemian and a staid bishop. In Barset, the new and the old continually jangle against each other, but somehow, the jarring of the past and future improves the quality of life.

Especially in his books written from 1853 to 1858, Trollope developed and became a master of the comedy of change. He liked to juxtapose radically different kinds of behavior in the face of changing conditions and to show the folly, the variety, and the joy of mid-Victorian life. His novels of the period have their black – sometimes very black – moments. We find in them, as in so much of Victorian literature, an elegiac note for a way of life that was passing. He made no attempt to gloss over the problems or the maladjustments of the times. But for the middle classes, at least, the decade was promising, and happy endings seemed realistically possible. The Barsetshire of these early books makes the phrase 'Victorian compromise' come clear; it is a place where the claims of the world and the individual conscience can be reconciled. . . .

I

'The function of the nineteenth century', writes G.M. Young, 'was to disengage the disinterested intelligence, to release it from the entanglements of party and sect . . . and to set it operating over the whole range of human life'.[2] We find a perfect example of Trollope's 'disinterested intelligence' in *The Warden* [pub. 1855 – Ed.]. He took the public controversy over ecclesiastical income and the larger issue of reform and turned it into a novel of poise and beauty. Journalistic reports – including one in Dickens's *Household Words*[3] – about Church abuse of endowment funds made him wonder just what impact an impersonal reform movement might have on the people directly affected. *The Warden* gets at the complexity of motives and feelings involved in reform. In his unassuming way Trollope makes clear the moral dilemma that progress can bring.

With all its light and sometimes awkward playfulness, *The Warden* is a very serious novel. Trollope barely does allow the comic possibilities in the story to win over its tragic potential. We have here, in its simplest form, the typical Trollopian situation of a man whose mode of life is suddenly challenged by changing conditions in his world. '[Harding] felt that he would give almost anything – much more than he knew he ought to do – to relieve himself from the storm which he feared was coming. It was so hard that the pleasant waters of his little stream should be disturbed and muddied by rough hands; that his quiet paths should be made a battlefield; that the unobtrusive corner of the world which had been allotted to him, as though by Providence, should be invaded and desecrated, and all within it made miserable and unsound.'[4] The problem which Trollope poses for Mr Harding lies at the heart of all of his best fiction: 'Now that I must rearrange my life, what should I do in these new circumstances?' How his characters go about resolving this question forms the most valuable part of his writing. *The Warden* is a prologue to all of Trollope's work in tone, subject matter, and particular concerns. The balance, the stress on conciliation, the fear of dehumanising utilitarianism, the celebration of modest private life that we find here, remain constant in his writing.

Harding, a clergyman and warden of Hiram's Hospital for old workingmen, is one of his great creations. He is both a unique figure and a kind of unheroic hero for modern times: an often ineffectual and ridiculous man who has little control over his era, but who conscientiously faces up to the necessity of making moral choices. The backers of reform charge that he unwittingly takes money which the Church ought to give his wards. Archdeacon Grantly, his domineering son-in-law, orders him to stand firm against this attack on Church privilege. Harding always tries to do the right thing, but ambitious men, irresistible social forces and his family constantly push and pull him about. Knowing that new times make new demands on one, he finally chooses, a bit wistfully, to do what best seems to reconcile his ethical standards with the world around him.

Not only Harding's plight, but the concrete difficulties of reform and change in the story give us a shock of recognition. Personal and party motives determine the sides over the hospital dispute, and the real merits of the case get lost. John Bold leads the attack on Harding's revenue. A young, enthusiastic reformer who loves ideal justice, he botches things because he knows nothing about the lives of those he wants to change. He understands neither himself nor the way he affects others. Trollope calls him a good man, but one characterised by 'arrogance of thought, unsustained by first-rate abilities, and that attempt at being better than his neighbours which jarred painfully on the feelings'.[5] The other moving spirit of change, Tom Towers, an editorial writer for *The Jupiter*, loves reform issues because they help him build his own power and the power of the press. On the other side of the question stand the worldly Grantly, who cares above all about family dignity and Church prerogative, and the ruthless, efficient attorney-general, Haphazard, who despises idealism of any kind. Trollope makes narrow-mindedness, selfishness, dogmatism, professionalism and the inability to sympathise with others the major obstacles in dealing properly with change.

Of all the Victorian novelists, Trollope best understands the relationship between a man and his work. The sanctification of work by the Victorian middle classes, and their professional pride, caused new problems. Neither Grantly nor Tom Towers, for example, can separate his opinion as a private citizen from what he considers to be good for his professional status. In *The Warden*, Trollope begins developing his theme that work comes more and more to determine identity, that what a man does tells him who he is. Clergymen in all the Barset novels are tempted to regard the ministry as a job rather than a calling and to see themselves as a worldly professional class. The drive for professional prestige muffles individual conscience. . . .

With his satire on the journalist Towers, Trollope declared his running war against a wayward press and the whole Victorian band of would-be mass-circulation sibyls and Cassandras. He realised both the potential force of public opinion and the tyrannical hold which the press was gaining on it. Towers says, 'The public is defrauded whenever private considerations are allowed to have weight', but Trollope continues in his own voice: 'Quite true, thou greatest oracle of the middle of the Nineteenth Century, thou sententious proclaimer of the purity of the press – the public is defrauded when it is purposely misled. Poor public! how often it is misled!'[6] . . . Tom Towers actually knows nothing about Harding's affair, but ignorance does not stop him from pronouncing judgement in *The Jupiter*. Trollope hated the press for its sensationalism, inaccuracy and arrogant pomposity.

His witty parodies of Carlyle and Dickens as Dr Pessimist Anticant and Mr Popular Sentiment also satirise the self-righteousness and oversimplified morality of the Victorian sages. Mr Sentiment writes a novel called *The Almshouse* with a caricature of Harding: 'What story was ever written without a demon? What novel, what history, what work of any sort, what world, would be perfect without existing principles of both good and evil? The demon of *The Almshouse* was the clerical owner of this comfortable abode. He was a man well stricken in years, but still strong to do evil: he was one who looked cruelly out of a hot, passionate, blood-shot eye.'[7]

Trollope is insisting in *The Warden* that moral questions in an age of transitions are not easy. The secular pundit for the masses forgets sometimes that he pontificates, not about abstractions or statistics, but about flesh and blood. In solving complex problems, it does no good to set up wicked straw men to hate or to propose simplistic answers. Trollope wanted to show the harm that the high priests of public opinion can do. The individual human being often gets lost in their generalisations, and polemics blur the uniqueness of each case.

What Anthony Cockshut calls Trollope's 'deep-rooted emotional conservatism'[8] shows through in his satire on the zealous reformers and most obviously in his fearful attitudes towards urban power. Bold, Towers, *The Jupiter*, the success-happy parvenu, Haphazard, and all the rest of the dynamic men who disrupt Harding's placid Barchester life come out of London. The growing influence of London over country life and the physical and moral ugliness of the city impressed Trollope. The city, with its horror, becomes a new Chapel Perilous through which Mr Harding must pass in trying to set his life in order. His visit to London turns into a comic nightmare:

A slipshod girl ushered him into a long back room, filled with boxes for the accommodation of parties, in one of which he took his seat. In a more miserably forlorn place he could not have found himself; the room smelt of fish and sawdust, and stale tobacco smoke, with a slight taint of escaped gas; everything was rough, and dirty, and disreputable; the cloth which they put before him was abominable; the knives and forks were bruised, and hacked, and filthy; and everything was impregnated with fish. He had one comfort, however, he was quite alone; there was no one there to look on his dismay; nor was it probable that any one would come to do so. It was a London supper-house.[9]

Harding passes his test of courage and is able to retreat into the comparatively wholesome life of Barset, but London power has changed Barset at the end of the book. It is not as cozy for Harding as it was in the beginning. *The Warden* has a touch of the pastorale about it, as do all the novels of this period. But the pastorale is a genre which blooms, after all, in times of urbanisation, and it almost always shows man's irrepressible will to fashion for himself 'the good old days'. Trollope's whole image of Barset shows that he both longs for the communal comforts of county provincialism and recognises the slow, inevitable suburbanisation of modern life.

The conservative's deepest fear is that change will be for the worse, and this sad kind of change takes place in the novel. At the beginning Trollope writes, 'Hiram's Hospital . . . is a picturesque building. . . . A broad gravel walk runs between the building and the river, which is always trim and cared for. . . . Further from the water . . . are the pretty oriel windows of Mr Harding's house, and his well-mown lawn.'[10] At the end, we get another view: 'The whole place has become disordered and ugly. The warden's garden is a wretched wilderness, the drive and paths are covered with weeds, the flower-beds are bare, and the unshorn lawn is now a mass of long damp grass and unwholesome moss. The beauty of the place is gone; its attractions have withered.'[11] The change in the landscape symbolises the change for the hospital residents. The ignorant workingmen find themselves at the close with no Mr Harding to take care of them. They have been mere pawns in a political controversy. No one has seen them as individual men, except Harding, and when he goes they become wretched, lonely, old people, still hoping vainly for more money, but finding only emptiness.

II

And yet despite the low-key tragedy of the hospital, the comic possibilities of this world *are* realised. The marriage of John Bold and Harding's daughter Eleanor shows human affection triumphing over party spirit. But the real comic affirmation in the novel is Harding himself. Mr Harding, a single man, matters more to Trollope than the hospital community, and *The Warden* becomes one of the best expressions of Victorian faith in individualism.

Harding's gain overshadows the communal loss. By resigning quietly when he does not have to, and giving up his income against the advice of Haphazard and Grantly, he gains self-respect and asserts the integrity of his conscience. The pressures of change give him the opportunity to live up to the ideals of his religion and put moral concerns before his own worldly interests. For Trollope, the health of society and peace of mind rest ultimately on the strength of personal conscience and the ability of men to act unselfishly. As long as he sees the force of changing circumstances leading to a victory of moral conscience, his comic vision prevails.

The rhetoric of Trollope's fiction works here in a delicate and effective way. It ought to convince us, in the end, how successful, if unlikely, a man Harding is in becoming what the existentialists call an 'authentic' human being. For a good part of the novel Trollope makes Harding a sometimes weak, bumbling and laughable creature. We tend to think of him as amusing and kind but ineffectual – his habit, when things go wrong, of letting his hands play imaginary dirges on an imaginary cello sums up his harmless futility. Yet by the end of the novel, if we understand what Trollope tells and shows us, we have to stop patronising Harding or we stand convicted of serious moral failings. If we think of him as inconsequential, then we identify ourselves with the point of view of the cold materialistic Haphazard, which reduces human worth to a matter of cash balances and *Who's Who* listings. If Harding seems too slight a figure to be significant, then we find ourselves agreeing with Tom Towers that only the sensational surfaces of life with headline potential count. If we think that Harding's qualms about staying at the hospital are foolish, then we take the dogmatic Grantly view that makes private conscience seem unimportant. Unlike Grantly, Harding can act against narrowly parochial interests; unlike Haphazard, he does not need worldly status and success to prove to himself that he is worthy; and unlike Towers, his ego does not require power over others: he can make his decision about the hospital without insisting that everyone else think as he does. Harding is sure enough of himself to respect the freedom and conscience of others.

Trollope's moral rhetoric works in two ways. First of all, it persuades us that almost anybody has, like Harding, the capacity for independent, conscientious moral action;

Harding, after all, is often ridiculous, and he has no great genius or force of character. But the rhetoric also shows us how hard it is for a man to resist outside pressures and *use* that capacity. To act independently and morally can mean upsetting the whole pattern of one's life. A passage that comes after Harding has just told Grantly that he is resigning reveals Trollope's subtle rhetoric: 'Had he not cause for triumph? Had he not been supremely successful? Had he not for the first time in his life held his own purpose against that of his son-in-law, and manfully combated against great odds – against the archdeacon's wife as well as the archdeacon? Had he not gained a great victory and was it not fit that he should step into his cab with triumph?'[12]

At first it appears that Trollope is being ironical. Standing up to Grantly may be a moral victory for timid little Harding, but for anyone else it would be a small triumph, and his pride is comic. Our next reaction ought to be to ask ourselves what kind of thing an act of conscience is. Moral courage does not usually mean making a grand gesture of universal significance or championing some cause that everyone around you believes in. Most often, it means upholding a point of view when those close to you, who have power to hurt you, disagree. Harding is funny – a few proud thoughts and a splurge on a cab can make a celebration for him – but he is also admirable. He can do that difficult thing of 'holding his own purpose'. In this characterisation, Trollope challenges and broadens our conception of what it is to be a superior person.

The problems of change loom large in *The Warden*, but he saw how the changing world could help to make a man aware of his individuality and free his 'disinterested intelligence'. Harding not only makes a satisfactory moral adjustment to the times, he positively changes his own life for the better. Out of the Barchester clash between impersonal reform and stand-pat rigidity comes his hard-won, faintly comic, yet beautiful serenity at the end.

Mr Harding is still precentor of Barchester; and it is very rarely the case that those who attend the Sunday morning service miss the gratification of hearing him chant the litany as no other man in England can do it. . . . Mr

Harding, we say, is not an unhappy man: he keeps his lodgings, but they are of little use to him, except as being the one spot on earth which he calls his own. His time is spent chiefly at his daughter's or at the palace; he is never left alone, even should he wish to be so; and within twelve months of Eleanor's marriage his determination to live at his own lodging had been broken so far through and abandoned, that he consented to have his violoncello permanently removed to his daughter's house.

Every other day a message is brought to him from the bishop. 'The bishop's compliments, and his lordship is not very well today, and he hopes Mr Harding will dine with him.' This bulletin as to the old man's health is a myth; for though he is over eighty he is never ill, and will probably die some day, as a spark goes out, gradually and without a struggle. Mr Harding does dine with him very often, which means going to the palace at three and remaining till ten; and whenever he does not the bishop whines, and says that the port wine is corked, and complains that nobody attends to him and frets himself off to bed an hour before his time.

It was long before the people of Barchester forgot to call Mr Harding by his long well-known name of Warden. It had become so customary to say Mr Warden, that it was not easily dropped. 'No, no', he always says when so addressed, 'not warden now, only precentor.'[13]

But he really is still warden – a self-deprecating warden now of the discriminating private conscience on which personal and communal happiness rest.

SOURCE: excerpted from chapter in *The Changing World of Anthony Trollope* (Berkeley, Cal., 1968; Cambridge, 1968), pp. 24–34.

NOTES

1. See *An Autobiography* (1883; new edition Oxford, 1980), p. 144.

2. G.M. Young, *Victorian England: Portrait of an Age* (1936; rev. ed., London, 1960), p. 186.

3. See Michael Sadleir, *Trollope: A Commentary* (1927; new edition London, 1951), pp. 164–5.

4. *The Warden* (new edition Oxford, 1980), ch. 5, p. 69.

5. *Barchester Towers* (new edition London, 1960), ch. 2, p. 13.

6. *The Warden*, ed. cit., ch. 15, p. 204.

7. Ibid., ch. 15, p. 207.

8. Anthony Cockshut, *Anthony Trollope: A Critical Study* (London, 1955), p. 177.

9. *The Warden*, ed. cit., ch. 16, p. 224.

10. Ibid., ch. 1, pp. 7–8.
11. Ibid., ch. 21, p. 281.
12. Ibid., ch. 19, p. 256.
13. Ibid., ch. 21, pp. 283–4.

2. *BARCHESTER TOWERS*

Pamela Hansford Johnson   'The Most
Amiable of Novelists'   (1952)

Anthony Trollope was a critic of human beings; he had no
complaint to make of society which, in the pattern of his time,
he found entirely satisfactory. Dickens had written *Hard Times*
and was writing *Little Dorrit* when Trollope, in 1857, published
Barchester Towers, the most urbane and shapely of his novels,
and his masterpiece.

Of all the great novelists Trollope is perhaps the most
amiable, a full man, calm, balanced, wise, taking as much
delight in observing the mechanics of living (the honourable
and necessary place-seeking, the financial aspects of
Preferment, the domestic complications of rearing fourteen
children) as in observing the emotional chances and
mischances of man. His sense of the absurd is all-embracing; he
can get as much fun from a discreet discussion of deanery
finances in the Bishop's library as from the preposterous
spectacle of Signora Vesey-Neroni's skidding sofa, as it rips half
the lace and all the dignity from the back of Mrs Proudie at the
latter's first palace reception.

Barchester Towers is a group novel, all the characters bound
together by the common interest of a special and reserved kind
of life. We see no society in Barchester but cathedral society,
unless we accept as more than figures on a backcloth the gentry
and the rustics at Miss Thorne's garden party. Everyone eats and
eats well, so there must be a butcher, a baker and a grocer; tables
are laid and beds made, so there must be servants. There is no
question of these characters being drawn in subservient shadow
to the major persons of the story; they simply do not exist.

Trollope's selective sense was acute. Judging precisely what was necessary to the unfolding of his tale, he never included a single character, a single incident, which was not. His book, for all its length, is tight-knit, a beautiful and intricate fabric unspoiled even by the 'Chapter the Last' which was a convention of the time.

These final chapters, enjoined by custom, served the purpose of tying up all the loose ends and pointing an acceptable moral. The Victorian reader always wanted to know exactly what happened to everybody *after* the end; and so the real end of most Victorian novels lies in the final paragraph of the penultimate chapter, the 'Conclusion' being no more than an addendum for the satisfaction of the reader's curiosity and for reassuring him of the ethical value of the work as a whole.

Trollope, who was bound as much by this convention as Dickens or Charlotte Brontë, used his 'Conclusion' to give an extra fillip to the book, a gratuitous and brilliant touch of the ridiculous. The Archdeacon's gift to Mr Harding of 'a magnificent violoncello with all the new-fashioned arrangements and expensive additions, which on account of these novelties that gentleman could never use with satisfaction to his audience or pleasure to himself', is one of the delights of the novel, and an example of Trollope's aesthetic prudence. He let nothing go to waste, not even the customary wasteland of Chapter the Last.

If he never criticised society, save to expound its faults and then accept them with equanimity, he could be profoundly critical of human beings, using for each one a distinctive method of analysis appropriate to the weight of his or her rôle in the story. Trollope's character studies are by no means made on a uniform level. The masterful Mrs Proudie, splendid and fearsome as she is, is drawn nevertheless on the plane of caricature; and Mr Slope has little more objective reality than a drawing by Phiz, a delineation rich with a life of its own, but not with the more complex life of breathing humanity. Slope is delightful because of his rôle: we are fascinated rather by what he does than by what he is. We are charmed by Mrs Proudie less because she is a recognisable individual than because, as the classic type of female bully (a weightier Xanthippe who at a lower stratum could have been a Mrs Gargery), she keeps us in constant anticipation of the defeats that must inevitably come her way. Neither she nor Mr Slope are creatures who could stand alone; their interest depends entirely upon their inter-relation with other people.

Eleanor Bold is, on the other hand, a careful and affectionate portrait of a young woman of considerable intelligence and force of character. We are allowed to study her when she is solitary, *for her own sake*: neither Mrs Proudie nor Mr Slope can be left for very long on their own and, in fact, seldom are. What happens to Eleanor is not really important, though we may feel Mr Arabin rather a dull fellow to replace the young and hot-headed John Bold, whose death occurred in *The Warden*: our interest is in herself, in what she *is* rather than in how she fares.

The most curious and most subtle of Trollope's female characterisations is, however, the Signora Vesey-Neroni, that dubious beauty condemned to lie for ever upon her sofa, and not minding her fate very much. On the surface this portrait has the conventional touch of caricature, the conventional splash and dash. The Signora, hungry for male attention and determined to have the whole of it, is at first a marmoreal figure of fun. Mother of 'the last of the blood of the emperors', she uses her infirmity to further her own ends. At Barchester receptions she is spectacular; everything comes to a standstill while she is borne in on her sofa and set down in the most conspicuous place in the room. All the gentlemen rush to attend her, and none of the fuming women dare criticise her lest they be charged with uncharitableness towards the afflicted. She is top dog and she knows it; and the reader's immediate reaction is merely a delighted but irritated amusement.

Gradually, however, the portrait begins to sharpen, and as it does so its audacity becomes apparent. It is a shrewd, mature study of a thoroughly shady woman with a really disreputable past. If the Signora had been drawn realistically, without the absurdity and the caricature, the Victorian reader would not have tolerated her for a moment. The 'Woman with a Past' of conventional fiction was seldom guilty of anything beyond a mild indiscretion, a rash letter or two, at most, perhaps, an illicit, but girlish embrace. Trollope, a man of the world, knew what the Vesey-Neronis were really like and what the precise circumstances of their Pasts had been. He then used his skill to present them in such a manner that though the truth was there for the sophisticated reader to discover, it was overcast by a deliberate heightening into the grotesque. No one who preferred not to see below a certain level was ever forced by Trollope to do so.

If the Signora is observed with fun, she is treated also with unexpected charity. Her generous gesture to Eleanor Bold is not merely a fine one, but one in psychological accord with her essential nature. Such women are selfish, but rarely mean. They know when to cut their losses. If they cannot play their own particular game any longer, they will often play with fervent good humour on the side of the undefeated rival. In the final scene with Eleanor the Signora is no longer ridiculous; for a moment, and a fleeting one, she assumes her full human significance.

Mr Slope is the only clerical character drawn with a farcical slant, a gangling and soapy man, embarrassingly pushful but of no mean intelligence, a man subtly repulsive of person, obviously repulsive of mind. He is the prototype of Rochester's curate with his 'low-soled high-lows', for when Rochester imagined St John Rivers he imagined Slope, and with the best will in the world one cannot feel that he was entirely wide of the mark. All the other people of *Barchester Towers* are conceived on a more human basis, are seen, if not precisely face to face, at least through a clear and not a distorting glass.

Bishop Proudie is the most surely imagined. Trollope, with his delicate knack of false direction, first presents him as a poor thing, then gradually makes it apparent that the Bishop is not quite so poor in spirit as might have been supposed. Two things sustain him in his fight against Mrs Proudie; a very real integrity where his work is concerned (in the last resort he will always put the Church before his wife) and a sporadic capacity for recognising an ally, even if it be Mr Slope, and using him very much in the manner of a man who holds a chair in front of him to ward off attack at close quarters.

He is a weak man rather than a silly one, and his affection for the tyrant is possibly more powerful than his fear of her. There is no indication whatsoever that Bishop Proudie has other than a deep and established fondness for his wife.

Archdeacon Grantly and Mr Harding are drawn plainly, humorously and with dignity, beautifully differentiated, the first more intensely observed than the other; yet they are, beyond doubt, cut diversely from a common cloth. Trollope's genius is nowhere more demonstrable than in this capacity to write quietly, with a deceptive simplicity, of persons to whom it would have been unseemly to apply too overt a satire.

His small scenes, his domestic conversation pieces, are intimate and precise. We hear men talking of parochial affairs, men of good will desirous of behaving decorously, even when it comes to discussing the new dean while the old one lies on his deathbed; but now and then there is the slip of the tongue, or perhaps no more than the slip of the breath, to indicate some little secret greed, some small eupeptic uprush of pleasure at a moment when pleasure is not quite in good taste.

His crowded scenes, usually given over to burlesque, he handles with ease, though the Gaffers at Mrs Thorne's party strike a doubtful note. The Bishop's reception is 'made' by the Signora and her elusive sofa; here Trollope is in high spirits, laughing as he writes. Admirably controlled, he has no difficulty in making the transition from burlesque to naturalism. There are no sudden jolts, no sudden speakings out of character; the mood is muted gradually, until the reader is ready to accept a new tone of voice, a new trend of ideas.

The plot of *Barchester Towers*, though essentially simple, is held in being by a fairly complex buttressing. It concerns the struggle for the control of a diocese and, more particularly, for the disposal of the wardenship of Hiram's Hospital. Later, there is the question of a deanery. The intrigues of Mrs Proudie on the one hand and Mr Slope on the other involve a great many interested parties and play their part in the admittedly rather turgid and conventional love story of Eleanor Bold and the worthy Mr Arabin. The latter is one of Trollope's failures, untouched by his revealing irony; even with the assistance of Eleanor, who is a living girl, he is unable to catch from the reader more than the sympathy which must be offered as a matter of decent routine to the juvenile lead or his dramatic equivalent. The passion of Mr Slope for Signora Vesey-Neroni, however repulsively comic, has more emotional truth in it than Mr Arabin's reticent and manly love for Eleanor.

Love, however, does not interest Trollope nearly so much as the manoeuvre for places in a closed society. It is by this manoeuvring that his people reveal their essential natures; a profound emotion may be brought into play in the pursuit of a petty object, and while romantic love displays personality only in a special aspect, the quiet and bitter fight to get on in the world reveals it in the round. Trollope liked to investigate man at his normal emotional temperature.

He is, for all his smoothly-smiling calm, his flawless taste, an audacious writer. The criticism levelled at various clerics is often severe, a ruthless humanising of what was considered, in 1857, the semi-sacred. Nowhere in his work is there anything more daring than the wonderful, incisive opening of *Barchester Towers*, in which Archdeacon Grantly ponders his chances of succeeding his father to the bishopric. It is a candid and very human study of a man who must, even in grief, have an eye to his prospects; and a lesser writer than Trollope might have soured it by an excess of irony or an insufficiency of compassionate understanding. That he never gave offence is due to the dualism of his writing. A good-natured caricature upsets no one; and readers who took Trollope's characterisations in this light were perfectly content to accept the friendly jesting at the man beneath the Cloth. The more sophisticated reader could, however, find the truth beneath the caricature, catch the half-hint, the inflection, the revelation of the real frailty of spirit.

Even so, he was not invited to condemn. Trollope, who was incapable of moral indignation of any kind, rarely condemned anyone or anything, and never passed a judgement save for the formal pat on the back demanded by the conventions of Chapter the Last. He was pleased to praise the good men, and did no more than make a little temperate fun of the not so worthy.

Judgment was not, in his view, the writer's business; one of his few outbreaks of hostility was directed towards Dickens, the

'Mr Popular Sentiment' of *The Warden*, who considered that it was. Trollope stated the facts as he found them, good or bad; and usually, good or bad, the way he found them was the way he liked them.

SOURCE: excerpted from 'Introduction' to Collins New Classics edition, (London 1952), pp. 13–19.

William Cadbury Character and the Mock-Heroic (1963)

Barchester Towers is one of the principal monuments of Victorian fiction, yet it has always been difficult to evaluate in terms of the Trollope canon, precisely because its excellences are of so different a kind from those of his other novels. In it Trollope's usual attempt to present characters in the round is subordinated to the attempt to present a unified world without involving us so deeply in any of his characters that they monopolise our attention. We are not to view the action only in terms of the aims and goals of the characters, as we do in such novels as *The Macdermots of Ballycloran* and *Phineas Finn*, but rather to see as a whole the social world they form. The technique of *Barchester Towers* is, in fact, a brilliant way of working out the ultimate aim of the novel of character, which is not only to elucidate character, 'but to give it in such variety as to suggest a picture of society'.[1]

If a picture of society as a unified world is to be maintained, it is necessary that we see all the characters from the outside, that they remain to us characters rather than selves, in Arthur Sewell's distinction. Sewell cautions us against treating the characters in drama as if they had selves: 'Dramatic draughtsmanship – to create the character in the round – is not concerned . . . with that kind of actuality we have for ourselves but with that kind of actuality other people have for us.'[2] The novelist who, like Trollope, attempts to create characters in the round, can present them either way; he can emphasise the kind of reality that others have in our eyes, or he can present us with characters who have the kind of reality we have for ourselves. The kinds of conflict he presents can be entirely internal, because the novelist has a privilege which exists for the dramatist only in the clumsy device of soliloquy, that of letting us see from the inside the make-up of his characters' minds, whether or not the conflicts they feel manifest themselves in action.[3] Hence there is no need for the novelist to present characters who are 'discovered for us in the mode in which the person of the play embodies . . . a distinctive address to the world',[4] or who, in Kenneth Burke's term, dance an attitude. Phineas Finn, for instance, has no attitude to dance; he merely is, without personality for himself as we are for ourselves. He has a self, the sense that he is, that he faces characters and situations, rather than a character, a conglomeration of personal attributes which may be contradictory and tangled, but which lead to a defined attitude to life, a personality. We can learn by observation of this self, but we do it from the inside.

The figures in *Barchester Towers*, on the other hand, are designed to be seen from the outside, to exhibit typical modes of behavior by which we can know them – to be, in short, characters. Warden Harding's mind, for all its complexity, is reducible to attributes by which we know him, and while we follow his thoughts with the greatest sympathy and understand his problems as problems, we never see him from the inside as we do Phineas Finn. There is always a kind of distance between us, and when we see his thoughts and sympathise with him as he faces his problems we say 'Yes, that is how someone with that character would feel', rather than 'I feel it with you'.

The special requirements of *Barchester Towers*, which, unlike most of Trollope's novels, is a detached, urbane, panoramic view of the operation of politics in social relations, dictate to Trollope the maintenance of distance from his characters. If he fails to keep it, the sense of character attributes is lost in a sense of personality, which at once restricts the boundaries of our attention to what the character feels and thinks, and keeps us from seeing him as an example of his type, with attributes and attitudes which we must judge. If we were to see any of these characters as we see ourselves, there would be danger of accepting their norms as ours, and thus danger of losing the panoramic view which is necessary to the comedy. All of the characters are to be ridiculous, and it is very seldom that we are ridiculous to ourselves. Trollope must keep us outside them, and the main achievement of *Barchester Towers* is the mastery of technical means for keeping us there.

But the sense of personality is of course precisely what Trollope does want in most of his novels. In the formulation of his principles of character creation in the *Autobiography* he tells us again and again that the novelist must live with his characters, must get inside and know exactly how they would respond in any situation. In a very famous passage, he tells us that the novelist 'desires to make his readers so intimately acquainted with his characters that the creations of his brain should be to them speaking, moving, living, human creatures. This he can never do unless he know those fictitious personages himself, and he can never know them well unless he can live with them in the full reality of established intimacy.'[5] . . . [Cadbury continues quotation from the passage, captioned as 'Imaginative Symbiosis', in section 1 of Part One, above – Ed.] And the operation of this aspect of the creative act must be reflected in the product. As he says in the essay 'On English Prose Fiction as a Rational Amusement', stories 'charm us . . . because we feel that men and women with flesh and blood, creatures with whom we can sympathise, are struggling amidst their woes. It all lies in that. No novel is anything, for purposes either of tragedy or of comedy, unless the reader can sympathise with the characters whose names he finds upon the page.'[6]

The kind of sympathy he here demands is clearly more involved with the characters than is the kind allowed by the outside view. And the contemporary reviewers find fault with the characterisation of *Barchester Towers* on just these grounds. The reviewer for the *North British Review* chides Trollope for not doing just what Trollope claims to do in the passage just quoted from the *Autobiography*. The reviewer says that 'if the character of a man is to be made fully known to us, it is from within that the artist must proceed'. Trollope does not do this enough for the reviewer's taste – 'he has not enabled us to form a conception of what his characters are like out of the four corners of Barchester Towers'.[7] And the *Saturday Review* critic of *Framley Parsonage* makes the general complaint that Trollope 'paints from the outside'. He is not strong at 'developing or creating, but . . . depicting the behaviour of drawing-room company'.[8] But the *National Review* critic of four early novels complains on the other hand (though it comes to much the same thing as the others) of too much subtlety, and says that Trollope should use 'stronger shades and brighter colours in the delineation of his fictitious personages', and that because he fails to do so he 'somewhat fails in awakening the sympathy of his readers'. In *Barchester Towers* and *The Warden* 'we are rather more inclined to be amused at than interested in the personages of the narrative'.[9]

Amusement at the personages is precisely what *Barchester Towers* is designed to supply, and the outside view of character, the lack of too deep involvement, is the way it is achieved. The novel does open, however, with an inside view, and it is partly this which sets off the old stable world of Bishop Grantly, in which selves could flourish, from the humor dominated world of power politics of Bishop Proudie. When we see Archdeacon Grantly at the bedside of his father, we see him as a self, not a character. His ability to pray for his father's life despite his own temporal needs is a triumph of his personality.

Thus he thought long and sadly, in deep silence, and then gazed at that still living face, and then at last dared to ask himself whether he really longed for his father's death.
  The effort was a salutary one, and the question was answered in a moment. The proud, wishful, worldly man, sank on his knees by the bedside, and . . . prayed eagerly that his sins might be forgiven him.[10]

When the bishop dies, too late, there is no longer any need for the archdeacon to search his own soul. As he engages in his politics and displays all the comic richness of his character in the rest of the novel, we see him from the outside. We sympathise, for we know from this first scene what he really is, but we are sympathetically amused at his character, not deeply involved with his self. It is his character we see, for instance, when he responds to the quite unexpected news of Eleanor's engagement in a way which demonstrates Trollope's technique of the outside view. All the archdeacon says is 'Good heavens!' and he says it five times, each time indicating a different state of mind, which Trollope explains. His progress from amazement to joy is thus immensely comic, because it is externalised in so characteristic a way [vol. II, pp. 246–7].[11]

The basic distinction between the outside and the inside view, then, is whether our attention is directed most strongly towards the singularising attributes or the universalising problems of a character. The characters in *Barchester Towers* who are most nearly presented from the inside are Harding and Arabin, because we are made to feel most deeply the complexity of the problems they face. But even here it is the eccentricity of the characters, their characteristic attitude to life, which is the main aim of the presentation. Harding is an extremely sympathetic character, yet his attitude to life is so individual that we think of him in terms of it – we could never see him as we see ourselves, as is possible with the archdeacon at his father's death-bed. After Harding has been told by Slope that he is 'rubbish', his governing attribute of scrupulous self-analysis forces him to characteristic reflection: 'Unfortunately for himself Mr Harding had little . . . self-reliance. When he heard himself designated as rubbish by the Slopes of the world, he had no other resource than to make inquiry within his own bosom as to the truth of the designation' [vol. I, p. 117]. Harding is intended to appear overscrupulous, and thus we cannot identify deeply with his moral quandary, though we sympathise with it.

Because *Barchester Towers* emphasises the outside view of character, when Trollope endows a character with a self it destroys the tone of the novel. In chapter 20, where Trollope presents what he calls an 'interior view' of Arabin's character, in which he emphasises Arabin's spiritual struggles, we lose sight of Arabin's attributes and become too much interested in the nature of the spiritual problems that he faces. Our involvement and identification with Arabin in this passage produce a disparity in tone between this and the rest of the novel, so that we never quite know how to take Arabin afterwards. But the chapter seems like a set-piece, having little to do with the rest of the book, and so when we see Arabin in action later, from the outside, we build up a separate picture of him from that of the 'interior view' of his character; there remains only a slight sense of strain, as if we have two characters mixed up in our minds.

Trollope's basic practice of character creation throughout *Barchester Towers* is similar to the way he presents Arabin, though in the rest of the characters he avoids the too-close analysis of the 'interior view'. He describes the characters in a set-piece, and then shows us the character in action, displaying the characteristics established in the description. Because Arabin and some others, particularly Madame Neroni, are such complex characters, this practice sometimes brings about the illusion of development in the characters. We tend to forget that they do not change, but rather unfold their full characters in action.[12] Eleanor Bold, for instance, learns as her pride is beaten out of her by circumstances, but she does not grow. In a workable though improbable analogy, like King Oedipus she finds out what was in her character all along, and unlike King Lear she does not find her character changing to fit her new circumstances. We sympathise with her, but remain aloof, and do not identify with her. Her pride particularises her, and we do not see her as we see ourselves. Thus when we are told of a character's thoughts in *Barchester Towers*, it is still, in terms of our definition, an outside view, because it reveals an attitude to life, a character rather than a self.

One of the most effective techniques of distancing a character from the reader is the creation of tension between the moral norms of the character and the moral norms of the implied author, which the reader shares.[13] Trollope retains the outside view when exposing his characters' feelings by imposing a sense of his own values on the values which the characters hold. In the presentation of the transmutation of Eleanor's grief for John Bold into love for her baby, we sympathise entirely with

Eleanor's feelings, but we perceive the gap between her feelings and the reality of the situation, and so we do not identify with her, but rather remain aloof. Trollope shows very clearly how she overreacts to the baby by emphasising Eleanor's worship of it and the perfect ordinariness of the child – 'The baby was really delightful; he took his food with a will, struck out his toes merrily whenever his legs were uncovered, and did not have fits. These are supposed to be the strongest points of baby perfection, and in all these our baby excelled' [vol. i, p. 16]. The kind of irony implicit in this contrast between the values of characters and audience is one of Trollope's favorite devices for making characters ridiculous. Mrs Proudie, for instance, answers Lady De Courcy's expression of amazement that Madeline has captured Slope: 'You don't know the intriguing villainy of that woman', said Mrs Proudie, remembering her torn flounces [vol. ii, p. 113]. She is responding to what was not actually Madeline's intriguing villainy at all, since she had nothing to do with tearing Mrs Proudie's dress, yet Mrs Proudie remembers with anger Madeline's laughter at her discomfiture. But it is still perfectly true that Madeline has been engaging in intrigue in captivating Slope – Mrs Proudie responds in terms of her own values, the reader in terms of the reality which Trollope has presented.

In the same way, there is a light irony involved when Madeline says, 'Parsons, I suppose, are much the same as other men, if you strip them of their black coats' [vol. i, p. 86]. The whole of *Barchester Towers* makes this very point, but the view of clerical character which the reader has is so much higher than Madeline's that for her to say it reveals more about her character than about parsons. She simply means that they can be made ridiculous by her blandishments, and she is mistaken in thinking it true of all clergymen, since Arabin remains true. To Trollope and to the reader, the remark means that parsons are as liable to be afflicted with narrowmindedness and jealousies as anyone else, but also as capable of nobility and truth.

These passages imply, since they demonstrate a difference in the responses of the characters and those of the audience, that there is a special relationship between the narrator and the audience, which itself helps to create the panoramic vision of life and to keep the reader distanced from the action. Trollope's well-known addresses and asides to the reader usually serve one of these purposes, although sometimes they can be merely petulant.[14] Mr Harding, for instance, is able to conceive of a marriage between Eleanor and Slope, partly because he is too easily convinced by Grantly, but partly too because 'it must be remembered that such a marriage ... did not appear so monstrous to Mr Harding, because in his charity he did not hate the chaplain as the archdeacon did, and as we do' [vol. i, p. 171]. The inclusion of the reader here is not ingenuous – Trollope is setting up a complex irony, of the type used by Thackeray, in which he blames Harding for too great charity, but blames the reader, too, for lack of charity. Slope certainly is bad, but Harding is right in seeing as little evil as possible in people. This irony, then, presents a vision of life – the sense that it is difficult to live in the world, and that the innocent is the most admirable man, though he is comic in his lack of grasp of reality.

The narrator's relationship to his novel, as well as his relationship to the reader, can be complicated, as when he discusses the character of Mrs Proudie:

Mrs Proudie has not been portrayed in these pages as an agreeable or an amiable lady. There has been no intention to impress the reader much in her favour. It is ordained that all novels should have a male and a female angel, and a male and a female devil. If it be considered that this rule is obeyed in these pages, the latter character must be supposed to have fallen to the lot of Mrs Proudie. But she was not all devil. There was a heart inside that stiff-ribbed bodice, though not, perhaps, of large dimensions, and certainly not easily accessible [vol. i, pp. 264–5].

This again is not ingenuous; by referring to a fictional character's place in the fictive world that he is creating, Trollope certainly violates the reality that critics of point of view have told us is necessary. But by contrasting Mrs Proudie's character with our conception of her place in the novel, Trollope enforces her reality – a sense is established of life in the novel on two planes, one highly conventional and established in terms of groupings of characters, and another in which the characters live absolutely, quite apart from their places in the pattern of angel and devil and the like. This sense of a double level of life keeps the reader removed from the action, surveying it with Trollope's panoramic eye, but also makes him believe in the world of the novel as an interaction of characters who have at least partially a life of their own. The technique enables *Barchester Towers* to be both artificial and literary, as behoves a comedy, and natural and lifelike, as behoves a novel.

Henry James, in a very famous passage, objected to the distortion of the novelistic world which authorial intrusion brings about, and upbraided Trollope for inconsistency in point of view: 'It is impossible to imagine what a novelist takes himself to be unless he regard himself as an historian and his narrative as a history. It is only as an historian that he has the smallest *locus standi*. As a narrator of fictitious events he is nowhere; to insert into his attempt a backbone of logic, he must relate events that are assumed to be real.'[15] Howells supported this view, and claimed that Trollope was 'warped from a wholesome ideal' by devotion to the Thackerayan method. He says that Trollope wishes 'to stand about in his scene, talking it over with his hands in his pockets, interrupting the action, and spoiling the illusion in which alone the truth of art resides.'[16] But the kind of illusion that James and Howells demand is precisely what Trollope does not want in *Barchester Towers*. As we have seen, the whole attempt is to keep the reader sympathetic to but uninvolved in the actions and responses of the characters. Successful creation of an illusion of reality guarantees a kind of focus on each scene and each character which would render the structure of *Barchester Towers* intolerable, as we are wrenched violently from one aspect of the plot to another. In a panoramic novel like *Barchester Towers* it is absolutely necessary to remain distant enough from the action for the mental eye to take in the panorama. As we have just seen, the illusion of reality is maintained with complete adequacy by the device of treating the characters as real people in a fictive setting – the life of the characters can occasionally break through their conventional groupings, and thus our interest in them is maintained as far as Trollope wants it.

In this way, then, Trollope's famous explanation of why he lets his readers know what is going to happen makes sense. He sets up a situation of trust between author and reader when he says of himself that he 'ventures to reprobate that system which goes so far to violate all proper confidence between the author and his readers, by maintaining . . . a mystery. . . . Nay, take the last chapter if you please – learn from its pages all the results of our troubled story, and the story shall have lost none of its interest, if indeed there be any interest in it to lose.' [vol. I, pp. 143–4]. This is all simply to say that suspense of the kind necessary to the dramatic novel, the simple eagerness to learn what happens, is a supremely unimportant quality in this kind of novel. Trollope is justified in speaking directly to the reader in *Barchester Towers*, since he does not need suspense and since he does need detachment from the action. If we became too involved in the characters or in the action, the trials of good characters and the disasters of bad would become too painful. Trollope wishes to show us what life is, but he does not let us mix up his comic portrayal with reality, in the manner of romance. Jamesian critics, looking to the novel for the best kind of romance, cannot cope with the antiromantic vision, just as F. R. Leavis cannot cope with the Trollopean values of detachment and urbanity, which lack the 'kind of reverent openness before life, and . . . marked moral intensity' that he feels necessary to the great tradition.[17] Different from the manner of Leavis's great tradition, 'Trollope's manner', as one critic puts it, 'is that of a skilled monologist speaking to an intimate, trusted and trusting individual or group' and we are asked to believe that he will 'work out the situations to our satisfaction'.[18]

The technique described here, then, provides a perfectly respectable *locus standi* which is not that of the historian. The relationship of the author to his audience which we have just seen in *Barchester Towers* is basically that of an epic bard to his. Trollope does not employ the radical of presentation of *epos*, the direct confrontation of the audience by the bard,[19] but the governing technical device, the mock heroic, is an imitation of it for the purposes of parody, and is still another way of keeping characters distanced from the reader. Trollope's device of giving an ironic commentary on the action, by means of mock-heroic apostrophes, substitutes for the use of a separate narrator – the tone of the apostrophes is so different from Trollope's normal narrative tone that a second narrative personality is implied. This narrator, the production of the implied author, comments on the realistic situation from the romantic point of view and thus achieves an ironic undercutting of the action.

When Trollope cries 'But how shall I sing the divine wrath of Mr Slope, or how invoke the tragic muse to describe the rage which swelled the celestial bosom of the bishop's chaplain?' [vol. ii, p. 146], he is clearly imitating the conventions of epic style, and laughing at Slope's absurdities by placing him in direct juxtaposition with Achilles. The main point of mock heroic is to give perspective, to place the tempest in the teapot, and the comparison of Trollope's clerical characters to the heroes of another tradition accomplishes this admirably.

Mrs Proudie, of course, presents wonderful opportunities for the exercise of this device, since pomposity is so central to her character: 'As Juno may have looked at Paris on Mount Ida, so did Mrs Proudie look on Ethelbert Stanhope when he pushed the leg of the sofa into her lace train' [vol. i, p. 96]. As she ponders her revenge on Slope, she is compared to Medea, another female character in the epic tradition [vol. ii, pp. 71–2], but sex is not limiting: 'As Achilles warmed at the sight of his armour, as Don Quixote's heart grew strong when he grasped his lance, so did Mrs Proudie look forward to fresh laurels, as her eye fell on her husband's pillow', and she thinks of the curtain lecture she can give [vol. i, p. 263].

The reversal of sexes for comic effect is applied the other way around, too: 'Dr Proudie was playing Venus to [Grantly's] Juno, and he was prepared to wage an internecine war against the owner of the wished-for apple, and all his satellites, private chaplains, and others' [vol. i, p. 37]. The image of the archdeacon as warrior is used again and again: 'And now, had I the pen of a mighty poet, would I sing in epic verse the noble wrath of the archdeacon' [vol. i, p. 41]. And when he has finally triumphed, he 'literally made presents to everybody':

'Twas thus that he sang his song of triumph over Mr Slope. This was his paean, his hymn of thanksgiving, his loud oration. He had girded himself with his sword, and gone forth to the war; now he was returning from the field laden with the spoils of the foe. The cob and the cameos, the violoncello and the pianoforte, were all as it were trophies reft from the tent of his now conquered enemy. [vol. II, pp. 267–8.]

The epic style is here used to let us imaginatively into the archdeacon's mind, for he clearly responds to his victory over Slope as if it were an epic victory; but the epic style is used to make fun of the whole struggle as well. As is plain from many of these examples, the imagery of war governs the treatment of the power-struggle. Arabin is consistently referred to in terms of knightly tourney – chapter 14 is entitled 'The New Champion', and this epithet is used again [vol. II, p. 218], where Grantly again demonstrates his own lack of sense of proportion about the ecclesiastical encounters with which he is so concerned. He thinks 'That paragon of a clergyman . . . that ecclesiastical knight before whose lance Mr Slope was to fall and bite the dust, that worthy bulwark of the church as it should be . . . was – misconducting himself' [vol. II, p. 218]. Most of the characters come in for such mocking treatment. Mrs Quiverful becomes Medea or Constance [vol. I, p. 247]; Eleanor Bold is Lucretia to Slope's Tarquin [vol. II, p. 5]. And the characters themselves, in an interesting variation of the device, are made to use the sense of conflict between the epic struggle and the reality of the situation to deflate each other. Madeline intends that the classical parallel deflate Slope when she tells him to avoid the example of Dido and not mix business with pleasure in his pursuit of Eleanor and herself [vol. I, p. 272], and the archdeacon feels an unfortunate lack of appropriateness between his vision of the real epic relationships of the antagonists and the reality of the situation:

Dr Gwynne was the *Deus ex machina* who was to come down upon the Barchester stage, and bring about deliverance from these terrible evils. But how can melodramatic *dénouements* be properly brought about, how can vice and Mr Slope be punished, and virtue and the archdeacon be rewarded, while the avenging god is laid up with the gout? [vol. II, p. 77.]

Barchester Towers demonstrates, then, a variety of techniques for keeping the reader distanced from the characters and from the action, a necessary condition in presenting a panoramic view of a given social world. The most important of these are the outside view of character established through description, the simultaneous presentation of the senses of value of the author and of the characters, and the parody of epic devices by a mock-epic bard in digressions and asides to the reader. All are devices for assuring that characters, rather than selves, be presented, and all are ways of placing the action of the novel in a context in which the reality of characters and situations is kept from becoming overpowering, since the panoramic novel is fragmented by a too great illusion of reality.

Source: article in *Texas Studies in Literature and Language*, v (1963), pp. 509–19.

NOTES

1. Edwin Muir, *The Structure of the Novel* (London, 1928), p. 32.
2. Arthur Sewell, *Character and Society in Shakespeare* (Oxford, 1951), p. 34.
3. For a full discussion of the varieties of distance the novelist can create between the narrator and his characters, see Wayne C. Booth, *The Rhetoric of Fiction* (Chicago, 1961), pp. 155–64.
4. Sewell, op. cit. pp. 26–7.
5. *An Autobiography* (1883; new edition Oxford, 1980), pp. 232–3.
6. Published in *Four Lectures*, ed. Morris L. Parrish (London 1938), p. 124.
7. *North British Review*, 40 (June 1864), pp. 383–4.
8. *Saturday Review*, 2 (May 1861), p. 451.
9. *National Review*, 7 (October, 1858), p. 419.
10. *Barchester Towers* (Oxford, 1980), vol. i, p. 4.
11. [Ed.] References in the text are to the pagination of the edition cited in Note 10.
12. Beatrice Curtis Brown points out that the characters in *Barchester Towers* are, unlike the figures in Trollope's later novels, 'ready formed figures, no longer developing'. *Anthony Trollope: The English Novelists* (London, 1950), p. 53.
13. For the distinction between implied author and narrator, see Booth, op. cit., pp. 67–77. On the necessity for agreement between implied author and reader, see Booth, p. 138.
14. See, for instance, *Barchester Towers*, vol. ii, pp. 251–2, where Trollope complains of the necessity of supplying happy endings.

162 WILLIAM CADBURY (1963)

15. 'Anthony Trollope, 1883', reprinted in *The House of Fiction*, ed. Leon Edel (New Haven, Conn. and London, 1957), p. 102. [Excerpted in Part Two of this selection – Ed.]

16. William Dean Howells, *Criticism and Fiction*, ed. Clara M. Kirk and Rudolph Kirk (New York, 1959), p. 39.

17. F.R. Leavis, *The Great Tradition* (1948; rev. edn London, 1954), p. 18.

18. Edd Winfield Parks, 'Trollope and the Defense of Exegesis', NCF, 8 (1953), p. 267.

19. Northrop Frye, *Anatomy of Criticism* (Princeton, N.J. and London, 1957), p. 248.

3. *DOCTOR THORNE*

Elizabeth Bowen 'Suspense Without Mystery' (1959)

... Almost no novel, to my mind, has a more unfavourable beginning than *Doctor Thorne*. Without an inkling of something better to come, few readers could stay the course of the first two chapters. Today, on the strength of the book's reputation, we just suffer them. The Victorian reader, supposedly, was inured or at least resigned to this kind of prosiness – longwinded explanation, categoric descriptiveness, and a trend to aggressive generalisation. Trollope gave himself over to every fault, from the point of view of an 'opening', that the present-day novelist schools himself to avoid. His technique, in this instance, might appear to be nil. By contrast, we are reminded of Dickens's openings, vivid, immediate, dramatic, concrete; of Thackeray's instant command of our thoughts and will; of the Brontës' sounding-out, from the very first. Trollope wrote fast, but moved into action slowly. Struck, himself, by this, he catches our eye disarmingly at the conscientious beginning of chapter II:

I quite feel that an apology is due for beginning a novel with two long dull chapters full of description. I am perfectly aware of the danger of such a course. In so doing I sin against the golden rule which requires us all to put our best foot foremost, the wisdom of which is fully recognised by novelists, myself among the number. It can hardly be expected that any one will consent to go through with a fiction that offers so little of allurement in its first pages; but twist it as I will I cannot do otherwise. I find that I cannot make poor Mr Gresham hem and haw and turn himself uneasily in his arm-chair in a natural manner till I have said why he is uneasy. I cannot bring in my doctor speaking his mind freely among the big-wigs till I have explained that it is in accordance with his usual character to do so. This is unartistic on my part, and shows want of imagination as well as want of skill. Whether or not I can atone for these faults by straightforward, simple, plain story telling – that, indeed, is very doubtful.

Those last words, so modest, are disingenuous. Our author, knowing what he was doing, did not doubt his ability to do it. Straightforward story telling exerts a spell; Trollope could well rely on that – he, himself, no less than ourselves, being under its power. He takes a risk, he admits, in unloading facts prior to the arousing of curiosity – the better procedure might be to withhold knowledge till there has been created, within the reader, a genuine appetite to know. But the risk is justified. Foe though he was to revision or blue-pencilling, he would not have left his opening chapters to stand were their effect likely to be disastrous – or, still more, if they had lacked function. Unaware of technique (as we think of it) he had method. Essential to the interest of *Doctor Thorne* is its complex preliminary lay-out. It was necessary to establish, without ado – or, shall we say, with what seemed the minimum of it – the topography of Greshamsbury and its neighbourhood; the agricultural nature of Barset county and the political bias that went with that; and not only the identity but the status of each of his central characters, and their consequent social relationships with each other. Gradations are part of the subject of *Doctor Thorne* – spin the plot love may, but not in a vacuum: does it ever? Though Trollope wrote for mid-Victorian English readers who took the social hierarchy for granted, certain special matters needed to be explained – for these were to be factors in his story. (The Thorne family's being more ancient in origin than the Gresham, and therefore by pedigree ruling 'better', is an example: hence the balance of power between Mr Gresham, the landed squire knit by marriage into the aristocracy, and Thorne, the free-lance dispensary doctor with nothing to live upon but his earnings.)

Nor was this all. The main *Doctor Thorne* characters – the doctor and his niece, the squire and his heir, the new-rich railway contractor Scatcherd – gain, immensely, in interest by being within the grip of what one might call an inherited situation. There have been stories before 'our' story opens. No one of those stories is finished; each runs its course, still, through its influence on the present drama. Consequently, each had to be imparted, in the nearest Trollope could find to foreshortened form. The scandalous secret attaching to Mary's birth, her father's death at the hands of her mother's brother, and the stigma left by the vengeance on the avenger: these (unknown by our heroine) are her background, her likely disqualification, her unjust handicap. The decline in the Greshams' fortunes, still more its cause, and with that their desperate objection to the heir Frank's romance, demand to be analysed and accounted for. No less, the blood-tie (of which both are ignorant) between deplorable Scatcherd and adorable Mary must be, and is, prominent in the reader's consciousness – it colours, makes complex and deepens our idea of them both.

Trollope's notion was this: that the reader should start by knowing more about every one of the characters than any one of them knew about themselves. (As to this, be it said, there is one exception: all-but omniscience is granted to Doctor Thorne. On the strength of his having to carry such dire weight, the good man is designated the novel's 'hero'.) Once all *was* known, the story could be set going, with the certainty of its producing the full effect. In slamming down at us, outright, all information, Trollope was in his own way adroit – he saved himself innumerable pauses which otherwise might have been necessary along the way. Also, from now on there were needed in *Doctor Thorne* no major flashbacks into the past. When we do find the author retracing his steps, it is to account for the sayings or doings of some character who has, for the time being, been lost to sight. One admires his conscientiousness in this matter – he had a large cast to keep in play, and a devious series of doings to chronicle.

Doctor Thorne is, thus, a novel without mystery – mystery either circumstantial or psychological. We are as clear as to the *character* of the characters as we are to their circumstances and likely destinies. Yet the interest relies, and successfully, on suspense. How does the author achieve suspense while discarding any support from mystery? That he succeeds in doing so seems the more remarkable when one sees that his plot (or rather, his brother's)[1] does not rely, for excitingness, on outside events – other, possibly, than the East Barset elections. No burning house, train wreck, robbery or cataclysm of Nature is introduced; the action springs, as it ideally should, out of the characters. The predicaments which continue to grip our interest are caused by the persons who must endure or surmount them. I suggest that the magnetism of *Doctor Thorne* resides in its author's power to keep us watching. We watch, and intently, the central characters to see how they will behave in the face of circumstance, how they will react to each new development – being what they are, feeling as they must. We are present at a series of 'revelations', each one producing a strong reflex: it is the reflex that we enjoy watching, though the actual matter is no surprise to us. In fact, the suspense-interest in *Doctor Thorne* is due to the author's system of keying up, gratifying, and then renewing (at still higher tenor) our expectations. The tale is a lengthy, pleasing progression from one to the next of a series of 'key' scenes – each one, by its force and after-effect, being guaranteed to beget another.

In principle (though not always, I think, in practice) a preface is read before one turns to the story. In principle, therefore, it is out of order for the preface to give away the plot, or make known, by comment or discussion, the way in which the central crisis is solved. In this case, Trollope does literally 'a tale unfold', and I should hesitate, even apart from scruples, to attempt to compress, into any paragraph, what by nature is leisurely and expansive. But the main situation, with which I would connect the 'idea' of the novel, is another matter. I repeat my belief that it was the idea, in the first place, which fired Trollope, inspired his handling of the plot, and eventuated into this masterpiece. The idea would seem to be, a finding of levels. In the story, the characters are as it were passing each other on a staircase; some going up, some down. By the end, each person has come to a stop where he or she belongs; that is, at his or her *right* level – or say, due level. What, in each case, *is* the right and the due is determined by virtue, integrity, moral character – or by the lack of them, where descents occur. Yet *Doctor Thorne*, as a story, by no means exalts the humble and meek. The hardworking country doctor and his penniless niece are, Trollope tells us outright, animated by pride – but it is a right pride. The weak squire, whose heir Frank courts Mary Thorne, fails to stand up against his overweening wife: Lady Arabella Gresham, an earl's daughter, is actuated by wrong or false pride, in which she is one with her relatives, the De Courcys. Sir Roger Scatcherd fails in the pride which should have rewarded his life's work; he sinks into squalour and alcoholism, and his son is to die of an inherited taint. The *Doctor Thorne* story indicts the abuse of privilege, the misuse of power, and the failure to be worthy of position – whether an achieved position, such as Scatcherd's, or an inherited one, such as the squire's. There is one idealised figure: good Doctor Thorne.

Trollope's ideal was this gentleman: uncompromising, 'speaking his mind freely among the big-wigs', unmercenary, fearless of the conventions (he shocks other doctors by mixing his own medicines), taking his stand wholly upon integrity – an integrity backed, as his creator reminds us, by awareness of honourable and ancient lineage. For such a man, a nagging problem of conscience could not but be created by Scatcherd's will, with its possible benefit to his niece Mary; by such a man, the battle against the Greshams, his former friends, on behalf of Mary could not be fought without sadness, regret, reluctance. The doctor despises pretension, honours, tradition. Taken all-in-all, he realises, I imagine, Trollope's sense of what a man not only should be but also *could* be. As a 'hero' he must have been more rewarding than Trollope can have ever been to himself, in dark days of solitary castle-building.

This hero exhibits what might be called the outstanding, best democratic qualities. Yet he is rooted in, and subscribes to, a society in character oligarchic. His figure depends for its true proportion on being seen within the frame and against the background of the English class system of Trollope's day and the doctor's. Puzzling or even shocking as that system may seem . . . it demands to be accepted, or at least recognised, for the duration of the reading of *Doctor Thorne*. A work of fiction, if worth reading at all, is entitled to its own landscape, its own climate, which may often be social no less than physical. Why, after his miserable schooldays, it may be wondered, did

Trollope not react against a system under whose pressures he had suffered? He was, clearly, neither poor-spirited nor subservient. But equally, he had not anywhere in him the makings of a dissident or a revolutionary; by temperament he was a romantic confirmist. He was a born admirer, and the existing order provided him with much that he could admire – that he *had* admired, even when he had no part in it. The figure ideal and absolute in its independence was, to him, the gentleman. He looked no higher; in fact he would have denied that there could be anything higher at which to look!

In so far as there is class conflict in *Doctor Thorne*, it is between the country gentlemen and the aristocracy – the latter represented by the De Courcys. There is no doubt where Trollope's sympathies lie; also no doubt, alas, that his antipathies misdirect his pen. The De Courcys, a tribe of caricatures, are portrayed with uneasy, facetious venom. Negligible as villains, they fail as comedy. As elements in the novel, their chief importance is their detrimental effect on the Gresham fortunes; and to their detestable influence is traced the squire's loss of prestige among fellow-gentry, and the ban upon the romance between Frank and Mary. Frank's long line of sisters, the Miss Greshams, live in peril of spinsterhood, for they dare take no mate discountenanced by their De Courcy cousins.

Barsetshire, the novel's landscape and setting, speaks for itself. This mellow county, by now so vivid to many that it becomes 'fictitious' in name only, may be taken to be a sort of abstract, or compost, of those south-west English counties travelled by Trollope, on horseback, in those 'happiest years' when he rode around for the Post Office. Somerset, Dorset, Wiltshire would be three which contributed very largely; though who knows if there were not an intake, too, from the east of Devon, the west of Gloucestershire? Generically, the scene is rural-English – wooded, rolling, with here and there a sculptured open skyline, small rivers meandering in the valleys, in which are sheltered also contented villages. Round the turns of lanes, at the heads of avenues, approached by bridges or set in orchards or ploughlands stand, great or small, the dwellings Trollope recalled – solitude their character, age their story. To

the Englishman home again from uncanny Ireland, this sedate
tapestried richness would have been speaking; so, after the
Irish slither to ruin, would the pretty prosperity of the villages.
Plotting his letter-carriers' courses, measuring byways,
walking his horse on field-paths, he had come to knowing such
regions like the palm of his hand; psychically it became his
property.

Part of the livingness of Barsetshire is its susceptibility to
change. Clouds and sunshine, summer and winter alternate
over the strong trees and the rich furrows. And in the year when
the story opens, 1854, 'progress' is already showing its suspect
hand. Young squire-to-be Frank Gresham's coming of age is, in
the scale and character of its celebration, a degree less feudal
than was his father's. A Radical is among the candidates at the
East Barset parliamentary elections; the Gresham-headed
Tories are on the wane. Also, this is the age of railway
expansion – prosperity is following the steel tracks; the
coaching roads and their hostelries are left desolate. Small
towns (such as Courcy, at the gates of the castle) are askance,
muted and high-and-dry.

And how changed has been the bustle of that once noisy inn to the present
death-like silence of its green court-yard! There, a lame ostler crawls about
with his hands thrust into the capacious pockets of his jacket, feeding on
memory. That weary pair of omnibus jades, and three sorry posters, are all
that now grace those stables where horses used to be stalled in close contiguity .
by the dozen; where twenty grains apiece, abstracted from every feed of oats
consumed during the day, would have afforded a daily quart to the lucky
pilferer. . . .

Oh, my friend! my poor lame friend! it will avail nothing to tell thee of
Liverpool and Manchester; of the glories of Glasgow, with her flourishing
banks; of London, with its third million of inhabitants; of the great things
commerce is doing for this nation of thine! What is commerce to thee, unless it
be a commerce in posting on that worn-out, all but useless great western
turnpike road! There is nothing left for thee but to be carted away as rubbish –
for thee and many of us in these now prosperous days; oh my melancholy,
care-ridden friend. [ch. xv.]

Our lame and care-ridden friend should have lived to laugh!
For a hundred years have brought the wheel to full circle. 'All
but useless', today, stretch the steel tracks, soon to be torn up,

grass sprouting between them as insolently as it did in the inn
courtyard. That courtyard, a car park, again booms. The great
western turnpike road is all but invisible under streaming
traffic.

One final word as to the topography. Salisbury, though the
first of the Barset novels was there conceived, is not to be
identified with Barchester. Smaller Wells, which, further to the
west, likewise has its close and cathedral, also claims a
connection with *The Warden*. One may take it that Barchester,
like the terrain surrounding it, is a compost – more truly *like* an
English cathedral city than any one real-life example could
hope to be. Fictitious places take on something from the at once
simplifying and concentrated imagination which has created
them – one may notice a sort of poverty in the atmosphere of a
scene which the novelist has no more than 'copied'. In creating
places, Trollope, one may be certain, worked as do others in his
craft – that is to say, he instinctively found it necessary to add,
snip, accentuate, modify, blend.

Doctor Thorne we have designated a love story. It follows the
fortunes of two young people on their difficult way to achieving
union. Like other novels of this kind, it has one disadvantage:
we part from the (now) happy pair at the church door. We are
denied a glimpse of them in the expanded relationship of
marriage – and indeed throughout the course of the story we
have had but too few glimpses of them in anything but a fleeting
harmony. Kisses are snatched, idyllic moments are interrupted
– perpetually they are in an atmosphere of emergency, or taking
part in hurried councils of war. The Greshamsbury Hall
attitude to the love affair is more than obstructive, it is militant.
There *is* considerable reason on the Gresham side: Trollope
admits the objections to the match, though he does not ask the
reader to share them. Frank is the heir to embarrassed
property; if he follows his heart and marries the doctor's niece,
the Greshams *as* Greshams will have to be written off. They are
faced by what, virtually, is extinction – that of a landed family
shorn of land.

Oddly enough, Trollope's divided sympathies do not detract

from the virtue of *Doctor Thorne*. He has built up, thanks to his plot, a first-rate predicament, out of which, with a patience allied with consummate skill, he goes on to extricate his characters. Were the scales too heavily weighted on either side, the tension would be less. Emotion is kept in balance against realism – and one must grant that no one scene in the book offends, in its content, against either. Love *is* to conquer all: but exactly how? Is it a fault that, quite early in the novel, you and I, the omniscient readers, see light ahead? Economic relief is to come from the Scatcherd quarter. Roger Scatcherd killed off by alcohol, only his sickly son stands between Mary and a large fortune. Louis Scatcherd's rate of drinking himself to death must be timed against the rapidly mounting pressure piled up against Frank's and Mary's love. How the race is to finish we do not doubt – throughout the lengthy final part of the book we are working to a foregone conclusion. Yet the excitement is never less.

Trollope sets and keeps burning in *Doctor Thorne* a fire no less formidable for being innocent. He creates in Mary a woman whose temperament is focussed upon a single devotion: Frank is the love of her life, there can be no other. Admirably, he matches Mary with Frank – boyish, wayward, naïvely the prey of vanity, but capable (as his adherence to Mary shows) of a sublime obstinacy, of courage, of a contempt for circumstance. Originally, Mary retreats from Frank, out of a dread of involvement – too much is at stake for her; she foresees disaster. She doubts – and one cannot wonder – that Frank is serious. They are of the same age (twenty-one, when the story starts), but he is a boy, she is a woman. Finally, after an all but speechless mutual declaration, it is to be she who involves him – part, she suggests they must; but they know they cannot. Trollope's touch on sexual love is tentative, awkwardly light, but unfailing – true. There are present in this blameless obstructed courtship the elements of a fatal illicit passion. Behind Mary's agonised offer of renunciation, towards the end, we feel the dire force of her character – she believes her letter likely to *be* the end. If we do not share her suspense, before Frank's reply, it is because we know that he cannot leave her. Once, he had been the happy type of young man who falls out of love as painlessly as he falls into it. But Mary is a woman who is not parted from.

The attractiveness of the doctor's niece may account for the eager reception of *Doctor Thorne*. Her effect on the Victorian reader may have been not unconnected with shock tactics: she was far from being the heroine then in fashion, limp with sweetness, pulpy with femininity. She *is*, in fact, a heroine in the greatest English tradition, from Shakespeare on – high-spirited, witty, resourceful, graceful and debonair. She is fearless, like Fielding's Sophia; she laughs and sparkles like Jane Austen's Elizabeth (if not quite so brightly); she is as vehement, as implacable, as outspoken with regard to her own feeling, as Charlotte Brontë's Jane Eyre. She has the merit of being not a person one is ever called upon to be wholly sorry for. In her relationship with her two friends, Beatrice Gresham and Patience Oriel, there is a touch of teasing, flirtatious gallantry – one delights in the scene where she kisses Beatrice's toe. She is proud; in that greatly her uncle's niece. She has grown up as the playmate of the Gresham children, daily in and out of the great house; her attitude to Greshamsbury Hall is untinted by over-gratitude or subservience – in this, she could not be more unlike the put-upon Fanny in *Mansfield Park*. Banished, after her fall from favour, she sustains her position without loss of face.

Mary Thorne's character has a darker inverse. It may be that we like her the better for suspecting that she is not naturally 'good'. Scatcherd, coarse and tormented, is (as we always remember) her other uncle. To her birth there attaches something worse than the stigma of illegitimacy – she is not to be called a love-child; she was the fruit of an outrage committed upon her mother. Our most revealing, and constant, view of Mary is in her companionship with her doctor uncle: an equalitarianism of tender confidence. In the scenes between them, Trollope is so much at his best that *Doctor Thorne* could twice over be called a love story.

The large-sized canvas of this novel is crowded around the edges with minor characters. Many owe their existence to sub-plots only; and, touched in hastily and to formula, they are for the most part no more than 'types'. An outstanding exception is Miss Dunstable, the plain but delightful heiress proffered to Frank by his aunt the countess in hopes of diverting him from Mary. We could do with more of Miss Dunstable than we are given; in her own right she is a major character, cramped for space by an inadequate role – though, with her affectionate shrewdness as to Frank, she is twice over permitted to act importantly: she compels him to see himself as he is, and she re-steels his will with regard to Mary. Also, there are present in *Doctor Thorne* two persons prominent in plot but imperfectly realised psychologically. Lady Arabella Gresham and Roger Scatcherd both of them demand to be on a scale of which Trollope, in their instances, was incapable. He perceives them, but still as aliens; he fails to cope with them. Both of them, though for exceedingly different reasons, are largely beyond the bounds of his understanding. One wishes that he could have leased them out to other novelists, better equipped to handle them – Lady Arabella to Balzac, Scatcherd to Dostoievsky. In extenuation of Trollope it must be said that his shortcomings were not peculiar to himself: nineteenth-century French and Russian novelists were better than their contemporaries in England in dealing with either aristocrats or tormented and difficult states of soul.

Trollope's disapproval of the De Courcys, of whose stock she came, starts him off with a bias against Lady Arabella. In the face of that, he tries hard to do moral justice to the proud, ambitious but far from heartless woman – Doctor Thorne's unbending, satirical yet clement view of her ladyship may be taken to be that of our author. In the case of Scatcherd, what does Trollope suggest as the cause of total disintegration? This former stone-mason, after a term in prison, has raised himself by sheer engineering genius: his rewards are abhorrent to him, all he does turns to dust. Scatcherd once killed a man, the friend of his youth – that he did so in vengeance, on behalf of his sister, cannot dislodge the horror from his mind. Is it to justify Scatcherd (at least, in part) that Trollope causes his heroine Mary Thorne to have been begotten in an atrocious manner? Scatcherd, due to play a large later part in the story, clearly could not be allowed to go to the gallows; at his trial, he had won the sympathy of the court, hence his being convicted of manslaughter, not murder. It may be feared, however, that Trollope had yet another reason for representing the mother of Mary Thorne as the unwilling victim of an enormity. Having failed to lure the girl from the path of virtue, Henry Thorne (the doctor's worthless young brother) had drugged her unconscious, then gone on to take possession. Thus, though sinned against, the unfortunate Mary Scatcherd still could be seen as sinless – 'pure' as to all but fact. Trollope, one must suspect, thought this better – thus his heroine did not originate from a stoop to folly! That the way in which he accounts for her antecedents would be far more repulsive to us, he did not foresee.

Nothing changes more than the notion of what is shocking. At more than one juncture in *Doctor Thorne* we may, today, charge the author with blind spots, timid shiftiness, ethical ambiguity. The second brotherly vengeance in the book is Frank's horse-whipping of Moffat, the fashionable tailor's son who has jilted one of the Gresham sisters. (Moffat, rich, had been a De Courcy *protégé*.) As to this scene, we feel Trollope himself uneasy: he resorts to a rhetorical facetiousness which makes the pages in question all but unreadable, apart even from their unpleasing content. Frank, he tries hard to persuade himself, *should* be 'manly' – we, alas, see the Gresham heir transformed (though briefly) into a fascist bully. Trollope, the mid-Victorian, was writing at a sort of transition point: behind him lay the unselfconscious rumbustiousness of the eighteenth century; ahead, a new world of scruples and sensibility. Fielding or Smollett could have got away, forthrightly, with the whipping scene, and still not offended us – Trollope wavers with regard to it, so is lost. This ambivalence of his was not, probably, evident to his early readers, for they shared it. His judgements, his acceptances, his solutions, with so very often their hint of compromise, are – *where* they show the hint of compromise – of his day. Frightened by abnormality in his youth, he breathed joyously the air of what seemed normality. Such deceptive air is not breathed in without a cost. He pays the cost in his art; we must see him pay it even in this his accepted masterpiece, *Doctor Thorne*. Yet somehow there remained, and remains, within him a creature of untouched, inveterate honesty. Such was the Trollope who has survived his day, the Trollope whom we consider now.

The question of artistry comes last. The idea of a novel's being a work of art not only never occurred to Trollope but would have been totally foreign, had it done so. The production of novels was an industry which he found himself happily able to carry on. How far this industry was rewarded, not only afterwards by cash but at the time by release and pleasure, his *Autobiography* never exactly tells us. He appends a list of his books, their dates, and the sums gained by them; into creative sensation he does not enter.[2] Like all authors, he thought more highly of some of his novels than he did of others; sometimes the public agreed with him, sometimes not. He worked to the clock, so many pages a day – a fact which, revealed by the *Autobiography*, was one cause of his absolute disrepute with a later, aesthetic generation. The *Autobiography*, by his expressed wish, was not published till one year after his death: he died in 1882. It is conceivable, indeed he faced the fact, that towards the end of his days he was less in fashion; he had not to live to witness his total banishment – 'ordinary' readers reacted, almost at once, to the cold wind blowing upon his name. That disgrace was temporary; it is a thing of yesterday. Anthony Trollope has reappeared. He is not merely back where he was; that would be impossible, for the world he first stood in relation to is no more. The twentieth century, having discovered that it requires him, calls him back. Inevitably, we rate what he has to give us in our own terms – which are not, and can not be, exactly his.

Speed and space-filling were the desideratum. He could not afford to be at a loss for a word; nor was he – the necessary words rushed in. (He stresses the writer's need for habituation.) He was grateful to any word so far as it served to help to establish a fact, add an attribute, or define a meaning – and 'help', I think, is here the correct verb: Trollope's words back one another up, bear one another out, and, collectively, do what has been desired. That there could be fewer of them did not worry him. Fining-down, selection would have demanded a concentration of which he was not capable – or, one had better say, a concentration he did not choose to apply. Take care of the sense, and the style will look after itself, could have been his axiom. He is intelligible; he makes point after point, though the reader's arrival at each may be laborious. Like all regular day-to-day writers, he shows great variation in his degrees of command and clearness: one is aware of his better days, and his worse ones – the worst to be said about his prose is, it lacks that precision we call distinction. As against that, his dialogue *can* be excellent; sufficiently clear-cut, dramatic and yet lifelike – this is borne out in all the important chapters in *Doctor Thorne*. The diversionary interludes are feebler, marred often by careless conventionality, or the facetiousness we have noted before. Why, we may ask, are such interludes here at all? – often they cast no light on the central story. Answer, Trollope deliberately fought a delaying action. *Doctor Thorne* was planned as a 'three-decker' (a three-volume novel). This form in his day was popular, and sold best. *The Warden*, he had decided, would have done better had it been bulkier. *Doctor Thorne* had to be spun out to the required length, and was. Inspiration could flag in him, but invention never. He was what he claimed to be, an unceasing worker.

Yet there can, I believe, be an artistry which is inadvertent – more than unconscious, all but unwilling. To this Trollope was subject; one is aware of its unmistakable action in *Doctor Thorne*. I spoke, at the outset of this preface, of his scenes' having a certain glow and rotundity; and there are moments when they have more. Something idyllic, if not poetic, is added to their intense likeliness; they become, if never piercingly beautiful, more nearly beautiful than is most reality – and when this happens there is a momentary transparency in his dense prose, as though by some magic the verbal sand reached a heat where it could run into glass. Elsewhere, at crises of emotion between the characters, that emotion not only commands us but austerely seems to command him, giving anonymous authority to his pen. An artist transmits more than he knows: in that sense we find Trollope to be an artist. On a level below that, he is a great conveyor of that to which he greatly reacted: charm – whether of face, person or manner, landscape, the visage or environment of a house. Aesthetically and fondly he loved girls, bevy-in-muslins, swinging their bonnets by the ribbons, dispersing over lawns liquid with sunset – he depicts floating pleasures, whose spell is in their evanescence, their slipping by. Had he been a painter, he would have been an inland Boudin. Also he took pleasure in masculine upright bearing and open countenance. Honour was his darling; grace, where he was concerned, went with strength in reserve or courage in play. *Doctor Thorne* as a novel has sterling merits – some I have touched on, others you will discover. But it acts on us most, perhaps, through some inner quality that only a warm and gentle word can define. It endears itself to us. For many, this is enough.

SOURCE: excerpted from 'Introduction' to Riverside Press edition, (Cambridge, Mass., 1959), pp. *xiii–xiv*.

NOTES

1. [Ed.] In *An Autobiography* (1883; new edition Oxford, 1980), p. 115, Trollope tells how his brother Tom was the instigator of the plot for *Doctor Thorne*. See 'Comment by Author' on the novel in section 2 of Part One, above.

2. [Ed.] But see indications of the pleasures writing gave to Trollope in the passages, captioned as 'Imaginative Symbiosis' and 'On Barchester', in section 1 of Part One, above.

4. *FRAMLEY PARSONAGE*

P. D. Edwards 'Broadening the Boundaries of Barset' (1978)

. . . Turning from *Doctor Thorne* to *Framley Parsonage* . . . we are inevitably struck by the comparative looseness of the latter's plot. Trollope himself characterises it as a mere 'hodge-podge' which he is reluctant even to call a plot. The novel was popular, he believed, simply because 'the characters were so well handled' and because the 'story was thoroughly English': 'a little fox-hunting and a little tuft-hunting, some Christian virtue and some Christian cant', 'no heroism and no villainy', 'much Church, but more love-making'.[1] In outline this is the formula for many of Trollope's domestic novels . . . and the popular success of *Framley Parsonage* must be held to have encouraged him in the belief that neither a coherent plot nor a unifying theme was essential. For such a formula implies both a dispersal of interest, to the extent that a number of stories offering different kinds of interest vie more or less equally for attention, and a substitution of the broadly realistic quality of 'Englishness' – or 'Englishry', as Michael Sadleir calls it[2] – for any more specific unifying idea. The result is that a novel like *Framley Parsonage* does seem to depend less on 'plot' and more on 'character' than one like *Doctor Thorne*: indeed, it strikingly attests the difficulty, for any novelist, of sustaining interest in characters who have no real part to play either in the story or in the total design of the novel.

Some of the characters who reappear in *Framley Parsonage*, after having been created for specific purposes in earlier Barset novels, are obvious cases in point: the Proudies and Greshams, for example, and Miss Dunstable and Doctor Thorne. Though none of these is completely redundant in *Framley Parsonage*, they are clearly allowed to hold more of the stage than their supernumerary role justifies; and even some of the reviewers, notwithstanding the Victorian love of 'characters' for their own sake, suspected that Trollope's imagination must be running out of steam.[3] The new collisions between the Grantlys and the Proudies on the subject of their respective daughters' matrimonial prospects [pp. 437–11, 490–2][4] are amusing enough and do show the Grantlys in a fresh light, cheerfully allying themselves with a Whig family. But both credulity and interest are strained by the frequent reappearances of, in particular, Mrs Proudie and Miss Dunstable, as part of the frivolous Whig establishment of London and West Barset.

Thus a long episode like that of Harold Smith's lecture [ch. 6], though effectively dramatising the extent to which frivolity and shallow cynicism of the 'Chaldicotes set' have seduced Mark Robarts from the virtue of old Barset (personified chiefly in Lady Lufton) and even from proper attention to his clerical duties, is obviously included mainly as a showcase for Mrs Proudie in one of her routine roles. As political satire, the lecture itself appears heavy-handed and flippant, like most of the other political satire in *Framley Parsonage*. But however grotesque its banalities and hyperboles, we are hardly prepared for the pointless farce of Mrs Proudie's disruption of it. The Proudies have earlier been brought before us at Chaldicotes in a series of skirmishes with Miss Dunstable and Mrs Harold Smith. Some of these, especially the one climaxed by Miss Dunstable's mischievous compliment to Mrs Proudie, 'Well, you've a gay set in the chapter, I must say' [p. 61], are pointed and entertaining; and in one the bishop is made to anticipate Mrs Proudie's objection to Mr Smith's lecture [p. 31] But much of the entertainment clearly derives from the familiarity of the performance: Miss Dunstable and the Proudies are jumping through the same hoops, repeating precisely the roles, and sometimes even the turns of phrase (Miss Dunstable's 'Oh – ah!', for instance), that characterised their encounters in *Doctor Thorne*. And similarly Mrs Proudie's terrific eruption at Mr Smith's lecture is on the face of it so maddeningly in character that our first impulse is to cheer from sheer joy of recognition. It is so nice and so typical a comment on her worldliness that she should insist on the power of Christianity to advance the material as well as the spiritual progress of the Solomon Islanders [pp. 66–7]. When, however, to Christianity she adds 'Sabbath-day observance' as a recipe for prosperity ('Let us never forget that these islanders can never prosper unless they keep the Sabbath holy'), the joke is surely being overdone. We already know all about Mrs Proudie's fanatical sabbatarianism, and her further indulgence of it here, so extravagant and out of place, simply accentuates a known eccentricity at the expense of the other, more sensible and practical, traits that leaven her absurdities. She is being coarsened into a caricature of herself.

Later Mrs Proudie is used more pointedly to illustrate the sterility of life in the circles frequented by the West Barset Whigs. At her 'conversazione' in London [ch. 17], Lord Dumbello and Griselda Grantly conduct an important part of their silent, passionless courtship, and Miss Dunstable engages in raillery so ill-natured that, though familiar enough to the reader, it seems for the first time to reveal itself in its true colours to Trollope. Miss Dunstable, he explains, 'was living now very much with people on whom kindness, generosity, and open-heartedness were thrown away' and, as a result, 'was gradually becoming irreverent, scornful, and prone to ridicule' [pp. 189–90]. Mrs Proudie herself must be one of these people, if being subjected to Miss Dunstable's irreverence and scorn is the test. But given Mrs Proudie's eccentricities, her essential dowdiness, and the blight that seems to be cast on all her projects – her daughter's marriage to a widower with three children, a friend of Mr Slope's, is a typical example – the attempt to assimilate her malice and worldly ambition with that of the Whig grandees of West Barset must be judged both pointless and unkind. Certainly, the novel is not equally unkind to Archdeacon Grantly's wife, whose worldly ambitions for her daughter show that high-and-dry Tory Barset is no more proof than low-church Whig Barset against the seductions of London, and no more scrupulous about hobnobbing with the enemy. But Mrs Grantly at least realises her ambitions and is allowed, into the bargain, to flaunt her triumph before Mrs

Proudie [pp. 437–41]. Indeed, by way of rubbing the Proudies' face finally in the mud, the bishop's daughter is made to stoop to the infamy of having a poison-pen letter sent to Griselda Grantly!

In contrast to Mrs Proudie, Martha Dunstable, who also tends to become more like a caricature of herself the more we see of her, is suddenly plucked back just as she seems about to tumble headlong in the mud. Her closest attachment, it is insisted, has always been to the 'old' Barset personified by Frank and Mary Gresham and Doctor Thorne. Her relish for fashionable frivolities, such as the puerile baiting of Harold Smith and the endless jokes at the expense of the Proudies, belongs only to the more superficial and impressionable side of her nature. In reality she finds exchanging dull pleasantries with Frank and Mary [pp. 79–81] much more congenial, and eventually, for no discernible reason except that she must be rescued from the descent of Avernus somehow, she is made to marry Doctor Thorne. But such is the hold the worldly pleasures of London have gained on her that she makes it a condition of the marriage that she be allowed to spend part of the year among them – with or without her husband. This suggests that, even to Trollope's mind, the couple are less than perfectly matched, and one can't help feeling that her absences in London will be a relief to them both: for to all outward appearances her vitality derives exclusively from her 'worldly' social talents. It is evident, however, that Trollope means the marriage to be a happy fulfilment for two characters whom he admits he is very fond of and who represent – though Miss Dunstable in her good qualities only – the values of good sense, simplicity, and respect for (but not worship of) money that the novel prizes most highly.

We also notice that, financially, the marriage is an unequal one. Miss Dunstable is the richest, or one of the richest, women in England. Doctor Thorne has only the income from his medical practice. Seen in this light their alliance offers a kind of parallel with the other three that are reported in the last chapter of the novel, all of which are unequal in one way or another: those of Lucy Robarts and Lord Lufton, Griselda Grantly and Lord Dumbello, and Olivia Proudie and Mr

Tickler. Perhaps, then, *Framley Parsonage* has some semblance of a coherent plot and of a unifying idea after all? If it has, however, the coherence and unity must be considered tenuous. For the four marriages convey little more than a general, conventional sense of the fluidity of society, with barriers of rank and fortune, and of political and social prejudice, toppling fast. But against this, and in such a way as to cast further doubt on the prominence given to old friends from earlier Barset novels, must be set the contradictory sense – which I believe emerges much more strongly – that at bottom the old Barset is growing increasingly resistant to change, increasingly less fluid. For Lady Lufton, who is old Barset's sturdiest champion in *Framley Parsonage*, is quite free of the 'democratic' leanings of Doctor Thorne and his niece, and is only superficially affected by the 'worldliness' of the De Courcys, the Grantlys, and to a lesser extent the Greshams. And although, from time to time, breaches are made to the defence of her citadel, they are nearly all closed by the end of the novel.

The most serious of such breaches is caused by Mark Robarts's entanglement with the 'Chaldicotes set'; but the danger of contamination from this source is short-lived. At the time of Harold Smith's lecture, Mark's character does show signs of deterioration; and his later acquiescence in 'simony', when he accepts a prebend's stall at Barchester, makes it clear that Sowerby is robbing him of his principles as well as his money. With his resignation of the stall, however, he cleanses himself. Not that he will be proof, even now, against minor backslidings: despite Mr Crawley's fervent admonitions, it is unlikely that he will for long devote more of his time to parochial duties and less to following the hunt – without participating in it. But there will be no danger of his being 'bought over' by the enemy [cf. p. 201].

Of the other weak spots in Lady Lufton's armour the worst is her own worldly ambition. This, however, is always rather bashful. It shows up first in her desire to have her son marry Griselda Grantly, and later in her refusal to sanction his marriage to Lucy Robarts. But at heart she is repelled by Griselda's cold worldliness, just as Lord Lufton himself is. Griselda's subsequent engagement to Lord Dumbello, scion of a Whig family whose iniquities are as black as any her imagination can conceive, is a sufficient warning to her of the brittleness of worldly splendour. Once free of the Grantly entanglement – which exerts itself on the side of worldliness throughout the Barset novels, until near the end in *The Last Chronicle* – there is never any doubt that she will finally accept Lucy. And there is no suggestion that in doing so she will have to compromise her own standards, for Lucy, unlike Mary Thorne, has no stain on her birth and is open to no more substantial objection than that of being 'so uncommonly brown' [p. 469]. The pretence that her marriage to Lord Lufton would be a misalliance is, as at least one contemporary reviewer protested,[5] an all-too-familiar expedient for stringing out the story rather than a pointer to any real conflict of principles or of class prejudices. Lucy's eligibility is clear to the reader long before Lady Lufton comes to recognise it. Her appearance and deportment are contrasted favourably, and pointedly, with those of Griselda Grantly; and the spirit and good sense she shows in stipulating that before she will accept Lord Lufton's offer of marriage his mother must endorse it, confirms that her accession will strengthen rather than weaken the defences of the Lufton citadel.

Lucy and Lord Lufton are perhaps the most impressive as well as the most likable of Trollope's lovers. Though he has been foolish in the past and is still a barbarian in his recreations, Lord Lufton courts Lucy, particularly at the outset, with delicacy and with convincing fervour; unlike most of Trollope's young heroes, he is also faithful to her, despite what seems a complete rebuff. And Lucy distinguishes herself among Trollope's heroines by being able to see her lover's faults and to love him without worshipping him as a 'god'. Her attitudes, and indeed her actual words, often remind us of some of Shakespeare's romantic heroines, notably Viola and Beatrice. When, for example, her sister-in-law asks her whether much harm has been done, either to Lord Lufton or to herself, by his attentions to her, she replies, 'Oh! by God's mercy, very little. As for me, I shall get over it in three or four years I don't doubt – that's if I can get ass's milk and change of air' [p. 231]. And her late confession of her love to her sister-in-law perfectly captures the slightly hysterical humour, embracing mockery of self, of lover, and of love itself, that is one of the characteristic notes of the Shakespearean heroine:

'I don't care for my heart. I'd let it go – with this young popinjay lord or any one else, so that I could read, and talk, and walk, and sleep, and eat, without always feeling that I was wrong here – here – here', and she pressed her hand vehemently against her side. 'What is it that I feel, Fanny? Why am I so weak in body that I cannot take exercise? Why cannot I keep my mind on a book for one moment? Why can I not write two sentences together? Why should every mouthful I eat stick in my throat? Oh, Fanny, is it his legs, think you, or his title?' [pp. 284–5].

Later again, when Fanny wonders why she does not languish under Lady Lufton's disapproval, she is as emphatic as Benedick that, whatever else may make her look pale, love will not: 'I ought to be pale, ought I not? and very thin, and to go mad by degrees? I have not the least intention of doing anything of the kind . . .' [p. 385]. Other Trollopean girls – Mary Thorne and Lily Dale, for instance – strike many of the same attitudes, but Lucy is unique in loving with her eyes fully open yet not unworthily. And although, as she is the first to admit, a man who 'devotes all his energies to riding after a fox or killing poor birds' can hardly be a 'hero' [p. 283], she and Lord Lufton on the whole seem a good deal better matched, morally and intellectually, and a good deal more likely to raise old Barset in the world's, and the reader's, estimation than Mr and Mrs Frank Gresham.

Lord Lufton, like Mark Robarts, is fleeced by Sowerby, the down-at-heels owner of Chaldicotes, and we may take it that he will in future be less complacent about exposing old Barset to the 'Whig' danger by hobnobbing with the enemy, by 'jeers and sneers at the old county doings', and by heresies such as his remark that, as far as he is concerned, 'Mr Bright may sit for the county, if he pleases' [p. 13]. But in any case the political threat to old Barset now seems remote. Happenings at Westminster do on occasion affect the fortunes of Mark Robarts, of Sowerby, and of Archdeacon Grantly. But in general the tiresome machinations of Harold Smith and Supplehouse and, needless to add, of Tom Towers and the *Jupiter*, now relate to a sphere of action apparently too far from old Barset to influence it much, or even to offer suggestive parallels: there is, for example, a degree of politicking in the 'alliance' of Lady Lufton and Mrs Grantly, but the implicit reminders of politicking at Westminster are at best broad and predictable. And even though the West Barset Whigs, headed by the Duke of Omnium, are sharply contrasted to Lady Lufton's circle in their manners, their sexual mores and their lust for money (the Duke's 'squeezing' of poor Sowerby), there is no suggestion that in parliament their behaviour is distinguishable from that of their enemies. On the contrary, the satirical presentation of Tories as 'giants' and Whigs as 'gods' has the aim and the effect – characteristic of Trollope's political novels – of playing down the differences between them. The differences that matter in the main plot of the novel are moral ones, and it is clear that these cut across party differences far more than Lady Lufton acknowledges. Arch-Tories like the Greshams visit Gatherum Castle, and the gaieties of Chaldicotes and Gatherum seduce the Grantlys no less than the worldly Whigs. Lady Lufton's real enemies are fashionable frivolity and money-hunger rather than a political creed.

That old Barset continues to hold its own against them is demonstrated most dramatically at the famous moment when Lady Lufton outfaces the Duke on his home ground, that of London, which is her enemies' capital as West Barset is their country seat:

Circumstances had so turned out that he had absolutely been pressed close against Lady Lufton, and she, when she heard the voice, and was made positively acquainted with the fact of the great man's presence by Miss Dunstable's words, turned round quickly, but still with much feminine dignity, removing her dress from the contact. In doing this she was brought absolutely face to face with the duke, so that each could not but look full at the other. 'I beg your pardon', said the duke. They were the only words that had ever passed between them, nor have they spoken to each other since; but simple as they were, accompanied by the little by-play of the speakers, they gave rise to a considerable amount of ferment in the fashionable world. Lady Lufton, as she retreated back on to Dr Easyman, curtsied low; she curtsied low and slowly, and with a haughty arrangement of her drapery that was all her own; but the curtsy, though it was eloquent, did not say half so much – did not reprobate the habitual iniquities of the duke with a voice nearly as potent, as that which was expressed in the gradual fall of her eye and the gradual pressure of her lips. When she commenced her curtsy she was looking full in her foe's face. By the time that she had completed it her eyes were turned upon the ground, but there was an ineffable amount of scorn expressed in the lines of her mouth. She spoke no word, and retreated, as modest virtue and feminine weakness must ever retreat, before barefaced vice and virile power; but nevertheless she was held by all the world to have had the best of the encounter [pp. 314–15].

It is ominous, however, that even after being publicly snubbed in this fashion the duke retains 'a slight smile of derision': his smile can be felt as a portent of the supplanting – in the political or Palliser novels which followed on from the Barsetshire chronicles – of the old Barset by the fashionable world, essentially a London world, of which the duke is leader.

Framley Parsonage thus continues the process by which the boundaries of Barset are broadened to include new social groups, and it is the first of the Barset novels to devote nearly as much attention to the activities of these groups outside Barset as inside. But at the same time, while West Barset is becoming less and less self-contained, the eastern half of the county, Lady Lufton's half, is contracting and consolidating, becoming more exclusive and intransigent. *Framley Parsonage*, in this respect, looks ahead to the remaining two novels in the series, as indeed it also does in the extent to which it takes us outside Barset altogether. And, in addition, it introduces us to Mr Crawley, who is to prove the last and staunchest champion of the old Barset and who, significantly, is able to awe even Lady Lufton by his strictness and fervour.

SOURCE: excerpted from *Anthony Trollope: His Art and Scope* (London, 1978), pp. 37–44.

NOTES

[Revised and renumbered from the original – Ed.]
1. *An Autobiography* (1883; new edition Oxford, 1980), p. 143. [See the fuller excerpt in section 2 of Part One, above – Ed.]

2. Michael Sadleir, *Trollope: A Commentary* (1927; rev. edition London, 1945), p. 398.

3. [Ed.] See, for example, the *Westminster Review* notice (July 1861) on the novel excerpted in section 2 of Part One, above.

4. [Ed.] Page references here and elsewhere in the text are to the World Classics edition (Oxford, 1926).

5. *Westminster Review*, xx (July 1861), p. 283.

5. *THE SMALL HOUSE AT ALLINGTON*

Bradford A. Booth   'The Weakest
Link in the Chain'   (1958)

... When in 1878 Trollope entered into protracted
negotiations with publishers to make possible a uniform edition
of 'The Chronicles of Barsetshire', he did not intend that *The
Small House at Allington* (1864) should be one of the novels in the
series. That it ultimately appeared in its proper place was
owing to the entirely reasonable insistence of Chapman & Hall.
Trollope's reluctance must be traced to his very precise
definition of a Barset novel. *The Small House* he always held in
high regard; indeed, he thought that he had never done better
work.[1] Yet it seemed to him not strictly a sequel to the earlier
novels. It is difficult to justify the distinction which he tried to
make. True, only two characters from *The Warden* appear at any
length: Griselda Grantly and Septimus Harding, and the latter
is brought in forcibly rather than naturally. But the de Courcys
are prominently introduced, and so many others are spoken
about (the Proudies, the Grantlys, Mrs Arabin) that the
Barsetshire atmosphere is strong. A definition of the series
which excludes *The Small House* must also, it seems to me,
exclude *Doctor Thorne*. Most readers will probably consider
Trollope's decision against *The Small House* as capricious.

Nevertheless, *The Small House* is perhaps the weakest link in
the chain.[2] There is a want of force, a lack of spark, in this
slow-paced narrative; in consequence, there are a number of
heavy chapters that can only be described as dull. This is the
judgement that one must render against the whole Lily
Dale–Crosbie romance. The Lily–Johnny Eames narrative is
much heartier and much livelier, not only because Johnny is

attractively and sympathetically presented (I cannot understand the judgement of the Stebbinses, who call him 'loud-mouthed' and 'boobish'[3]), but also because Trollope was perceptive enough and strong enough to resist the sentimental Victorian plot stereotype. Trollope tells us that many demands were made by frivolous or immature readers that Johnny be rewarded for his constancy. A reply to one such correspondent has recently come to light.

> You were angry with me because I did not make my pet happy with a husband, but you would have been more angry if I had made it all smooth, and supposed her capable of loving a second man while the wound of her first love was still so fresh. Indeed the object of the story was to show that a girl under such circumstances should bear the effects of her own impudence & not rid herself of her sorrow too easily. . . .[4]

This answer suffices for the dénouement of *The Small House*, but it does not suffice for *The Last Chronicle of Barset*, where Lily is indeed the French prig that Trollope describes in the *Autobiography*, nursing her wounded feelings and taking out her aggressions on the faithful Johnny, who is by this time, one suspects, too good for *her*.

The interest of Johnny lies initially in Trollope's own life, but the sustaining power of the characterisation is intrinsic in the concept of his humanity. Trollope saw him as a typical junior clerk, somewhat at loose ends in the city – swaggering a bit at times, perhaps, but more often grave and self-conscious. He has his moods of easy confidence and exuberance and his moods of blackness and impotent despair; is not this the pattern of most young men on their own in an impersonal society? One imagines that Johnny came easily to Trollope, for he has the authenticity of observed and recollected experience. Perhaps because Trollope slipped naturally into self-identification with Johnny, he never showed so firm a grasp of psychology. Consider, for example, the scene immediately following Lily's rejection of Johnny's proposal.

> He made his way out by the front door, and through the churchyard, and in this way on to the field through which he asked Lily to walk with him. He

hardly began to think of what had passed till he had left the squire's house behind him. As he made his way through the tomb-stones he paused and read one, as though it interested him. He stood a moment under the tower looking up at the clock, and then pulled out his own watch as though to verify the one by the other. He made, unconsciously, a struggle to drive away from his thoughts the facts of the last scene, and for some five or ten minutes he succeeded. He said to himself a word or two about Sir Raffle and his letters, and laughed inwardly as he remembered the figure of Rafferty bringing in the knight's shoes: He had gone some half mile upon his way before he ventured to stand still and tell himself that he had failed in the great object of his life.[5]

This is masterly in its simplicity and in its truth. So too is the meeting a few moments later with Lady Julia de Guest, who comes upon Johnny as he is cutting out Lily's name from the wooden rail on which he had carved it some time before.

> 'She has refused me, and it is all over.'
> 'It may be that she has refused you, and that yet it need not be all over. I am sorry that you have cut out the name, John. Do you mean to cut it out from your heart?'
> 'Never. I would if I could, but I never shall.'
> 'Keep to it as to a great treasure. It will be a joy to you in after years, and not a sorrow. To have loved truly, even though you shall have loved in vain, will be a consolation when you are as old as I am. It is something to have had a heart.'[6]

No doubt many modern readers put down *The Small House* with something of the amused incredulity of the reviewer for the *Illustrated Times:* 'How *does* the man contrive to make his stories so interesting, while he keeps so very near the surface of things? What magic is this which gets such a heap of entertainment out of next to nothing?'[7] The questions are actually relevant and fundamental, for their implications touch the bases of Trollope's purposes and techniques in the novel. Precise and detailed answers are difficult, but perhaps some suggestions of the Trollopian *modus operandi* can be made.

Trollope's world is one of complicated social strategy, of the drawing-room tactics of hint, innuendo and concealed artifice. It is one of contending forces, pressing shades of advantage offered both by character and by circumstance. One remembers the cool skill with which the impassive Lady

Dumbello contrives through her frigid beauty to achieve social position; or the soft-spoken power of the old Duke of Omnium, who, disapproving of Plantagenet Palliser's tentative advances to Lady Dumbello, has only to drop a word to his man of business; or the clever stratagem by which Lily is enabled to meet on advantageous terms Hopkins, her masterful gardener.

> . . . Hopkins appeared at the parlour window, and signified his desire for a conference.
>
> 'You must come round', said Lily. 'It's too cold for the window to be opened. [To Mrs Dale:] I always like to get him into the house, because he feels himself a little abashed by the chairs and tables; or, perhaps, it is the carpet that is too much for him. Out on the gravel-walks he is such a terrible tyrant, and in the greenhouse he almost tramples upon one.'[8]

If Trollope's imagination plays only over the surface, as the critic contends, so likewise does Oscar Wilde's. The writer of the comedy of manners can scarcely be asked to do more. Of these two practitioners of different varieties of the form, Wilde is, of course, the more sparkling. Trollope is no phrase-maker. But Trollope's humor is more subtle. Some of the nuances of character relationship in *The Small House* are incomparably delicate: that moment at which Crosbie recognises what must forever be his position in the eyes of the Countess de Courcy, when he suddenly finds himself 'enveloped in the fumes of an affectionate but somewhat contemptuous patronage'; or the uneasy balance of power between Crosbie and Lady Julia de Guest, who first triumphs over the young man's worldliness but then cannot stand against his bold assurance; or the shrewd way in which Lily asserts the claims of grief and martyrdom to assume a tyrannic control (no less powerful for its semi-playful touch) over the conduct of her mother and sister. Trollope is particularly skillful, as the *Spectator* reviewer saw,[9] in suggesting how one person may dominate another by the clever exercise of a vague unexpended resource, an unexpressed hint of menace, a totally unfair play upon good will and known sympathies.

All these evidences of a clear-sighted perception of human motives, of their origin and their expression, are to be found in *The Small House*. If the novel remains, nevertheless, one of the

192

least interesting of the Barsetshire series, we have additional proof of the richness of Trollope's gift.

SOURCE: *Anthony Trollope: Aspects of His Life and Art* (New York, and London, 1958), pp. 51–5.

NOTES

1. *An Autobiography* (1883; new edition, 1980), p. 175.
2. [Ed.] Professor Booth appends here a note giving a table of sales of 'The World's Classics' volumes of Trollope. *The Small House at Allington* does not figure among the first twelve of these, though all the other Barsetshire novels do.
3. L.P. Stebbins and R.P. Stebbins, *The Trollopes: The Chronicle of a Writing Family* (New York, 1945), p. 217.
4. *Letters*, ed. Bradford A. Booth (1951; new edition, 1980), pp. 152–3.
5. *The Small House at Allington*, vol. II, p. 338.
6. Ibid., pp. 340–1.
7. *Illustrated Times* (2 April 1864), p. 222.
8. *The Small House at Allington*, vol. II, p. 319. Walpole calls Hopkins 'one of the best gardeners in fiction' (*Anthony Trollope*, p. 62).
9. *Spectator*, XXXVII (9 April 1864), pp. 421–3. [Excerpted in section 2 of Part One of this selection – Ed.]

6. *THE LAST CHRONICLE OF BARSET*

Laurence Lerner   'Near to Greatness' (1967)

... *The Last Chronicle of Barset* (1867), is the last and darkest of the Barsetshire novels. It conducts us into the familiar world of the close, the deanery and the lawyer's office, but that world is no longer taken so completely on its own terms. The emphasis has shifted, morally, financially, even geographically. There is more distress, more despair and more poverty; we spend less time in the close, and more in the parish of Hogglestock, a cold bleak place where nothing is pretty; and even in Hogglestock, our time is divided between the resigned poverty of the brickmakers at Hoggle End, and the bitter poverty of the clergyman's house. The familiar Barsetshire figures are all here to delight the Trollopian – Dr and Mrs Proudie, old Mr Harding, Dr Grantly the Archdeacon; but among them stalks a 'lean, slim, meagre man, with shoulders slightly curved, and pale, lank, long locks of ragged hair' – the Rev. Josiah Crawley, perpetual curate of Hogglestock. The two extremes of Trollope's range meet in this novel, the finest he ever wrote.

There are four or five stories in this novel, interwoven with the casualness that the Victorians (who liked their novels long) were well used to. As we arrange them in our memory after reading, we can see that each story corresponds to a different part of Trollope's personality, and uses a different side of his talent. His social and political preferences, for instance, are seen most clearly in the Grantly story. Theophilus Grantly, Archdeacon and Rector of Plumstead Episcopi, is an old Barchester favourite. He first appeared in *The Warden* as the obstinate defender of unjust clerical privileges: a hard, fierce, unattractive man, and something of a hypocrite. When he reappeared in *Barchester Towers* his character had softened: he was still hot-tempered, obstinate and fond of worldly possessions, but an apologetic note has crept in, and an assurance that he was affectionate enough under the fierce outside. If he was to remain interesting over several novels he could not be the mere bully of *The Warden*; and the Dr Grantly of *Barchester Towers* is more or less the Dr Grantly of *The Last Chronicle of Barset*. He loves 'the temporalities of the church as temporalities'; he does not care to see abuses reformed, or even much discussed; but he once more has a soft heart under the quick temper, and it is crucial to the story.

The Archdeacon is probably nearer to his author than any of Trollope's characters. He loves money, as Trollope did; he is generous and impulsive, as Trollope was; being a cleric, he may not hunt, but he knows the whereabouts of every fox in Plumstead. He is the squire as well as the parson of Plumstead, and loves to think of his son Henry as a landed gentleman. Trollope, for whom hunting was 'one of the great joys of my life', must have pitied so vigorous a man his inability to hunt. He makes it clear that Henry's concern over the foxes was something that endeared him to the Archdeacon through the worst of their quarrel, and I think that the Archdeacon's concern for the foxes endeared him steadily to his author, through his most selfish and pompous remarks.

The Archdeacon appealed to Trollope as a man; and interested him as a social force. He represents the unrepentant conservatism of a propertied church, and the political assertiveness of an established church. If he failed to become bishop when his father died, it was not for want of trying. Most of the country gentry of Barsetshire would have preferred him to Dr Proudie, and so would Trollope; but whether you think he would have made a good bishop depends on your point of view. He would not have responded to the wind of change: not because he did not feel it, but because he hated and despised those who set it blowing. Like so many tolerant men, Trollope is ambivalent in his attitude to this intransigence. He was a liberal in politics, and he did not share the Archdeacon's diehard resistance to reform. Yet though in his head he is often on the side of the reformers, in his heart he too is charmed that 'one man by interest might have a thousand a year, while another man equally good, but without interest, could only have a hundred'. He attacked ecclesiastical abuse in *The Warden*, but at the same time made splendid fun of the denunciations of Mr Popular Sentiment and Mr Pessimist Anticant, who are clearly Dickens and Carlyle. Carlyle was fond of reminding his readers that nothing was theirs absolutely, that they owed gratitude and duty for whatever the world allowed them; Trollope, solid and property-loving paterfamilias, was proud of his ability to earn, and would not have liked the thought that anyone could tell him what to do with his £68,939 17s. 5d.

This Grantly streak in Trollope was a benefit to him artistically. It checked any danger of didactic zeal; if there is didacticism, it is nicely tamed.

Mr Thumble called to mind the fact that Mr Crawley was a very poor man indeed – so poor that he owed money all round the country to butchers and bakers, and the other fact, that he, Mr Thumble, himself, did not owe money to anyone, his wife luckily having a little income of her own.

It was not simply natural subtlety that kept Trollope's propaganda down to this cool ironic level; the irony is what comes out when Dr Grantly is keeping a fierce eye on Mr Anticant.

The Archdeacon's son is much less interesting than his father; and the son's sweetheart is less interesting still. In this they are like all Trollope's young lovers: virtuous, handsome, oozing decency and high sentiments. Trollope's formula for a love story is a simple one: to put some obstacle in the way that will enable one of the lovers, usually the girl, to be high-minded. Sometimes (as in *Orley Farm*) he cannot even be bothered to put an obstacle in the way, and he delays the happy ending with a lengthy account of the young man's plucking up courage to propose. The formula is common enough and we would not mind it if there was any quality of real experience, any felt life, in the love scenes themselves. 'Mamma, what am I to say to him?' says Grace Crawley when her lover comes at last to claim her. What she does say is, 'I do not know why you should be so good to me. ... I am such a poor thing for a man like you to love.' It is a slight improvement on Nellie Bold and Mr Arabin ('When the ivy has found its tower, when the delicate creeper has found its strong wall, we know how the parasite plants grow and prosper. ...'); but Grace Crawley, like all Trollope's young ladies, is a sugarstick. Nellie, Lucy Robarts, Lily Dale: through book after book they simper, the fine young man saying 'my wife, my own', the girl running off 'like a roe' to lock the door (the man outside) and enjoy the 'full luxury of her love' – all the girls indistinguishable, all the stories written with the same dreadful competence.

Lily Dale is a bit more interesting than the others. Not that the love scenes are any better, and Lily talking to her mama after the letter has come from Mr Crosbie bids fair to be the worst scene in this novel. But Lily comes to life when she is being pestered by her friends: the unmarried girl's resentment at the world's reluctance to leave her alone is very well caught.

She had received the same advice from her mother, from her sister, from her uncle, and from Lady Julia, till she was sick of it. ... Her secret had been published, as it were, by the town-crier in the High Street. Everybody knew that she had been jilted by Adolphus Crosbie, and that it was intended that she should be consoled by John Eames. And people seemed to think that they had a right to rebuke her if she expressed an unwillingness to carry out this intention which the public had so kindly arranged for her.

Lily is less convincing when Mrs Arabin is talking to her, for Mrs Arabin had once been the heroine of a novel herself, and she must not be sullied with so much frankness; and she is less convincing still – she is made of pure wood – when Johnny Eames is with her. At these moments she joins the indistinguishable, the alas not anonymous, throng of pretty and sexless dolls.

Trollope's heroines are of their time in being sexless. None of the great Victorian novelists tells us anything of the sex life of his heroines, but we do not need to condemn them alike for this.

There are those who leave out the bedroom scenes because convention demanded that they be left out, but who make you feel they could have written them had they chosen: Thackeray, George Eliot, Samuel Butler. And there are those whose coy heroines are attractive in a way that is more sexual than the author admits, those for whom the convention of reticence is a convenient device for their own evasiveness. Dickens is the worst offender here; and Trollope is not guiltless. The suggestion that Lily will not marry John because she is frightened of sex seems so obvious to us, that we must ask if it had occurred to Trollope; and it looks as if it hadn't. When she refuses him for the last time, she does so in a flurry of frankness: 'she had described her feelings more plainly to her lover than she had ever done to anyone.' But the plain description, with its central image of the shattered tree, is about a disembodied emotional life. When she says 'He could not ask me to do a single thing for him – except the one thing – that I would refuse', the one thing is only the wedding, not its consequences. Lily seems to have weighed the whole thing up without thinking about physical contact with John. No doubt we ought not to blame Trollope for the conventions of his time: but we have to blame someone.

The least admired of the stories is that concerning the Dobbs Broughtons, Madalina Desmoulines and Clara Van Siever. Most of its effects are achieved by juxtaposing the incongruous – the method of comedy and of melodrama. It does not often achieve the plain style of Trollope's best realism. One scene, however, in which it does is that in which Mrs Dobbs Broughton has to be told the news of her husband's death. This is written with characteristic Trollope frankness: 'Then she dropped his hands and walked away from him to the window – and stood there looking out upon the stuccoed turret of a huge house that stood opposite. As she did so she was employing herself in counting the windows.' This is frankness of the eye: Trollope takes a quiet pride in telling us what she saw, not what she'd have claimed to see. There is a similar frankness of the emotions, when Conway has to answer Mrs Dobbs

Broughton's remark 'I know that you despise me.' He is behaving well in the crisis, and tells her that he doesn't; but 'as he descended the stairs he could not refrain from telling himself that he did despise her'.

If we compare the ruin and suicide of Dobbs Broughton with the ruin and suicide of Merdle in *Little Dorrit*, it is obvious that Trollope has none of the symbolic power, none of the imaginative vision of Dickens; but he has a scrupulousness in reporting the consequences that can make Dickens, in contrast, look strident. Trollope at his most honest is often Trollope at his best: true, it is a very simple honesty, neither probing nor subtle, nor frank beyond a certain point, and perhaps he is a little self-satisfied about it. But the chapter is a memorable one, and surely the best in a story that is mostly in the mode of comedy, even farce. Trollope might have had a fine entertainer's talent if he had written for the stage: there is richly farcical material in, for instance, Johnny Eames's last escape from Madalina, watched by the astonished policeman. Madalina has found her way into the novel from farce, Mrs Dobbs Broughton from something between farce and melodrama. There is an attempt to turn Clara into a more serious character, but it is merely perfunctory.

If we want to reflect on the nature of Trollope's talent, however, they are worth a moment's longer attention: for they show him at the extreme of comedy. They offer neat an element that is present in the more complex presentation of Mrs Proudie. The browbeating wife is a stock figure of farce, and Mrs Proudie has, in some scenes, the crude shape of a comic character. When Trollope sees her like this, he drops into metaphors of battle. He tells us endlessly that there is a war (it is a cold war, of course) between the Proudie faction and the Archdeacon's faction. Dr Tempest's breakfast conversation with Mrs Proudie is a battle in which he is 'rather proud of his success'; when she reappears in the bishop's study he is lost in admiration: 'He had left her, as he thought, utterly vanquished and prostrated by his determined but uncourteous usage of her; and here she was, present again on the field of battle as though she had never even been wounded.'

There had been another meeting in the Bishop's study, in

which Mrs Proudie was put down by Mr Crawley; and it too is
seen as a battle:

> Then Mr Crawley stalked on, clutching and crushing in his hand the bishop,
> and the bishop's wife, and the whole diocese – and all the Church of England.
> Dirty shoes, indeed! Whose was the fault that there were in the church so
> many feet soiled by unmerited poverty, and so many hands soiled by
> undeserved wealth? if the bishop did not like his shoes, let the bishop dare to
> tell him so! So he walked on through the thick of the mud, by no means
> picking his way.

The same metaphor, but we are in another world. When
Trollope writes of Mrs Proudie the metaphor is his own, used as
a way of thrusting before us the one comic element in the
situation: he sees her as an army, and does not trouble to see
her as a person. When he writes of Mr Crawley the metaphor is
not his but Crawley's, the simplification is Crawley's –
the inevitable simplifying result of his fierce, proud
self-justification, that drives him tireless over the muddy lanes,
enacting and re-enacting the scene with the bishop, boasting of
the shame of poverty, crushing him with his fist. The one is
metaphor for mere effect, the other is metaphor as an
expression of character.

Mrs Proudie is too simple to be really interesting, and too
conventional to be an archetypal figure: the scenes in which she
figures are delightful, but they have the simplifications of
comedy. One can understand the impatience of the two
clergymen who had her killed. It is one of the best stories in
Trollope's *Autobiography*. . . . [Lerner quotes the passage
excepted in section 2 of Part One, above – Ed.] That shows us
the kind of novelist Trollope was: his plots are meant to have
the unpredictability of life, in which people do die un-
expectedly; not the planned sequence in which each scene is
allotted its careful place and written with an eye to what the
reader does and does not know. It is impossible to imagine the
great plotters – Jane Austen, Conrad, James – responding so
obligingly to the clergymen; they'd have had to throw away
what they'd written, and start again at the beginning.

And the incident shows us, too, that Mrs Proudie's death is

not the real climax of the story: the breaking of the bishop's heart is that. If Trollope killed Mrs Proudie within a week of the conversation, he could not have had her death in mind when writing chapter 47 ('Dr Tempest at the Palace') or chapter 54, the opening pages of which show the broken spirit of Dr Proudie. These pages are sad and impressive; they modulate out of comedy into a kind of sub-tragedy, as if the victim who fell on the banana skin of Mrs Proudie were to get up and rub his wounds ruefully, and we remember that it must really have hurt.

As for him, he hardly left his own sitting-room in these days, except when he joined the family at breakfast and at dinner. And in his study he did little or nothing. He would smile when his chaplain went to him, and give some trifling verbal directions; but for days he scarcely ever took a pen in his hands, and though he took up many books, he read hardly a page. How often he told his wife in those days that he was broken-hearted, no-one but his wife ever knew.

This is Trollope near his best: a firm and rueful honesty, a scrupulous psychological analysis, not probing deep, but seeing steadily as far as it goes. Mrs Proudie's death was not needed for the story to have taken on this more serious tone: indeed, with its rather brassy unexpectedness, its unconvincing claim that the Crawley incident caused the death, it lowers the level slightly, taking us back to the kind of startling incident that Trollope so often builds round Mrs Proudie for his readers' entertainment.

Immediately after the death we move back to the bishop; and the novel returns from broad effects to plain ones. The paragraphs that end chapter 66 and begin 67 are surely the best of all the Proudie story. There is a fine dramatic sense in the bishop's reception of the news, cross, unwashed, querulous about his dinner; and there is something more in the broken-backed train of thought that follows, the 'slight irregular movement of his fingers on the top of his bald head' (how rare in Trollope is a behaviourist's eye as keen as this), and the vague, automatic prayer: 'I think he was praying that God might save him from being glad that his wife was dead.'

How easily this brilliant sentence could have been worked up into a strong comic effect: how wise Trollope was to use the hesitant, probing tone.

Mrs Proudie deserved her fame: and she deserved her startling death. The poor henpecked bishop outlived her, and perhaps outlives her, quietly and persistently, in the minds of many readers.

And so, finally, to Mr Crawley: the central character of the novel, and the finest: probably the finest Trollope ever created. Like most of the characters of *The Last Chronicle of Barset*, he was taken from an earlier novel. He occupies only two or three chapters in *Framley Parsonage*, where his wife's illness gives Lucy Robarts, the heroine, a chance to be heroic; but he dominates that book as he does this. He is already the Mr Crawley we know – 'a strict, stern, unpleasant man, and one who feared God and his own conscience'. In *The Last Chronicle of Barset* Mr Crawley is not called 'unpleasant' in the very first sentence that describes him, as he was in *Framley Parsonage*; and the difference is a sign of how Trollope's attitude has shifted. He is more severe on Mr Crawley in *Framley Parsonage*, more intent on contrasting him with his wife, to her advantage. 'She was made of the sterner metal of the two', says Trollope. 'How much higher toned is her mind than his', says Lucy, and Trollope clearly agrees; 'how weak he is in many things, and how strong she is in everything'. The tone has altered in *The Last Chronicle of Barset*, but not in the way that the treatment of Dr Grantly changed from *The Warden* to *Barchester Towers*. Here we have neither inconsistency nor sentimentalising, but a longer, closer, deeper look at the same character, a stronger sympathy that comes from a close enacting of his own inner struggle.

When Trollope discussed *The Last Chronicle of Barset* in his *Autobiography*, he confessed that he did not think the plot altogether plausible: 'I cannot quite make myself believe that even such a man as Mr Crawley could have forgotten how he got the cheque; nor would the generous friend who was anxious to supply his wants have supplied them by tendering the cheque of a third person.' [Lerner continues with the passage excerpted in section 2 of Part One, above – Ed.] It is the voice of the craftsman: afraid he has done a botched job, and more concerned with that fear than with the intense power of what he has, though imperfectly, created. It may be true that Mr Crawley's uncertainty is implausible, though if so Trollope has done a skilful job of covering up that implausibility – skilful in plot (the Arabins are not together, the Dean did not know of the cheque, Eleanor was not asked till her grandfather wrote), and skilful in psychology (Mr Crawley thought he had got the cheque from the Dean; when the Dean denied it he refused, after his first mistake, and with his mad honesty, to insist that he was right). But even if this initial premise is implausible, we soon forget this in the power of Mr Crawley's tragedy.

Mr Crawley is a man in whom pride and integrity are inextricable. Such total integrity is not easy to bear, and the main aim of Trollope's study is to show its discomforts: for the world, for his family, for himself. Barsetshire is full of people whom Mr Crawley has made uncomfortable – Mr Robarts, Lady Lufton, Mr Thumble, the Proudies. Some of these discomforts are almost comic; the portrait of Mr Crawley, for all its serious plainness, is trimmed with comedy – with a perception of odd juxtapositions, that never undercuts the seriousness, but is very much alive to the incongruities it can lead to. We have to admire the control of tone that can see the ridiculousness of Mr Thumble contrasted with Mr Crawley, without allowing Mr Crawley himself to be invaded by that ridiculousness.

The discomfort for his family was, as I have suggested, more emphasised in *Framley Parsonage*. Not that they suffer less in this novel. Grace's suffering, it is true, forms part of her own insipid story, but that of Mrs Crawley is real enough. Yet somehow she is more firmly an appendage to her husband than she was in *Framley Parsonage*. Mr Crawley, we are told in *The Last Chronicle of Barset*, 'never permitted the slightest interference with his own word in his own family', and Trollope likes him all the better for it; we see him adding to his letter of resignation after she has read it, a sentence in which he praises his wife, and Trollope likes him for the delicacy. There is less about smuggling food into the parsonage without his knowledge than there had been in *Framley Parsonage*. Mr Crawley is master in his own house, and that, in Trollope's view, makes for a happy house. And when he prepares to inflict on them the greatest suffering of all, the destitution that may fall on them if he resigns the living, he does so with full knowledge of what he is doing, and with an almost mystical intensity that impressed Trollope, impresses us, and impresses his wife. He knows so clearly what he is doing that it is hard to see him as inflicting any cruelty: when Mr Robarts suggests that he is doing wrong in not considering them, he answers in a flood of integrity, and any reader must feel he has the best of it.

The suffering Mr Crawley brings on his family is never so profound – never so profoundly described, at any rate – as that he brings on himself. It is this that makes him an almost tragic figure: he is prepared to destroy himself in his integrity. For an instant, under the spell of old Giles Hoggett, he becomes an archetypal tragic sufferer: 'there ain't nowt a man can't bear if he'll only be dogged'. It is wierdly impressive, this cutting away of all the sound arguments for staying in the living, by his sheer determination to suffer the worst because he believes he can bear it. It is stoicism run mad, but it is the madness of tragic dignity.

For most of the time, however, we must speak of Mr Crawley as 'almost' a tragic figure. The almost is not – or not directly – a sign of Trollope's limited powers; but rather of a difference of intention. It may be there is an element of self-pity in every tragic hero, but it must be kept out of sight: if it is thrust too much on our attention, then our attitude will be too critical for full tragic identification. Trollope's intention was to make us critical, by thrusting the element in front of our noses.

She had been quite right when she had accused him of over-indulgence in his grief. He did give way to it till it became a luxury to him – a luxury which she would not have had the heart to deny him, had she not felt it to be of all luxuries the most pernicious.

And when he sits on the gate in the rain at Hoggle End, uncertain what to do, not yet dogged, Trollope reminds us how deserving of better things he is, and reminds us that this is what he himself is thinking. The bitterness of grief can drift easily into a fury of self-assertion.

Trollope respects Mr Crawley too much to score cheap points off him, whether angry or comic; without this respect he could not have built him up to such stature. Yet he did not like him. Perhaps he even disliked him as much as Archdeacon Grantly did. Trollope's ideal clergymen are not sober and angry enthusiasts, they are gentle, kindly men like old Mr Harding, or the deceased Bishop Grantly, whose whist-drives at the Palace are remembered with affection. This mixture of dislike and respect, this uneasy admiration, is the cause of the power with which Mr Crawley has been created. Few writers are at their best when they are comfortable; even Trollope, who is more comfortable than most, only rises to his heights when he has disturbing material. Mr Crawley disturbed him enough to drive him deeper than he usually explored; but left him the vein of sensible moralising that continually refuses to accept Mr Crawley's view of himself. The result is a sober strength that takes us as near to greatness as the virtue of early rising can unassisted come.

Source: excerpted from 'Introduction' to the Penguin English Library edition, (Harmondsworth, 1967), pp. 9–24.

Ruth ApRoberts   'Trollope and the Contrariety of Man'   (1971)

[The] contrariety of man is one of Trollope's recurrent themes. At times he will take it up lovingly, as mere frailty: 'The parish parson', he writes in *The Clergymen of the Church of England*, 'generally has a grievance and is much attached to it – in which he is like all other men in all other walks of life.' In the case of Louis Trevelyan [in *He Knew He Was Right* (1868)], he takes up the contrariety in its purest because most extreme form, where the unreason, present in all men to some extent, becomes a force of self-destruction. There can be no doubt as to the general significance Trollope attaches to the study of Trevelyan's case; at one stage he observes: 'They who do not understand that a man may be brought to hope that which of all things is the most grievous to him, have not observed with sufficient closeness the perversity of the human mind.'[1]

Josiah Crawley, in *The Last Chronicle of Barset*, who is probably his most brilliant achievement in a single character, is also, I think, his most careful study of human perversity. He is not mad, like Trevelyan, but feels himself threatened with madness, and is frequently referred to as 'half-mad'. Trollope places him in circumstances that push his endurance very near the breaking point. Although a spiritually dedicated man, Crawley suffers acutely from poverty: as he himself says to his poor parishioners, 'Poverty makes the spirit poor, and the hands weak, and the heart sore – and too often makes the conscience dull' [ch. LXIX]. It is painful for him to receive charity from his peer, and so he would indeed be liable to forget just where or how the cheque he is accused of having appropriated did come from. One might call it Freudian forgetting. But anyway he is so dedicated in his vocation that he is inclined to slight temporal matters for spiritual. Elijah does not keep accounts with the ravens. All this is not perversity in itself, but it all puts him in circumstances that force his perversity. We find him, in all his wonderfully indicated complexity, to have a gift for suffering; he courts destruction, he persistently denies his own best good, denies help, denies the support of the kind Robarts. He is forever atoning for a very problematical crime, even in those small things which surprise us into amusement: at the hotel on his way to London, 'They did their best to make him comfortable, and, I think, almost disappointed him in not heaping further misfortunes on his head' [ch. XXXII]. In a chapter where Trollope describes him in his very nadir [XLI] – and surely it is one of the most acute pieces of psychological description of the century – he is somehow able to relate Crawley's extreme irrationality to our own ordinary human-ness. We find him contemplating suicide, and then even for a fleeting instant, the murder of his wife and children, for 'only that was wanting to make him of all men the most unfortunate'. Still more remarkable, this man himself knows his own perversity, sees himself revelling in his suffering, dramatising it in that pompous way of his. He seeks to see himself as 'of all men, the most unfortunate', because he has a propensity to be the scapegoat of humanity. When his friend Arabin tells him of the Holy Land, and how the exact location of the crucifixion is uncertain, Crawley says *he* would know, *he* would know and recognise the actual place of Calvary! [ch. LXXIX].

In this same novel we re-encounter Archdeacon Grantly who is himself a fine study in another kind of perversity. When Trollope observes – as Grantly has been losing an argument to his wife – that Grantly 'was apt at such moments to think that she took an unfair advantage of him by keeping her temper' [ch. LVI], the observation is funny, really just because it is a brilliant discovery of a psychological truth. *À propos* of the Grantlys again, he demonstrates the more ordinary contrariness of a family quarrel. 'It would be wrong to say that love produces quarrels; *but* . . .' and he goes on to anatomise this common occurrence, showing how we 'nurse our wrath lest it cool', against someone we love best of all, and are supremely wretched in doing so, and yet the beloved one is never more beloved than then! [ch. XLIX]. In a more general comment, he declares 'the cross-grainedness of men is so great that things will often be forced to go wrong, even when they have the strongest possible natural tendency of their own to go right' [ch. LVIII].

There is an interesting irony even in the fact that Crawley, this most 'gross-grained' of men, is also one of the most brilliant of men, the most learned, not only in literature and theology but also in that 'true philosophy' of morals. We know him as the peer or superior of the distinguished Dean Arabin; he dowers his otherwise portionless daughters with the knowledge of Greek drama, and his own self-knowledge is almost unbearably acute. Yet it would seem that in this case the brilliance has functioned to find out new turns in contrariety, new discoveries of moral paradox, new virtuosity in the appreciation of ethical dilemmas. Crawley denies 'common' sense, the easy-going practical ethics of such men as Robarts, and of such 'sensible' people as his wife. The more agile the mind, the more ingenious to find new ways of unreason.

Even Trollope's interest in suicide is part of his interest in man's cross-grainedness – it is surprisingly frequent in his work. In this very novel, there is one actual suicide, that of Dobbs-Broughton, and suicide is considered by Crawley, by the Bishop, by Crosbie – a rather high frequency for a good-humoured Victorian novel. . . .

SOURCE: excerpted from *Anthony Trollope: Artist and Moralist* (London, 1971), pp. 103–5.

NOTE

1. *He Knew He Was Right*, ch. XXXVIII.

SELECT BIBLIOGRAPHY

Students are advised to consult the complete books from which extracts have
been reproduced in this collection. In addition, the following studies contain
at least substantial references to Barsetshire or comment on individual novels
within the cycle.

Tony Bareham (ed.), *Anthony Trollope* (London, 1980).
John W. Clark, *The Language and Style of Anthony Trollope* (London, 1975).
N. John Hall (ed.), *The Trollope Critics* (London and Basingstoke, 1981).
John Halperin (ed.), *Trollope Centenary Essays* (London and Basingstoke, 1982).
Geoffrey Harvey, *The Art of Anthony Trollope* (London, 1980).
James Pope Hennessy, *Anthony Trollope* (London, 1971).
J. R. Kincaid, *The Novels of Anthony Trollope* (Oxford, 1977).
Bill Overton, *The Unofficial Trollope* (Brighton, 1982).
C. P. Snow, *Trollope* (London and Basingstoke, 1975).
R. C. Terry, *Anthony Trollope: The Novelist in Hiding* (London and Basingstoke, 1977).
Hugh Walpole, *Anthony Trollope*, 'English Men of Letters' series (London, 1929).

The best collection of contemporary comment and criticism on the novels is in
Donald Smalley, *Trollope: The Critical Heritage* (London, 1969).

NOTES ON CONTRIBUTORS

RUTH ApROBERTS: Professor of English, University of California; in addition to work on Trollope, her publications include *Arnold and God* (1972).

BRADFORD A. BOOTH: American scholar and critic; editor of Trollope's *Letters* and of *An Autobiography*.

ELIZABETH BOWEN (1899–1973): Anglo-Irish novelist and short-story writer; her novels include *Death of the Heart* and *The Heat of the Day*.

WILLIAM CADBURY: American scholar, formerly teaching at the University of Oregon.

ANTHONY COCKSHUT: G.M. Young Lecturer in Nineteenth-Century English Literature, University of Oxford; his publications include, in addition to his work on Trollope, studies of Dickens and Walter Scott, and *Anglican Attitudes: Victorian Religious Controversies* (1959), *The Unbelievers: English Agnostic Thought* (1964) and *Man and Woman: Love in the Novel* (1977).

E. S. DALLAS (1828–79): journalist, author and critic.

P. D. EDWARDS: Professor of English, University of Queensland; in addition to numerous studies on Trollope, his publications include *Some Mid-Victorian Thrillers* (1971).

M. A. GOLDBERG: his publications include, in addition to work on Trollope, *The Poetics of Romanticism: Towards a Reading of John Keats* (1968).

FREDERIC HARRISON (1831–1923): man of letters and Positivist thinker.

R. H. HUTTON (1826–97): theologian and man of letters; joint editor of the *Spectator* and of the *National Review*.

HENRY JAMES (1843–1916): novelist and critic; many of his critical studies are included in the collection, *The House of Fiction*, ed. L. Edel (New Haven, Conn., and London, 1957).

PAMELA HANSFORD JOHNSON, Lady Snow (1912–82): novelist, playwright, literary critic and poet.

RONALD KNOX (1888–1958): scholar and priest; a leading figure in Roman Catholic intellectual life and in academic circles at Oxford.

LAURENCE LERNER: novelist, poet and literary critic; Professor of English at the University of Sussex. His publications include *The Truth-Tellers: Jane Austen, George Eliot and D.H. Lawrence* (1967).

FRANK O'CONNOR (1903–66): born Michael O'Donovan; short-story writer, critic and biographer. His publications include *The Big Fellow: A Life of Michael Collins* (1937, rev. edn 1965) and *The Backward Look: A Survey of Irish Literature* (1967).

MARGARET OLIPHANT (1828–97): novelist and literary critic.

R. M. POLHEMUS: Professor of English, Stanford University; besides his authoritative studies on Trollope, his publications include *Comic Faith: The Great Comic Tradition* (1980).

ARTHUR POLLARD: Professor of English Literature, University of Hull; his publications include, in addition to his work on Trollope, studies on Mrs Gaskell and Charlotte Brontë, *Satire* (1970) and the Casebooks on Thackeray: *Vanity Fair* (1978) and on Marvell, *Poems* (1980).

SIR ARTHUR QUILLER-COUCH (1863–1944): man of letters, novelist and King Edward VII Professor of English Literature, Cambridge, 1912–44. He was knighted in 1910.

SIR LESLIE STEPHEN (1832–1904): man of letters, philosopher and critic, and first editor of the *Dictionary of National Biography*. He was knighted in 1904. Father of Virginia Woolf and Vanessa Bell.

GEOFFREY TILLOTSON (1905–69): Professor of English Literature, Birkbeck College, University of London. His publications include studies on Pope and other eighteenth-century writers.

INDEX

Section I lists Trollope's writings and novel-characters. Section II is a general index of names, including commentators and critics. Page numbers in bold type denote essays or excerpts in this Casebook.

I TROLLOPE'S WORKS AND CHARACTERS

II GENERAL